We got the neutron bomb

MARC SPITZ

and

BRENDAN MULLEN

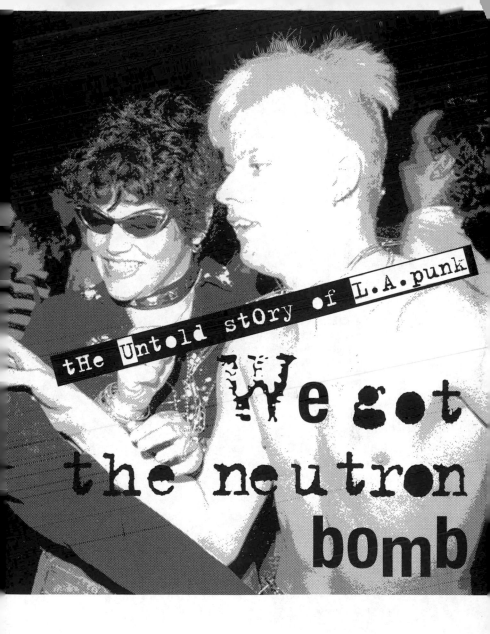

tHe Untold stoRy of L.A. punk

We got the neutron bomb

THREE RIVERS PRESS • NEW YORK

Title page: Hellin Killer, Pleasant Gehman, and Bobby Pyn at the Starwood Club, 1977. Photo Credit: Jenny Lens

Published by Three Rivers Press, New York, New York.
Member of the Crown Publishing Group.

Random House, Inc. New York, Toronto, London, Sydney, Auckland
www.randomhouse.com

THREE RIVERS PRESS is a registered trademark and the Three Rivers Press colophon is a trademark of Random House, Inc.

PHOTO RESEARCH BY LISA CORSON
DESIGN BY ELINA D. NUDELMAN

Library of Congress Cataloging-in-Publication Data

Spitz, Marc.
    We got the neutron bomb : the untold story of L.A. Punk / by Marc Spitz and Brendan Mullen.— 1st ed.
    1. Punk rock music—California—Los Angeles—History and criticism.
    2. Punk rock musicians—Interviews.   3. Punk culture.   I. Mullen, Brendan.   II. Title.

    ML3534 .S656   2001
    781.66—dc21   2001049137

    ISBN 0-609-80774-9

First Edition

146119709

contents

acknowledgments

Marc Spitz would like to thank Jim Fitzgerald and everyone at Carol Mann, Carrie Thornton, Jim Walsh, Amelia Zalcman, and everyone at Three Rivers Press, Brendan Mullen, Lisa Corson, Matt Ellis, the world-famous Danny Athlete, Jim Carberry, Sid Spitz, Ricki and Al Josephberg, Alan Light, Tracey Pepper, Maureen Callahan, Sia Michel, Ron Richardson and everyone at *Spin,* Kari Bauce, Jackie Pants, Johnny Lisecki, James and Camille Habacker, Ultragrrrl, Jaan Uhelszki, Charles M. Young, the Weirdos (for the title), Johanna Went, Ron Shavers, The Library, Pleasant Gehman, Jenny Lens, Cat Tyc, Paige Lipman, Jennifer Schwartz, Amra Brooks, Emma Forrest, Lisa Derrick, Legs McNeil, Susan Clary, John Roecker, "Phast Phreddle" Patterson, Steven Darrow, Jennifer Black, Omid Yaminiand, Ben Edmonds, Greg Shaw, and everyone who offered encouragement and helped us keep our shit together when it was coming apart.

Brendan Mullen would like to thank Kateri Butler, Jim Carberry, Deborah Drooz, Marc Spitz, Lisa Corson, Doug Cavanaugh, Jim Walsh at Three Rivers Press (for patience and going the extra two miles), and all those who generously contributed their time and memory or allowed us to use source material and photographs. Also shouts to Ron Stringer, Kristine McKenna, John Payne, Adam Parfrey, Kerry Colonna, Dave Alvin, Alan Rudolph, Jerry Stahl, Johanna Went, Stuart Cornfeld, Don Snowden, Europa, and others from the Mullen, Gallagher, Earley, McKeown, and Rainford clans who encouraged me to write things down.

We aren't experts. We're basically two record-collecting music geeks, born twenty years and an ocean apart. One of us was there, the other spent the '70s watching the Muppets. But we shared a common goal: to give Los Angeles punk rock the respect and consideration that it's due (even if it doesn't want it anymore). This book was a hard sell. Many editors figured they knew the full story of punk rock because they were able to name-check CBGB and Sid Vicious. This, because too many times the so-called founding punk scenes of New York and London have been autopsied, then crudely sewn and suited up for the big funeral ceremony, where everybody wants to be a pallbearer to seal their own legacy and sustain a quasi-mainstream career as a "professional punk." To let anybody else in on it, especially a surfer or a skater, would stall the gravy train. See, the aging punker's shtick is reminiscent of their pre-Elvis forefathers, old men who endlessly recounted their yarns about fighting in World War II. Once punk revisionism hit in the '90s, the post-Vietnam blank generation was eager to tell their progeny that they fought in a cultural world war whose long-term implications are still surfacing in today's mainstream. They are right. They did fight in a war . . . and the kids who can now safely stagger across the food court with their spiked hair and tattoos owe them one. But they didn't fight alone.

This book was no easy road. Most old L.A. punks have not mellowed, for good reason. They know that their relatively ignored history will remain pure until pesky pop morticians like us come around to dress up the corpse, collect our fee and our cred before targeting the next movement to plunder (hip hop? grunge?). We knew that with this project, we might pollute the whole thing. But the need to record the history of Los Angeles punk remained, if only to combat those who still deny its existence. So we opted for oral testimony: a forum that gives these fucked-up, brilliant, neglected souls a chance to get it right or wrong along with us. To expose their warts or clam up (and have them exposed by another punk). Primarily, we labored to keep the content as appropriately pure as the requisite editing for space and time allowed (call us enlightened vampires). Still, we admit that our story remains an endless work in progress. A first step toward getting the balance right. There are many bands and key figures missing (the Alley Cats, the Deadbeats, the Decadents, and Spazz Attack come to mind), and to them we offer our apology up front (send your angry e-mail to markyspin@aol.com or madscot21 @aol.com and we'll have it out and labor to include you in volume two). A definitive work is impossible. Our objective was to simply begin the process of reparation. To get people talking again. To show others what they've been missing. To put together enough to inspire a reader to do a Web search on the Screamers, or add a copy of the Germs' *GI* to their angry, nu-metal CD collection.

Did we mention this was not easy? Many original punks guarded their heirlooms, the anecdotes, the gossip, the cabalistic history, and the rare photos with shotguns full of attitude. To those, we say we understand your point of view . . . and please feel free to write your own fucking book (hard). Others were angels. Those who believed that our project was possible and necessary drank with us. Smoked with us. Supported us. Opened their scrapbooks and diaries for us, and because of them, you are reading this. Some were simply impossible to find. We knocked on strange (and wrong) doors and frightened old women. We drove to Pasadena at night with no headlights to corner Peter Case and Dave Alvin backstage at a sold-out gig. We staked out a tag sale on a Sunday morning at a notorious Hollywood drug pad in search of Rick Wilder of the Berlin Brats (later the Mau Maus) only to find it canceled for fear of hurricanes and tornadoes.

With the exception of Black Flag's Greg Ginn and the Germs' Pat Smear and Lorna Doom, who refused to cooperate with us directly, the rest, the Darby Crashes, Black Randys, Jeffrey Lee Pierces, Tomata Du Plentys, and Claude Bessys, are deceased. Really dead. We include their testimony as respectfully as we can, but realize that they do not have the privilege of hindsight or revisionism (as several of our beloved subjects attempted). Some, like Rik L. Rik and Top Jimmy, passed away shortly after giving us their final interviews, which we are proud to include.

If you're still asking, "Why this book? Why now?" read on. Many of the stories we heard and now report stand independent of our thesis. Forget it's L.A. Forget it's punk. Appreciate them because they represent the full spectrum of wild youth: from the extreme darkness of original prankster Black Randy and ultraviolent Jack Grisham of TSOL to the pop-sunshine world of the Go-Go's. If that doesn't get you either, consider this dubious endorsement from the great demented rock-and-roll carny barker–poet Kim Fowley, "If you have some good photos, you'll sell some books and everybody will jack off, and smoke a joint and shoot up and there'll be a couple of ODs. And more kids will be inspired to go onstage and be horrible. It will be wonderful and everybody will cum even more viciously." Enjoy.

Marc Spitz and Brendan Mullen
Los Angeles, California, June 2001

We got the neutron bomb

Jim Morrison sound checks at the Hollywood Bowl, July 4, 1968. Photo Credit: Kerry Colonna.

HARVEY KUBERNIK: I always thought Phil Spector was the first L.A. punk because of the rebel aspect. The attitude first and foremost. He didn't answer to anybody. It was also the clothing, the hair, the costumes, and he was a tiny little runt. He was the guy at Fairfax High that people told you, "Don't be like Phil Spector. He dresses weird. You don't wanna be some weird-assed punk like Phil." And that only attracted us young'uns more to him, especially when he showed up on the Stones' first album as a songwriter.

DENNY BRUCE: There were as many iconoclasts here during the '60s as there were in New York. The Velvet Underground weren't the only proto punks. Look at Frank Zappa, who utterly savaged flower power culture on *We're Only in It for the Money*. Look at Captain Beefheart, an untrained musician who blew free-form bass clarinet solos without even being able to play, or even more extreme . . . look at Charlie Manson, for God's sake. Not that I'm comparing Frank or Don (Van Vliet, aka Captain Beefheart) to a lunatic . . . but these were not hippie love people, nor were they cranks hammering out folk songs in the East Village about transsexuality and shooting dope.

DON WALLER: L.A. was full of punks in the '60s. The Music Machine, the Standells, Arthur Lee and Love, Black Pearl—Sky Saxon and Jim Morrison. My definition of punk rock Mach 1 is basically '60s American garage bands like the Sonics that wanna be a combination of the London bands like the Yardbirds, the Pretty Things, and the early Stones.

SKY SAXON: My band, the Seeds, was a balance between chaos and wonderland. Music was and always will be the great escape from when there is too much reality. "Pushin' Too Hard" was a battle cry for the young, that we weren't going to take it anymore.

JIM MORRISON (FIRST ELEKTRA RECORDS BIO, 1967): I am primarily an American, second, a Californian, third, a Los Angeles resident.

SKY SAXON: I loved the Doors. The Doors opened for the Seeds in the '60s. I remember Jim coming to hear the Seeds at the Bido Lito's club in '66.

JIM MORRISON (FIRST ELEKTRA BIO): I've always been attracted to ideas that were about revolt against authority. I like ideas about the breaking away or overthrowing of established order. I am interested in anything about revolt, disorder, chaos—especially activity that seems to have no meaning.

DANNY SUGERMAN: Most people associate punk with mindless mayhem, but Jim was a true original artist who refused to compromise for anyone for any reason. It was that attitude that made him a punk, because supposedly he didn't know what was good for him. Not listening to good advice has always been a characteristic of a punk, I'd say.

HARVEY KUBERNIK: Morrison was obviously much more rebellious and outrageous and more chemically induced and alcohol driven than Spector was. There was Jim the poet and artist and then there was li'l ol' Jimbo . . . and ol' Jimbo drank way too much. I thought it was extremely rebellious during Doors concerts to tell everybody to shut up or to scream "Fuck you!" from the stage . . . even to ask "Anybody got a cigarette?" And somebody would come up to the stage and give him one. I always saw that as a major rebellious thing, the leering drunken swagger, the sheer whimsical insolence of asking for a cigarette from a seated audience while they're yelling for "Light My Fire."

DANNY SUGERMAN: Jim certainly was the first rock singer to front off an audience, to tell them to go get fucked . . . that's what happened at Cobo Hall when Iggy saw Jim for the first time and decided to be a singer instead of a drummer. He loved what he saw Morrison doing, flipping the audience the finger for screaming out "Light My Fire" while the band was going off into "Celebration of the Lizard" instead.

RAY MANZAREK: Iggy Pop, whom many consider the godfather of punk, loved the Doors, especially Morrison. When Iggy was still Jim Osterberg he checked us out when we played at the University of Michigan. We didn't know till we got there that it was homecoming weekend. We thought, "This is entirely wrong, this is going to be such a disaster." The audience was thick-necked young men in tuxedos with their girls in ball gowns. We're playing in their gymnasium and Morrison is drunk as a skunk, knowing full well what we had gotten ourselves into, and he was just gonna obliterate himself. We played the worst fucking show ever. John and Robbie were so fed up. Finally John tossed his sticks into the audience and walked offstage. We tried to do a simple blues, but Jim was all over the place. Then Robbie left the stage, too. All they wanted to hear was "Light My Fire," but Jim kept on hollering freeform, so I picked up the guitar and played a slow blues and the audience started booing. He was shouting, "Hey, this is what we play, man. This is the fucking blues. Keep on, Ray. Hey, fuck you! Fuck you!" Huge refrigerator-sized football players began lunging toward us. Then the dean came out and said, "That's it, that's it . . . show's over. Would you boys leave the stage? Just leave the stage." And Morrison's screaming, "Fuck, we don't wanna leave the stage. You people wanna hear more music, dontcha?" And they're going, "Boo! Boo!" We got paid and got out of there by the skin of our teeth before they pulverized us. Afterward Iggy said: "Holy fuck, true anarchy prevailed. You guys were great. I loved it." Who knows what that night did to Iggy Pop's head, 'cause he's been doing that show ever since. Soon the Stooges were brought to Elektra, the Doors' label, with the thinking: "The Doors are a band with a wild-man singer that has pop hits, let's get another hit with these guys."

RON ASHETON: Iggy watched Morrison and learned how to use and abuse the audience and get them into the act. Morrison wore a pair of brown leather pants, so Iggy had a pair of brown vinyl pants made 'cause he couldn't quite afford the leather, you know.

DANNY SUGERMAN: Morrison had no interest in the Stooges. They were playing the Whisky and I wanted him to take me to see them, but he said: "No, Bo Diddley's going to be there next month, I'll take you to see him instead."

JOHN DOE: Jim Morrison had to be one of the first punks because he was just as shit-faced as the rest of us and alcohol has a way of loosening your tongue—and the same thing about demons, having all these personal problems and working them out. I was attracted to the Doors as a teen because of the dark imagery.

EXENE CERVENKA: I liked the Doors' version of the ocean, which was dark and scary. It wasn't the sunny beach that the other people liked, especially those who liked roller skating.

JIM MORRISON (FIRST ELEKTRA BIO): We are from the West/The whole thing is like an invitation to the West. The world we suggest is of a new wild west. A sensuous evil world.

DANNY SUGERMAN: The Velvet Underground get more credit than the Doors for dark and somber themes. The Doors' being from the Sunshine State didn't help, but certainly songs like "End of the Night," "You're Lost Little Girl," and "The End," are as dark and foreboding as anything the Velvets did. I'm a fan of both bands, but the darkness seemed to be the Velvets' entire raison d'être. New York street poets writing about the dark side of life, whereas the Doors did that, too, but they had a greater, wider range, emotionally and musically.

Lou was more street than Jim. Jim never sang about putting a spike into his vein but he did sing "Father, I want to kill you." I'd say the Velvets had the street sewn up but the Doors have forever staked out the domain around the abyss.

DON WALLER: It's pretty hard to top the Velvets' "Heroin"—although the Doors' "The End" comes close. I think the Doors don't get some of the credit for being a voice of darkness in a world of flower power that the Velvets do because the Doors sold a lot more records and the Velvets came from New York. New York is a parochial town run by a publishing media that likes to think it invented everything.

SKY SAXON: L.A. was very groovy in the '60s. I believed that flower power was the way, although the record industry completely destroyed the message of love and peace. The '70s should have been a rebirth of spirit for all; instead there was a war.

RAY MANZAREK: At some point white men took over, the impulse to whiteness took over in L.A. Black jazz and black soul were taken out of rock music. It went country, a shift in radio programming which represented the triumph of country music over psychedelic hippie rock. The country rock of Linda Ronstadt, Jackson Browne, and the Eagles reigned supreme. It was nice enough radio music, nice tunesmithing and all that, but the whole country rock period was all a little too mellow for me. No runaway passion. No Dionysian impulse. If the Doors had still been active, would the country rock stuff have happened? Depends on who you talk to. There's always something to fill a vacuum; usually it's the lowest common denominator.

HARVEY KUBERNIK: By '71, the Elektra/Asylum Records singer song-writer type music was all that this town was offering. They were social climbers, very locked into the traditional Brill Building verse/chorus/verse style. They wore flannel shirts, long hair, beards. When Morrison died, I said to Manzarek, 'Well, maybe Jim wasn't supposed to see all this singer-songwriter shit take over his label.'

chapter 1

Captain Zory Zenith of Zolar X says; "This is the Zorian Zorman mediator, Model 11-000, at your service." Photo Credit: Mark Sullivan

GREG SHAW: The lull in pop culture in 1970–71 was maddening. The decline in radio play from the likes of the Yardbirds to someone like Gordon Lightfoot was ghastly, and it drove me and a lot of my friends into oldies. I started listening to practically nothing but rockabilly, doo-wop, old country, bluegrass, and jazz. There was no college radio, no fanzines, no indie record labels, and no local bands, for the most part. There was nothing! It was very depressing. There were few if any local bands. Nothing amounting to a scene. There was Christopher Milk. And Sparks.

HEATHER HARRIS: Doug Weston banned Christopher Milk for life in 1970 after lead singer Mr. Twister [aka Kurt Ingham] wreaked havoc during the Troubadour's Monday "Hoot Night." Kurt wrecked a bunch of microphones and was pouring hot wax all over himself and running out into the audience and biting people . . . . he was overturning tables and spilling drinks into customers' laps . . . before Iggy Pop ever got to L.A. , and don't forget . . . this was right at the beginning of the mellow solo singer-songwriter era . . . the audience gawked in horror.

HARVEY KUBERNIK: If that wasn't punk rock personified, who or what was?

KURT INGHAM: Christopher Milk stood for theater and drama as opposed to droning introspection, and sure enough, our hideous platform boots and make-up clashed with denim and fringe buckskin jackets. We were 86'd from the Troub for life.

RUSSELL MAEL: Sparks was not involved in any particular music scene in L.A. pre-glam since we were living in England through the early '70s and saw it all from a more British perspective. We felt alienated from L.A. since what we were doing had more in common with what was going on in Europe. Most people assumed that Sparks was from some unspecified European nation. We got no local support at first. We'd play the Whisky for the four waitresses who worked there. We didn't recognize the apparently extreme nature of our band's music at the time. We thought we were kind of like the Rolling Stones live, but I think we missed the mark in that respect and didn't know how pretty quirky and offbeat we really were for a pop band. Listen to *A Woofer in Tweeter's Clothing* today and imagine what the audience would think if you were playing those songs on the same bill as Little Feat!

ZORY ZENITH: Shady Lady was the beginning of the L.A. underground—well, not the beginning, but the beginning of the glam part of it. I was like this 19-year-old Keith Moon prodigy drummer, the first to play clear plastic drums, and I'd just answered a musician wanted ad and found these very weird guys who lived about a half a block from me. They had super long scraggly Alice Cooper–Rod Stewart cropped hair and they were wearing skintight satin pants with snakeskin boots. I thought, "Wow, this is pretty cool." I thought they might have been from England or something, so we started rehearsing. After we signed with Robert Fitzpatrick we lived all over the fuckin' hills. We got signed by

Sceptre Records, but Sceptre didn't come through on their part of the deal. We rented three or four houses during a coupla years that Shady Lady was happening. There were lots of parties there. That's when I first met Rodney. Shady Lady ended because John Christian, our guitar player, was on too many drugs, but by that time I'd already met Zany and Y-Garr and we got the Zolar-X concept up and running.

GREG SHAW: Rodney Bingenheimer was practically the first person I met when I arrived in L.A. He was enthusiastic, friendly, full of news and gossip, and he knew everybody. He also had very good taste; the bands he liked tended to be the best ones. Though inarticulate and not well educated, Rodney is in fact a lot sharper than he gets credit for.

HARVEY KUBERNIK: My mother worked for Raybert Productions, which did the Monkees. I met Rodney Bingenheimer at the Monkees' press conference when they made their world debut in '66. He was short, with a bowl cut like Davy Jones—in fact he was once a stand-in for Davy Jones. At the time he had a column for *Go* magazine, but he couldn't type. To this day he doesn't type. We've all had stints being Rodney's typist.

RODNEY BINGENHEIMER: Before *Go* magazine, I had a column in *What's Happening* magazine, called "It's All Happening." I always used those phrases: "What's happening?" "It's all happening!" I had another column called "If It's Trendy, I'll Print It." When I wrote the *Go* column, I couldn't type, so Edie Sedgwick did it for me. She was working at Charlie Green and Brian Stone's office. They managed Sonny and Cher and Iron Butterfly and Buffalo Springfield.

PAMELA DES BARRES: Rodney Bingenheimer was my peer. He was one of the first guys I met when I hitchhiked over the hill to Hollywood in 1966. And he hit on me, of course, but we actually wound up just being friends. He helped me out of my Valley-ness. Took me all over the place and introduced me to every-one. There was certainly no one like him at Cleveland High in Reseda.

HARVEY KUBERNIK: A guy named Al Hernandez had the first copy of *Space Oddity* on the West Coast. And believe me, you went to somebody's house if they had that album.

RODNEY BINGENHEIMER: Al Hernandez was totally into Bowie real early and had turned me on to the *Space Oddity* record. He had pictures of Bowie all over the walls of his house. He was probably already the biggest Bowie fan in the U.S. at the time.

PAMELA DES BARRES: Rodney got into Bowie very early, before almost anybody else in this country.

ANGELA BOWIE: The first time David met Rodney was on his radio tour of the U.S.—pre–*Ziggy Stardust*—the first tour when he just took his acoustic guitars and entertained key people as a solo folk singer in a dress and sang songs from *Space Oddity* and *The Man Who Sold the World*.

RODNEY BINGENHEIMER: In 1971 I was working FM promotion at Mercury Records doing stuff for Uriah Heep, Rod Stewart, and the Sir Douglas Quintet. *The Man Who Sold the World* was out, and so Bowie came over here to promote it. He was unknown. He had very long hair and he was wearing a dress.

RICHARD CROMELIN: I interviewed Bowie on *The Man Who Sold the World* promotional tour. I think the piece ran in the *L.A. Free Press.* There was no doubt in my mind that it was just a matter of time before he'd be recognized as a major rock artist. Bowie was extremely charismatic, and musically I thought it was a strong album.

DAVID BOWIE: Alone in L.A., Rodney seemed like myself, an island of Anglo "nowness." He even knew British singles and bands that I wasn't aware of. Rodney single-handedly cut a path through the treacle of the 1960s, allowing all us "avants" to parade the sounds of tomorrow dressed in our clothes of derision.

RODNEY BINGENHEIMER: When I took David around to radio stations, they were put off. These stations in Santa Ana and Long Beach didn't know what to make of this British guy in a dress.

MICHAEL DES BARRES: Nobody had seen that shit before . . . boys dressed as girls. It really was absolutely shocking.

HARVEY KUBERNIK: Everybody had a beard and they gave Rodney and Bowie shit. Bowie showed up in a dress, and in a Nixon world that didn't go down very well. It was analagous to the way some people react to gangsta rap today. U.K. glitter rock hits like T. Rex's "Hot Love" weren't gonna get heavy rotation next to "Suite Judy Blue Eyes" by Crosby Stills and Nash on this station's playlist. After a few awkwardly polite handshakes, Bowie and Rodney were aggressively vibed out of the building.

LISA FANCHER: Bowie and Marc Bolan had it easy. Jobriath was the real thing. He really was gay. He wasn't just wearing the clothes. When English glam started gathering steam, Elektra Records signed him for around $300,000, which was a lot of money in those days. Jobriath had some kind of career in New York, but he started out in Los Angeles. He was a fabulous dancer and singer who wrote his own material. He was going to be the next big thing. The American Bowie.

HARVEY KUBERNIK: Jobriath was supposed to be the rock and roll Judy Garland. I saw Judy Garland with my mother when I was a teenager. Jobriath was no Judy Garland.

ZORY ZENITH: Elektra Records signed this new artist who was pretty much on the same wavelength as my band Zolar-X were. He snatched a lot of stuff from Bowie, but he was an incredible classical piano player and a decent singer and his whole on-stage thing was a pink skin-tight suit with a bubble helmet and Zolar-X eyebrows like Spock. He had a pompadour thing and makeup and he came out with a clear plastic bubble on his head and then he'd pull a pin out of the top and the thing would fall apart and rose petals came out. It was very bizarre. Musically we were in awe of Jobriath. We did a two-week run at the Troubadour with Zolar-X and him. About the second or third night into it I stopped by his dressing room and he was wearing this black tuxedo-cut satin suit and a red shirt. I said, "Jo, where's your suit?" and he said, "I just really want to concentrate on the album and the music right now, and we're sounding good, and you guys have the space thing wrapped up and it's ridiculous for us both to do that."

LISA FANCHER: There was this unbelievable hype around him. He was on the sides of buses, full-page ads in *Rolling Stone*. But he was just so flamboyantly gay, and rock fans just weren't really digging it, so Jobriath was just wiped off the face of the earth. He was just stunned and depressed to be rejected like that. He died of AIDS in 1983.

KIM FOWLEY: England dictated glam rock. England invented glam rock. If you weren't English, you were dog shit.

RODNEY BINGENHEIMER: In America it was called glitter rock. It wasn't "glam."

HARVEY KUBERNIK: Rodney had the records that you would read about in *Melody Maker*. He had stacks of the stuff. He'd play this music and you'd wonder, "Who is this Eno guy? Who's this Bryan Ferry guy?"

RODNEY BINGENHEIMER: After Bowie left L.A., I went to London to meet this girl named Melanie McDonald who was gonna be my girlfriend. By now David was recording the *Hunky Dory* album, so we'd hang out. We went to see the Warhol play *Pork*. During the sessions my girlfriend got chummy with David's manager Tony DeFries and they ended up going off and getting married! During that same trip I stayed in Ealing and there was a little club there called the Cellar. It was like a pub with lots of teens. You could legally drink at eighteen in England. Downstairs there was amazing music: T. Rex, Slade, and the Sweet. I told Bowie about it, and he said, "You should open a place like that in L.A." And I said, "That's a good idea," so I bought up a lot of the 45's. When I came back to L.A., I was staying at Tom Ayres' house and we'd go driving around late at night in Hollywood and I'd tell him these fantastic stories about Bowie and London. And Tom said, "We should open up a club."

TOM AYRES: Rodney and I opened our first club in Hollywood in a building that had formerly been a peep show. It was October of '72 and we called it the E Club. Bowie was one of our first customers.

RODNEY BINGENHEIMER: *E* stood for *English*, I guess.

PAMELA DES BARRES: At Rodney's E Club patrons could hear the latest glam pop sounds from England and catch a glimpse of real-life rock stars. Rodney had found his niche. It was like being in a small English pub, masked by mirrors and Hollywood artifice.

TERRY ATKINSON: I was DJ'ing the night Bowie first came by the E Club. I knew he liked Elvis, so I put on the King doing "If you're looking for trouble, you're in the right place . . ." and the dance floor emptied. All of a sudden Bowie jumped up and did this incredible dance—striking all these poses alone on the dance floor, watching his reflection in the mirrors on the back wall. If they'd had a name for what he was doing back then it would have been voguing. The crowd was blown away.

TOM AYRES: Later Bowie took me and Rodney into the men's room and said "You guys have done so much for me, what can I do for you?" Rodney pulls out this piece of paper and says "Be a member of the board of this club." While he was standing at the urinal taking a piss, Bowie signed it. Then he told us to put lots more mirrors around the dance floor. Things went real well at the E Club those first couple of months—except for one thing—the owner failed to come up with any money for us. So one night I said to Rodney "Let's get out!"

RODNEY BINGENHEIMER: We did the E Club for a few months and then Barry Barnholtz said, "Why don't you do your own club?" And that's when we moved it. The E Club was a lot smaller. We had lines. People couldn't get in. Bowie came, Roxy Music came by. These amazing girls like Lori Lightning and Sabel Star made the scene.

BARRY BARNHOLTZ: Rodney's vision foresaw this entire new wave of music that was picking up on and continuing that Anglophilic direction which had begun here in the '60s with the first British Invasion groups. Music had been a big part of my past. I had been involved in promoting concerts and bands at frat parties out in Victorville and Barstow. Now I saw an opportunity to get together with Rodney to open a club. I formed a business partnership with Rodney as the front man and Tom Ayres, the record producer, to help oversee the day-to-day operation of this new club, which I would finance. The new place would pick up where the E Club left off. We found the real estate together.

TOM AYRES: We were driving down Sunset Boulevard and we passed this club called the Ooh Poo Pah Doo, which was kind of down on its luck. So on December 15, Rodney's birthday, we turned it into the English Disco and quite early on all the kids started dressing up and coming in.

BARRY BARNHOLTZ: I was gun-shy about putting in a lot of dough, so we looked for a small place because we thought if you take a hundred people and put them in a place the size of the Whisky, it would be like, "Yeah, the place is nice, but nobody's there." But if you take eight people and shove them in a closet and turn the sound system up, it's like, "Wow, the place is jammin'." We hoped to be able to turn the crowd over two or three times a night. The legal occupancy was only 135 or something. The rent was minimal, like $225 or $325 a month. I was mainly the business end and I put up the cash for the lease and got the permits, the licenses, and the other paperwork stuff together. It was beer and wine only. It was very expensive to get a full liquor license, and we reckoned that if it was just beer and wine, different city agencies might not be so concerned about people being over twenty-one. We sold British-style steak-and-kidney pies because serving food allowed us to bring people in under twenty-one.

TOM AYRES: We had turkey, meat pies, bowls of potato salad, all you wanted for a dollar. It was like a soup line, except the faces went on to become famous people.

KRISTIAN HOFFMAN: Above the DJ booth there was a sign that said RODNEY BINGENHEIMER'S—in glitter, of course—and over the bar was the most prized possession in the club—a copy of *The Man Who Sold the World,* the original cover with Bowie wearing a dress. Everyone used to try to figure out ways to steal it.

CHUCK E. STARR: Architecturally, Rodney's English Disco was just an empty store with a bar. Oh, but it was the most beautiful bar you've ever seen, this hand-carved wooden bar from some old tavern overseas. It had beveled glass mirrors in it. The backdrop was all the same wood. I'm sure it was older than the whole building. The rest of the joint was el tack: red indoor-outdoor carpeting and a bunch of folding chairs up against the wall. The mirrors were at the back of the club on the dance floor, the same mirrors from the E Club. The DJ booth also had mirrors on it.

BARRY BARNHOLTZ: The opening night of the English Disco was planned around the Rolling Stones playing the Forum. We made up flyers that said, "After the concert the Stones will be partying at our new nightclub on Sunset." We got a limo and parked it in front of the club after the concert to create the perception that the Stones were inside! Sure enough, after the concert a line of Stones fans started in front of the club and went down a block or so and then up three more blocks around the corner.

RODNEY BINGENHEIMER: Opening night was so packed that we kept running out of beer and we'd have to run to the liquor store to buy six-packs.

BARRY BARNHOLTZ: The perception was that Bowie was a partner or some kind of investor in the English Disco too, but Bowie never put in any of the money and we never signed any legally binding documents showing any proprietary involvement, although we did have one of his gold records behind the bar and a framed picture showing him reclining on a sofa in a dress . . . and his music was heard there all the time.

LORI LIGHTNING: I was twelve and a half when I started going to Rodney's. The first time, David Bowie said, "Lori, come with us." I was terrified. I was still a virgin.

RODNEY BINGENHEIMER: There was a strict door policy: girls a dollar, guys two dollars.

STEVE PRIEST: The groupies were pretty obvious. They were just underage girls who wore red sequins and that's about all. And they weren't timid. They all acted like Mae West.

MICHAEL DES BARRES: Sixties groupies like the GTOs were these flowery girls, whereas Sabel and Lori were that much more sophisticated, as evolution would dictate. Sabel was a true rock-and-roll girl: fearless, sexy, and ready for anything, not in a crude beans-in-the-bath-with-the-shark way. I found them incredibly inspiring. They were as inspirational to me as Chuck Berry 'cause they loved the scene and they nurtured it and they believed in it and they made you believe in it more. Those girls created the ambience in which the lifestyle could be lived and the songs could be written and the music could be recorded . . . it was one fantastic sort of orgasmic organism.

AMY FREEMAN: My friends and I were wannabe groupies. Back then, we thought that the older musicians just liked to have us around. Today we'd probably look at them as potential child molesters and perverts.

ANGELA BOWIE: Rodney liked young girls, and his club was full of them. Visiting rock stars off the leash from their wives in England would go to the English Disco to look for young girls under the auspices of arranging record promotion with Rodney. The club was Rodney's storefront, where he did his business. Knowing Rodney or being prepared to interact with Rodney was a prerequisite to going to Rodney's English Disco.

KID CONGO POWERS: How come they let so many underage young people into the English Disco, I was always wondering. Very young girls and young boys. You know the movie *Almost Famous*, where there were all the young girls running around? Well, at Rodney's there were also little boys running around. I was one of those young glitter kids scurrying around like that.

RODNEY BINGENHEIMER: Soon celebrities like Led Zeppelin, Shaun Cassidy, Keith Moon, and Linda Blair came. We had wild record release parties for Bolan, Slade, Suzi Quatro. There was a VIP booth. Jobriath would be up there with Michael des Barres and Silverhead and all the people down below could watch you.

MICHAEL DES BARRES: When my band Silverhead came to Los Angeles in 1972, we were met by the legendary and messianic Rodney Bingenheimer, who actually arrived at the airport clutching our album. So we thought we were Elvis, really. We thought we had conquered America already. Rodney made us feel like we had, and that was the important thing. The club was twenty feet by thirty feet, and fifteen feet of that was the VIP booth. It was this absurd ratio of the entire Led Zeppelin band's table and Pamela and me and then two hundred groupies compressed into five feet.

TOBY MAMIS: The revelry was nightly. Rodney's was an epicenter. From the rock stars and would-be rock stars to the industry-ites to the teen girls and boys, it was the place to see and be seen. It was much more exciting to me than the Max's scene in New York I had come out of.

MICHAEL DES BARRES: Los Angeles was the Babylon that we were looking for. We were looking for the playground, and it was here. There's a simple reason for that—the weather. You can't have a girl running around with two sequins on her tits and a Silverhead sticker on her pussy in twenty-below London! The other reason is this is the place of Errol Flynn's ghost, the collective consciousness of Irving Thalberg, Clara Bow, and Errol Flynn . . . it's here, in the bricks and the mortar and the concrete. Hollywood's been the birth of fantasy, man, since 1914. It's in the fucking air. It's the mecca, the holy grail for beauty. It's the magnet that attracts the cheekbones and great asses, and you put all that together with three chords and some pancake and you rock the fuck out, know what I mean?

LORI LIGHTNING: In the back of the VIP booth at Rodney's there was this big poster of Mick Jagger . . .

AMY FREEMAN: . . . with lots of red lipstick marks—Mary Quant Black Cherry, that was what we wore to Rodney's—all around Mick's crotch.

HARVEY KUBERNIK: The groupies even had their own magazine. *Star* magazine. It didn't have a long run, but girls were so enthralled to get into the magazine, they all so badly wanted to be *Star* girls of the month, that they'd show up at Rodney's with their own eight-by-tens.

SYLVAIN SYLVAIN: There were two magazines. On the East Coast we used to get *Rock Scene*, and on the West Coast there was *Star* magazine, which used to feature all the Hollywood starlets. Me and Johnny Thunders used to get import copies of *Star* and there'd be pictures of Sabel Star in it, and he'd say, "Wow, this girl Sabel, I love her. When I go out to L.A. she'll be my girlfriend."

RODNEY BINGENHEIMER: Tom Snyder did a *Tomorrow* show on the club. He interviewed me and Chuck E. and Zolar X. The show was all about the Strip and glitter rock.

BARRY BARNHOLTZ: We were in *Newsweek* twice in one month, and we made a centerfold in *People*. These national publications weren't writing about any other clubs in the U.S. until Studio 54, which came at a much later date.

CHUCK E. STARR: One night Rod Stewart came in and Bianca Jagger. Bianca was wearing a three-thousand-dollar ensemble and the toilets were overflowing, running out onto the dance floor, and she was trying to step over stools to get through to the bathroom. It was wonderful. I was there when Elvis was there, Bowie, and Mick Jagger . . . all at different times, of course. You had to make a name for yourself in that environment, honey, so I became Chuck E. Starr, legend. I added another *r*. I didn't want to be mixed up with Sabel.

ANGELA BOWIE: The L.A. groupies greeted me, and we had a dance and a good laugh. The scene was like L.A. is now. Lots of girls holding on to each other and plenty of public French kissing.

RICK WILDER: Rodney's was a drunken cuss-and-fuss place, and the big thing was peacocking and dancing with yourself in front of these stupid mirrors . . . you'd wind up doing crazy drugs and getting into pointless fights with people. One time Chuckie whatever-his-name-was got mad at me for something, I had worn the same platforms as him or something, and we got in some dumb fight, and I put his head through one of those mirrors.

RODNEY BINGENHEIMER: We rarely had live bands. On special occasions we'd have Zolar X, who dressed in space suits and played original songs about life in outer space. They'd go everywhere dressed like that. They'd go to Ralph's Supermarket dressed up like that.

ZORY ZENITH: We were cruising the parking lots and back alleys of the movie studios and major department stores and you'd be surprised what you'd find on the loading docks. I can't imagine what I spent in just those few years on silver aluminum spray paint. When we put that shit up at Rodney's it was fuckin' glowing!

JACKIE FOX: Zolar X had prosthetic ears and heads . . . but I couldn't name a single one of their songs.

ANDY SEVEN: They were terrible . . . the guitar was constantly going into an Echoplex.

ZORY ZENITH: Since Zolar-X was so loud and the clubs of the time didn't have onstage monitor systems we couldn't hear ourselves when we played. Everyone thought it was weird that we decorated the mike stands with acrylics and plastics and we were wearing antennae and all that space stuff. I also hooked a wire around my head, attached to this clear plastic tube. I took the tip end off of a transistor radio earplug and put it into the tube and stuck a wire through it and sent it around to my mouth so that no matter where I moved on stage, however loud it was, I had my voice coming directly into my right ear like a homemade monitor. This setup became my costume trademark. Now all the stadium acts use high-tech headsets.

RODNEY BINGENHEIMER: The first real L.A. homegrown glam rock band were the Berlin Brats. They were great.

RICK WILDER: The Berlin Brats were me and Matt Campbell. We started in like '72 in the bedroom of my mom's house . . . that's where Rodney discovered us. He walked up to my bedroom and saw us drinking Rainier Ale, and we told him we got it at the Lido liquor store, where if you were tall enough to reach the counter, they'd sell it to you.

ROBERT LOPEZ: The Berlin Brats were New York Dolls–esque. They were trashy like the Dolls but not as shiny. They didn't wear women's clothes, but to us they were the bridge from glam to punk . . . the in-between.

RODNEY BINGENHEIMER: The Brats were accused of being a New York Dolls rip-off, but they were totally original. Nobody looked like Rick Wilder, the lead singer. He was way over six feet tall, and he wore platforms on top of that. And he was the skinniest person you'd ever seen in your life. And they had great songs like "Tropically Hot."

RICK WILDER: The Dolls weren't a factor in the Brats forming at all, but we did have a lot of the same influences, which made it seem that way—early R&B Stones, the Standells and other '60s garage bands, weird Chuck Berry B-sides, and Blind Lemon Jefferson. It was two different coasts. Sure, I loved the Dolls and what Johnny Thunders was doing, but look, I had a guitar player, Matt Campbell, who at fourteen was as good as Johnny's big idol, Keith Richards.

ANDY SEVEN: The Berlin Brats were great. They had that whole raw early Stones R&B thing going on, but Rick Wilder looked more like Peter Wolf than Mick Jagger, and the band were actually pretty decent musicians.

HARVEY KUBERNIK: The one thing the New York Dolls and the Berlin Brats had in common, besides heroin, was that they were glam but not at all femme. They were hardly pretty like David Bowie or Marc Bolan. And they didn't experiment with bisexuality. It was girls, girls, girls, all the way.

MICHAEL DES BARRES: Androgyny didn't necessarily mean that you sucked cocks if you were a guy.

SKOT ARMSTRONG: By the mid-'70s Hollywood was decadence-drunk, and the scene was wide open for clever street-level situationists to gain entry and turn freeloading and nose-thumbing into art. Enter Les Petites Bon-Bons led by Jerry Dreva and Bobby Lambert, former art students, guys who were as much energized by the post-Warhol Pop aesthetic, the Stonewall riots of '69, and CORE, the Congress of Racial Equality, as they were by catty English rock disco gossip.

HARVEY KUBERNIK: The Bon-Bons actualized the new music, this glitter dance pop, if you will. They were the antithesis of the Laurel Canyon buckskin-jacket country rock people. They were into clothing, they were into art, they were into makeup and drag, they were into the cutup method . . . they were scene makers and tastemakers who happened to dress outrageously with shaved heads, jewelry, dresses, boas, stuff you just didn't see.

RICHARD CROMELIN: There was a party at Peter Lawford's mansion on the beach in Malibu after an Eagles concert at Santa Monica Civic. Jerry, Bobby, and I were leaving and we were walking back down PCH [the Pacific Coast Highway] toward Bobby's car when these three dudes asked us, "You got any cocaine?" And suddenly they were running after us. There was fisticuffs, but we escaped with our skins.

HARVEY KUBERNIK: The party scene was a buncha newly moneyed, womanizing cowboys hassling cross-dressed glitter street trash. There weren't gonna be any faggy freaks looking like Divine at their big New West rock-and-roll party. They couldn't stand the idea of a guy in makeup or even wearing a velvet jacket. I remember them calling Rodney and his constituency "pussies."

RICHARD CROMELIN: Glam filled the role as an alternative to your more proper and corporate kind of music. It was renegade, it was dangerous, it was fun, exciting . . . glamorous. A lot of things that the mainstream had stopped being.

HARVEY KUBERNIK: Here were these people that were threatened by clothing, by Rodney and his friends or even chicks with cool minidresses? Most of them seemed to come out of the bar scene at the Troubadour and they liked those earth-mama girls. Those Laurel Canyon chicks in Levi's overalls. They couldn't understand self-expression of women then, women who were looking to be with the band or just dug the music and liked to dance to Slade. The poor glitter critters would be mocked constantly, and more than one of them got beaten up. These "L.A. Sound" clowns were so used to being cock of the walk. I've got nothing but animosity toward those people.

RICHARD CROMELIN: My interpretation of Les Petites Bon-Bons was "Everybody is a star." It was all about being flamboyant and cultivating a fascination with fame, no matter how minute, no matter how fleeting or tenuous the connection. Warhol was an obvious strong influence in that regard, and Jerry Dreva frequently cited Warhol. Les Bon Bons worked their way onto every guest list there was. Just being on the scene was part of their aesthetic. They wanted to be part of the social landscape. It was sort of male-groupie-ish, but at the same time serious artists who met Jerry were always taken by him, especially Bowie. Jerry was no dumb ornamental diva queen—he could converse with the best of them on politics, art, and culture. He had a brilliant mind.

GENESIS P. ORRIDGE: Jerry Dreva and the other Bon-Bons people gave Bowie a whole lot of extra credibility through the L.A. gay underground and the mail arts scene and helped him cross over into an audience he might have taken longer to access. In England he had Lindsay Kemp and everyone behind him before he took to working Warhol and the Factory scene in New York and Rodney Bingenheimer out west.

BOBBY LAMBERT: Huge promo parties were being thrown all the time by major record companies, and they were always pretty easy to crash. Catered banquets and open-hosted bars made it possible to subsist on one meal a day. We routinely infiltrated any party for any band. Even funky old rural hard rockers Black Oak Arkansas weren't beneath us!

HARVEY KUBERNIK: Rodney and I lived on press parties four times a week. "There's a steak dinner at the Black Oak Arkansas party!" I felt bad I usually didn't like the guy's music, but there was always great rib eye steak!

chapter **2**

Iggy (*left*) with Michael Des Barres, crica 1974. Photo Credit: Mark Sullivan.

MICHAEL DES BARRES: As far as decadence goes, the Continental Hyatt House on the Sunset Strip, better known as the Riot House, was the court absolute of this Babylonian kingdom.

RON ASHETON: Los Angeles was the glam capital of America, not New York, so of course the Stooges relocated to L.A. right after we recorded the *Raw Power* record in London. MainMan, Bowie's management company, opened their West Coast offices in this big house on Mulholland Drive. Iggy and our guitar player, James Williamson, lived there. I stayed at the Hyatt House on Sunset Strip, where I was able to enjoy the perks of living there for a while . . . signing for everything and getting to know all the house detectives and the vice cops and the prostitutes who'd hang in the bar every night. There were all these high rollers that seemed to live there all year round, like this guy Mr. Thompson, who was some big wheeler-dealer in God knows what. I'd slide into the bar at the Hyatt and sit right next to a hooker on one side and a vice cop on the other and Mr. Thompson'd be across the way yelling, "Have drinks on me!" and he'd buy the whole bar a drink. It was a great time . . . until MainMan dropped us, and then it all went to hell, everything turned into a bad nightmare.

DANNY SUGERMAN: Iggy's career was still washed up despite the energy and goodwill of the glitter rock scene in L.A. *Raw Power* looked glam, but it didn't sound "glam." Sales bombed badly. It wasn't Sweet or Suzi Quatro. Rodney didn't play it very much at all. But people knew Iggy had worked with Bowie and that carried a lot of legitimacy, so he was able to depend on the generosity of strangers quite a bit. Iggy had no money. He was set on self-destruct. There was nothing happening to give him any hope. He took drugs to numb himself to the reality.

HARVEY KUBERNIK: The Dolls realized they could get better gigs out here. In New York, they were playing art galleries. Then they came out to stay at the Riot House and play a couple of shows at the Whisky. They were downtown-New-York, swaggering, looking-for-a-party types, but I don't know if they bargained for the level of decadence going on here. At the time they loved it, though. They were not anti-L.A. at all, like the Velvets were. I do remember David Johansen was mad he couldn't find hand-cut pastrami in L.A. He was like, "Where's Nathan's?" I said, "There's one in the Valley." We had to do a hot dog run to Nathan's with him. I'd never seen anybody put sauerkraut on a hot dog. I was like, "Wait a minute, you eat this at ten in the morning?" He said, "Oh yeah. Anytime." He was always going, "Where's the vendor carts?" I never knew you could get a hot dog on the street.

SABEL STAR: [When the Dolls came to town to play the Whisky] we got them all something. Syl got some crotchless underwear, David [Johansen] this cocksucker thing, and I got Johnny some silver Fredrick's of Hollywood underwear, which was my favorite. I gave Johnny his present and he goes, "Why don't you come upstairs with me?" It was so weird because I knew he was going to be mine. For a week, we never left that room.

SYLVAIN SYLVAIN: Johnny and Sabel went into the hotel bedroom. She gives him a blow job and that's it, they were married in the eyes of God. He was hers and she was his.

SABEL STAR: Johnny was so sweet and innocent and so cute. That first week was magical. I just fell in love with him. During the day, we'd hang around Hollywood Boulevard, we went to all the shops and we got our picture taken in a little photo booth, it was so much fun. Johnny and I just went off on our own, then there'd be the gigs at night. I thought I'd died and gone to heaven.

LEEE "BLACK" CHILDERS: Iggy set out to turn people onto heroin. I don't know for sure what his reasons were, but I lived with him for eight or nine months and I watched him do it. We had this really nice big house in the Hollywood Hills, he was with Corel then, and he'd invite people up to the house. It gave him something in his head, it was like sex, I guess, he'd tie them off and shoot 'em up, watch the blood bloom in the syringe. Watch them have their first high, and that's what he got off on.

SYLVAIN SYLVAIN: Johnny was a big Iggy fan and the four of them were always together, and one thing led to another. Johnny's the kind of guy you turn him onto one joint and the next day he's got a whole pound. So they'd fix together and that's when that started. Johnny began using. Not regularly at first, just a little bit here and a little bit there. It turned out to be the worst thing you could ever introduce Johnny to, with all his problems, all the sexual confusion. "Am I a boy or a girl?" Heroin was perfect 'cause it puts you at rest with all that.

LEEE BLACK CHILDERS: There was this groupie [at the Hyatt House where the Dolls were staying] who was being really pushy and annoying. Apparently she was behaving really badly so they put her in a chair naked. Then they wrapped her in tape, taped her to the chair so she couldn't get out, then they covered her naked body with slices of baloney. They carried the whole taped package out, put it in the elevator, and punched for the lobby. The doors closed and down she went. The doors opened in the lobby and there was a naked girl covered in baloney.

MICHAEL DES BARRES: Abusing groupies and the room service guy was not my thing. Unfortunately for some bands, the rock-and-roll wild nights at the Hyatt consisted of beating and sodomizing some poor infatuated midteen girl with an absent father complex or throwing the room service guy out the window. The Caligula rock-and-roll cliché. I wasn't into any of that. I hated it. Why would I want to do that when I could be off with some beautiful woman in the hills with great wine, good conversation, and wonderful sex.

HARVEY KUBERNIK: The party ended, pretty quickly. Iggy got hooked on heroin and *Raw Power* didn't take off immediately, so there you go. So long, Iggy. Goodbye and good luck, you know? It's been fun.

DANNY SUGERMAN: After Columbia dumped the Stooges, Iggy owed MainMan a hundred grand, so Tony DeFries used the Columbia advance from *Raw Power* to make Bowie a star in Japan, and Iggy was pissed. He'd been used. He had nowhere to go. Being a fan, I felt an obligation to help him out. There was a guest room where I lived in this house in Laurel Canyon owned by Manzarek, who used the downstairs living room for his rehearsal studio, and Iggy stayed there. He was pretty strung out. Pamela Morrison was hanging around, also strung out. Both were at a pretty low place in their lives and I was just 18, 19, a kid trying to help them, but Pamela was not impressed with Iggy. He once showed his dick to her and she said, "Put that toy away."

RAY MANZAREK: Iggy was crashing at my rehearsal space and Danny's living quarters on Wonderland Avenue. We were trying to put a band together, but Iggy had a failure of will . . . and couldn't see himself going in the direction I wanted to take it in. He said, "I can't abandon my audience." I said "What audience? What the fuck are you talking about? You don't have an audience!" He just couldn't do it. He had to have the Stooges guitarist James Williamson come in. So James came by and cranked his guitar up to 11 and I said, "Well, you don't need me. There's no sonic space for a keyboard."

DANNY SUGERMAN: I wanted to reform the Doors with Iggy singing. I think Iggy wanted it, too. He himself started the rumor, first printed in *Creem* magazine, that he was auditioning for Morrison's role in the Doors. Unfortunately, the other ex-Doors, Robby Krieger and John Densmore, failed to perceive his genius. Still, Ray and Iggy jammed a lot, and they played on the third anniversary of Jim's death at the Whisky. Iggy got up at the end of Ray's set and did "L.A. Woman," "Backdoor Man," and "Maggie McGill." The crowd loved it, but John and Robby hated it and walked out on him.

RON ASHETON: When MainMan dropped us we just went out and played our butts off. We still lived in L.A., but Bowie and his manager, Tony DeFries, were gone. We played the Whisky a lot . . . that was down and ugly and dirty times . . . we had nothing happening . . . it was hand-to-mouth living in the Riviera Motel on Sunset. Those guys had no money, so I got to pay for Iggy's room and my brother's room and we were just going from one weekly hotel to another. Boy, that was the true, bizarre kind of fear-and-loathing side of being in L.A., something I wouldn't wish on an enemy. We were playing for just enough money to survive. It was a bad time. Bad feelings. Bad drugs.

PLEASANT GEHMAN: You'd buy Quaaludes at the Rainbow parking lot. Everybody would be there. Everybody knew that's where you could get them. They cost a dollar. Quaaludes were like the Ecstasy of the time, a downer version of E.

HAL NEGRO: If you wanted Quaaludes, you could always go to the Rainbow. But don't go there for them now 'cause they don't sell them anymore. They don't even make them anymore.

CHUCK E. STARR: Quaaludes were wonderful. You didn't have to drink that bottle of Boone's Farm before you went in. You'd just take half a Quaalude, and you were smashed. It was better living through chemistry. That was the best drug ever because you didn't have to drink. God forbid you drank with them, 'cause you went right to sleep. People would do them with wine and get in their cars and wake up—if they were lucky—wrapped around a telephone pole.

JUDITH BELL: It was Quaaludes and malt liquor. You'd do a half a lude and sink a can of Goldfrog malt liquor, guzzle that thing as fast as you could. On Quaaludes, you'd fuck a doorknob. They made people just want to have sex. I remember watching Dan Rather call them "disco pillows" on the news. After that we called them disco pillows, too. God!

RON ASHETON: After the Stooges broke up in L.A. I was starving—'74, '75 was all about trying to fall asleep with a clenched fist in my stomach. And I got no shoes. Then somebody said to me, "I can give you a pair of platforms." I loathe platforms. It's a hundred degrees out and it's 1975, the glam rock thing is way over, and I'm wearing blue platforms. And I hate the color blue.

ANDY SEVEN: I remember seeing Iggy at Rodney's after the Stooges broke up when he still had the platinum rinse, and Michael Des Barres, the singer for Silverhead. Stan Lee, who later started the Dickies, used to go there. He was this short, pushy little puffed-out guy with a big Marc Bolan poodle shag, and he claimed he had the leopard jacket that Iggy wore on the back cover of *Raw Power,* he told me he got it from Iggy for dope collateral.

RON ASHETON: Oh, yeah, Iggy would trade his possessions all the time for drugs. That's how he lost some of those great clothes, like that plastic jacket on the back of *Raw Power* with the tiger's head . . . that got traded to somebody for drugs or whatever.

STAN LEE: When I was sixteen I used to hang out with Iggy. I got his *Raw Power* jacket in a drug deal that went down in the Whisky parking lot. It was used as collateral, and thankfully I kept it.

CHUCK E. STARR: One night at Rodney's Iggy took a Sparklett's water bottle, threw it onto the floor, and it broke into a million pieces, then he dove onto the glass. Another time he was wearing this dress and he kept pulling it up and he wasn't wearing anything under it and he was scaring the customers. One time he came over to my house and called David Bowie in London and I got like a sixty-dollar phone bill. That would be like a coupla hundred dollars by today's standards. When he started making money in the '80s, I should have called him and said, "Hi, can you give me the money for that bill now?"

ANDY SEVEN: Iggy once showed up at Rodney's all luded out and he kept jumping up and down at the DJ booth wanting to sing along to side two of *Raw Power.* Rodney played the entire side of the album for him and Iggy tried to sing along over the DJ's announcer mic, but he was so fucked up he couldn't remember the words. He was in full drag, complete with dress, high heels, makeup, and this really scary gingham straw hat like girls wore in the '30s. He was totally blasted out of his mind, and I heard the next day he got picked up for impersonating a woman.

TOM AYRES: One time, Iggy actually played live at the English Disco. Just before the show, it was rumored that he was planning to kill himself onstage at the end of the act. Sure enough, when the set was coming to a close, Iggy got out a butcher knife and went wild, man, all across his chest. The security guards had to jump onstage and literally carry him off.

RON ASHETON: One day Iggy said, "Hey, you got any of those Nazi uniforms of yours with you in L.A.?" And I said, "Yeah, I got a couple of things." And he said, "Well, we're doing this show at Rodney's and I want you to dress up in the Nazi uniform and whip me. We'll get you some beers and stuff." So I took a couple of my buddies down there and that's what I did. I just showed up in my brown shirt. Iggy had a bass player and a drummer and they were just playing this weird rhythmic music and Iggy was trying to incite people. Iggy got up in this black dude's face and was really trying to provoke him, and I thought, "God, if I was that guy, I would fucking deck him." Then he got out a rusty pocketknife and started cutting himself up.

DON WALLER: That night I went backstage at Rodney's and found Iggy lying on his back on a couch with Sabel Star holding him and Ron Asheton was standing around in his Nazi uniform and there was Williamson and Scott Asheton and Scotty Thurston just hangin' around . . . they were givin' Iggy a half a gram of coke just to get up the energy to go onstage, he was so junked out.

RON ASHETON: It was a fake whip, but you could still hurt somebody with it, but it wasn't hard enough for Iggy. He was like, "Come on . . . thrash me more, really do it." I guess he thought that I would really just lay into him, but there was no way, man. No way I was just gonna whip the hell out of him. But my two buddies came in and they had belts . . . my one buddy had taken one of those high-tension wires, a big round cable wire in a heavy rubber casing, and he'd made a blackjack thing out of it, and my buddy said, "Fuck it, I'll hit him!" and they came out and started beating on him. They were hitting him a lot harder than me, and he did get a little wound up and that's when he started cutting himself. He wanted to be put in a gunnysack and dragged through the club and put outside in the gutters of Sunset Boulevard. So that's what we did. We drug him out, kicking him in the bag, and then we dumped him out on the street.

MICHAEL DES BARRES: Iggy just went on an absolute mutilation spree . . . kind of like, "I'm going to hurt myself before you hurt me."

DANNY SUGERMAN: Iggy wanted me to call every writer in L.A. and tell them he was going to kill himself on stage that night. I didn't want to make that call, but I did—to my eternal regret. It was a mess, no staging, no rehearsal. The "piece" was called "Murder of a Virgin," I believe. I drove him to the ocean afterward, where he washed off his wounds in the moonlight.

HARVEY KUBERNIK: Bowie weathered the gradual glitter rock decline by shrewdly retiring Ziggy in late '73 and reemerging the following year with the *Diamond Dogs* stage show, which sold out about six thousand tickets at the Universal Amphitheater. He escaped with his career intact. The rest of them—the Dolls, the Stooges—were smacked out and stuck in the glitter ditch. Stuck in the quicksand, and sinking fast.

CHUCK E. STARR: In late '74, suddenly this new type of dance music was happening with songs like "Lady Marmalade." You know, "Voulez-vous coucher avec moi?" People were just going nuts over this new stuff. Times change. By then Rodney's was much nicer. They'd built these cool wooden booths and a VIP section. They'd moved in these old 1920s couches. And they put glitter on everything and painted Rodney's name on it. They really made it nice. But then the scene started to change. Platforms were still popular, but kids started wearing bell bottoms over them. Groups like Disco Tex and the Sex-O-Lettes appeared. Gradually this new music came to be called disco. Newcomers would ask me: "Well, this is a disco, isn't it?" The sign outside said RODNEY'S ENGLISH DISCO, so they'd come in looking for a disco as they knew it, and so the new people were totally confused by the name. They'd bug me to play new disco and I'd oblige with a few tracks, but glam was dying anyway. Bowie had taken off his orange haircut and had started wearing these butch suits and was going for an R&B sound. Mott the Hoople and the Sweet hadn't done anything new for years. Gary Glitter was getting fat in England. It all just ended.

DON WALLER: Rodney's support of the Dolls certainly helped them out in L.A., but they still couldn't get it together. The Dolls played the

Santa Monica Civic with Silverhead, and two-thirds of the crowd walked out 'cause they were even sloppier and their overall sound was even worse than usual.

PAMELA DES BARRES: Silverhead and the GTOs played the last big glam show at the Hollywood Palladium. The New York Dolls, or Iggy, one of them didn't show up at the last minute. It was all haywire. The scene was getting very debauched at that point. A little too decadent for my taste. Too many hard narcotics. I'm actually a flower child.

CHUCK E. STARR: They had a big end-of-glitter party at the Palladium. Oh, honey, they carried me through in a coffin. I was throwing glitter and plastic nails at everybody. I was the glitter corpse. That was the end of it.

RAY MANZAREK: I thought glam was totally absurd. Men in makeup and spandex and soft feathers and eyeliner. It was the ultimate degeneracy. The worst of Rome. I thought it was most distasteful and absolutely the wrong direction to go in. That was the falling apart of everything for me.

TOM AYRES: The English Disco went strong from the end of '72 to almost the end of '74. People were just insatiable for it. Then suddenly it was all over.

MICHAEL DES BARRES: I think it fell apart for us not because we had a choice but because we were so fucked up and it caught up with us and then you had to either clean up or not. The makeup had faded and you either put some more on or you went natural.

LEEE "BLACK" CHILDERS: I just kinda faded out of MainMan like everybody else. It all just kind of faded away. Iggy helped me realize that glam was over. He taught me the difference between glam and cool. Iggy always made fun of David [Bowie] and the whole glitter voguing routine, even though for a while there he went along with it, 'cause he could have a fabulous place to live and a lot of money, but Iggy was always saying, "Who do they think they are? They're so awful looking, look at those shoes!" I began to realize that just having a lot of glitter on your clothes was eventually gonna wear real thin, which it did. Iggy got fired from MainMan first and then I was let go, too. Everything has its moments and then it doesn't anymore, especially in California.

chapter 3

The premiere issue of *Back Door Man* fanzine, published March 1975.
Flyer: Courtesy Freddie Paterson

MICHAEL DES BARRES: It went from fuck music to fuck-you music.

RON ASHETON: I'd made contact in L.A. with Dennis Thompson of the
MC5 and we put New Order together. I found a backer and guys
started filtering in and we found a place to practice. The downside
was the trend of music was changing so dramatically that we got
caught in the middle of a shit storm. It was disco time, and people
weren't going for the hard-rock shit anymore, so it was like, "Uh-
oh, screwed again." Plus, we'd play gigs in front of my big
swastika flag. I wasn't a Nazi, the flag was just part of my collection . . . I had Jewish girlfriends and black buddies. It had nothing
to do with promoting Nazism or condoning it. I just enjoyed the
flash uniforms. But other people freaked—they were like, "It's

fascist." New Order didn't mean to put out a Nazi vibe at all. I knew it was probably a bad idea . . . how not to get a record deal in an industry run by Jewish people. "New Order? Let's sign 'em up right now."

HARVEY KUBERNIK: You couldn't read about bands like New Order in the mainstream rock press, of course. Even the English press wasn't writing about a band like New Order, but if you went looking, you'd come across a bunch of small fanzines that were starting up in the early-to-mid '70s. Greg Shaw's *Who Put the Bomp*, later just *Bomp*, was the first, then there was *Back Door Man*.

GREG SHAW: I had published a rock mag earlier, in '66–'67, because I loved music. Then I got the urge to try it again with *Who Put the Bomp*. At first the readership [circa 1969–71] was former subscribers of my old zine, sci-fi fans I knew, and other rock critics, who used the zine as a sort of forum for things they didn't feel they could say elsewhere, about the state of music and the rock press in general.

LISA FANCHER: I started my fanzine called *Records/Street Life*, probably because of my leftover Roxy Music obsession, while I was in high school in 1973, but nothing held a candle to *Back Door Man*. Who would even try? They had a whole staff of cool people! And the best parties at Phast Phreddie's house.

PHAST PHREDDIE (FRED PATTERSON): *Back Door Man* began mainly out of frustration with the mainstream music press. My friends and I were listening to records that were not getting reviewed, and we cared about artists who were not getting the coverage that we felt they deserved. The Patti Smith show at the Whisky in November '74 was the catalyst. Don Waller dragged me there.

DON WALLER: Paul Therrio, the guitar player in my band, the Imperial Dogs, and I, plus a couple of other people, were living in Hermosa Beach in late '72, early '73, when Fred Patterson came over and we all just skronked around and talked about music and played records till two, three o'clock in the morning. It was Fred who brought the "Piss Factory"/"Hey Joe" single over one afternoon. We knew of Patti's writing from reading *Creem*. And it just blew the room into silence. We played "Piss Factory" about three times in a row. Everybody in the room was working shitty jobs—Paul and I worked at Armco Steel. Those sentiments were very real to us.

PHAST PHREDDIE: The Roxy was empty at the Patti Smith show. There was hardly anybody there, but to me and my friends this was a major event unheralded by the public. By January 1975 I was asking friends to write articles for this magazine I was planning. All of us cared deeply about the music. If we heard Aerosmith, the Sweet, or Mott the Hoople on the radio, it was a good day. We covered the local scene, the South Bay first, because that's where we're all from, then Hollywood, because that's where the action was.

DON WALLER: Phreddie said, "I'm going to start a magazine and it's gonna be called *Back Door Man* and I want you to write for it." This was 1975. I said yeah—I'd written since I was in high school and college—and I said let's get D.D. Faye (my girlfriend at the time) and Thom Gardner (who I'd met through Phreddie in 1973) and Bob Meyers, a neighbor from when I was a kid in Torrance, and Don Underwood (who we met when Phreddie and I taught a rock-and-roll class at a UCLA extension program) 'cause they're all real good writers and let's do it. That, plus Underwood's wife, Liz, who was a photographer, was the original staff. A few dropped out, a few more came on over the years. We put out fifteen issues in three and a half years. Everybody worked. Record stores. Machine shops. I think we all pooled a hundred bucks each when we became more of a collective after deposing Phreddie as editor.

PHAST PHREDDIE: The premier issue of *Back Door Man* came out in March '75. It had a warning on the cover: "For hardcore rock 'n' rollers only." Iggy was our first cover star. We included a feature on the South Bay scene and reviewed records by Roxy Music and Brian Eno. All this set the information-starved hard-rock fan back thirty-five cents.

DON WALLER: Our concept for *Back Door Man* was to make a magazine that we would want to read ourselves. To cover the kinds of music we liked. From blues to garage rock to Eno. To write about local bands. To tell the truth. To be funny. To get up people's noses. *Bomp* had gone dormant, or at least infrequent. And it was mostly about cataloguing older records—I still have the English Invasion issue—but we saw ourselves as more broad-based than *Bomp*. We wrote about Howlin' Wolf *and* Pere Ubu.

D.D. FAYE: We crashed this house party in Carson for a bunch of Montgomery Ward department store employees soon after the first issue of *Back Door Man* came out, and Phreddie took over the turntable and blasted "Search and Destroy" by the Stooges as loudly as possible . . . the hostess freaked and had us all turfed out. Phreddie had consumed an uncanny amount of alcohol and wasn't about to leave without a struggle. Two of the guests kept saying: "We're peaceful people, man." They were trying to calm Phreddie down. All we could hear was him yelling, "No, I won't be cool! I'm not cool! I've never been mellow! Play some Stooges, goddammit!"

KID CONGO POWERS: Phast Phreddie and Don Waller and D.D. Faye, yeah. There was a little bit of a scene surrounding these people that was my first exposure to punk. *Back Door Man* was where I first read about Pere Ubu, and they'd print essays on rebelliousness and other things. *Back Door Man* was seedy but smart. I felt lucky that I'd discovered it.

RON ASHETON: New Order got a lot of support in *Back Door Man*. They were ahead of their time, knowing the music scene, and they weren't afraid to say, "This sucks!" "This is cool." They were nearly always right, and they covered the kind of music that I liked. I had a box of Stooges promo discs from Elektra, a bunch of 45's for "I Wanna Be Your Dog," and so I had my brother Scott autograph a bunch of them, and got Iggy to autograph some, and told *Back Door Man* that they could give them away with subscriptions. Nowadays they're worth a few bucks—autographed "I Wanna Be Your Dog" singles with the song on both sides—but that's how much I enjoyed and believed in those guys. *Back Door Man* was a really cool bunch of guys and gals.

chapter 4

WORTH $3.50

FREE ADMISSION

with coupon

SUGAR SHACK

A DAZZLING DISCO AND LIGHT SHOW THAT WILL BLOW

YOUR MIND

AGES 14-20

HOURS: WEDNESDAY-SUNDAY
8 p.m.-2 a.m.
12456 Magnolia Blvd. at Whitsett
North Hollywood
980-9743

COUPON
ONE FREE ADMITTANCE

TO THE
SUGAR SHACK
Good any night

Expires End of April

UNDER NEW MANAGEMENT

The Sugar Shack, no grown-ups allowed, circa 1975. Flyer: Courtesy Steven Darrow

MICHAEL DES BARRES: Of course, L.A. retained the glamour after glam died, because L.A. *is* glamour . . . it's gLAmour. Cherie Currie was as glamorous as anybody with that little shag.

RODNEY BINGENHEIMER: Toward the end of the English Disco some of the kids who would go on to become the punks started coming around. Maybe they were too young when we first opened. Because everybody had names like Chuck E. Starr or Sabel Star, Lori Lightning . . . these new kids all eventually changed their names too.

CHRIS ASHFORD: I was working as a clerk at Licorice Pizza in West L.A. when Paul Beahm and George Ruthenberg [who later became Darby Crash and Pat Smear] came in one day and we started talk-

ing about *Raw Power* and Iggy. I said, "I know where Iggy lives."
And we all jumped in my car and went to this apartment where
Iggy was staying with James Williamson, right next to the Continental Hyatt House on Sunset. The first time we went nobody
answered. Then they went back themselves later and Iggy let them
in and they talked for a while, but if James was there by himself, he
wouldn't let us in and he'd tell Iggy, "Your little hippie hoodlum
friends came by." This was around 1976. Iggy and James had just
finished up doing the *Kill City* record with the Sales Brothers for
Bomp Records. That was like the beginning of our becoming
friends . . . trying to go see Iggy. They were still Paul and George
then. To us, going to see Iggy was what it would be like for someone from the previous generation going to see Elvis.

PAT SMEAR: We would look through the cut-out bins and look at
records and buy them for the cover and that's how we discovered
Raw Power by Iggy and the Stooges. The cover had this horror style
dripping letters and showed Iggy with his shirt off with makeup
and platinum hair. The record was cool, but it didn't even matter,
the cover made it, it wouldn't have mattered what it sounded like.

CHRIS ASHFORD: *Raw Power* was discovered and became the godhead
album for these new post-glitter kids.

JOAN JETT: A defining moment for any teen misfit is finding others
like yourself, even if the only thing you share is the feeling of not
belonging anywhere else.

BELINDA CARLISLE: I was born and raised in southern California. Growing up, I listened to schlocky radio—Doobie Brothers and Chicago,
pop music. One day I walked into a record store and I saw the
cover of *Raw Power*. And I said, "Who's that?" And I bought the
album and it opened up a whole new world that I didn't know
existed. Discovering Iggy led to discovering the Velvet Underground and Roxy Music. I started going into L.A. to see bands.
Post-glitter bands.

JANE WIEDLIN: I'd go to Rodney's with my girlfriends, and we'd all try
to get laid. We were all virgins. It was a lot of fantasy. But then
we'd go back to school and in gym class, we'd talk really loud
about how we fucked Mick Jagger, and we fucked Bowie, and we
fucked so-and-so, and how great they were in bed.

TRUDIE ARGUELLES: My friend Helen, who later became Hellin Killer, and I were a duo at school in Palos Verdes. We wore platforms. People thought we were a bit strange.

MARY RAT: I was always kind of a loner person. I remember people throwing things at me for wearing a Queen T-shirt. I had a pair of silver boots but I only wore them to school once because I got totally ridiculed. But I was always friends with Trudie. We'd known each other since the sixth grade. Then Trudie met this other kind of weird girl, Hellin, and we all started hanging out. They started to go to Rodney's Disco, but I never went. My parents weren't as lenient as theirs.

HELLIN KILLER: High school was bad. I didn't have any friends. In eleventh grade I made friends with Trudie. We were both into the same music, the New York Dolls and Iggy Pop. We started going out together to Rodney's. . . .

TRUDIE ARGUELLES: We used Hellin's mom's car to drive to Rodney's, about forty-five miles away. We got all decked out . . . I wore Mary Rat's grandmother's beaded dress from the twenties. We put glitter on our hair . . . and we walked in, made our grand entrance, and Chuck E. Starr rolled his eyes and glared at us and said, "Gawd, I thought glitter was dead." We knew it wasn't the heyday, . . . 'cause we didn't see Iggy or Bowie anywhere. Then we met Rodney and Kim Fowley—any girl that walked in there met them immediately. We also met all these trashy Hollywood kids from broken families, runaways or kids from abused homes . . . a real sleazy kind of a scene . . . some of them were really young . . . and we fit in somehow. Everybody looked really glamorous, but it turned out that they were all wounded kids inside.

NICKEY BEAT: I heard about Rodney's disco when I lived in San Pedro, but I never went there. I was basically this yokel from the sticks, so I thought, "Hmmm, I can't go there. Out of my league. You have to be some big star like Rod Stewart or Elton John." You had to be in Led Zeppelin, or in Bad Company at least, and I was useless at faking an English accent.

ALICE BAG: I went to Sacred Heart of Mary, an all-girl Catholic school in Montebello. I was really into Elton John, so I had huge rhinestone glasses. I'd cut my hair in the girls' bathroom. It was a few inches long, dyed red. I'd wear platform tennis shoes with my uniform. I was reading a lot of *Creem* and *Circus*. It was during the tail end of the glitter rock period that I started to read about early New York protopunk. I'd missed Rodney's club during its heyday when it was really happening. I remember seeing Trudie at a Kiss concert at Long Beach Arena. We looked at each other long enough to say hi. I ran across many different people like that on the same wavelength who'd reappear later on in the early Hollywood punk scene.

CHUCK E. STARR: Rodney hated the funkier new music I was bringing in, straight off the bat. I'll never forget him saying: "No wah-wah pedals in my club." There wasn't enough good dance stuff yet, so I was playing both . . . the glam hits mixed with some funky new R&B. Disco, as it became known at the height of the big hype, hadn't happened yet. Everybody at Rodney's was going for this new funky stuff. The response was immediate, it was exactly what the newer crowds wanted to hear. I never force-fed it to anyone. I was only a club DJ doing my job: working the dance floor. The end finally came one night while Rodney was playing and nobody was dancing. "Suffragette City" and "Rebel, Rebel" just weren't happening anymore. These tunes had been so completely beaten to death it was embarrassing. We'd had like three years of "Suffragette City" and "Ballroom Blitz," and the whole crowd was just chanting, "Let Chuck E. play the records." And that was it. Rodney quit. He walked out.

RODNEY BINGENHEIMER: We closed in '75 after Chuck E. Starr, our DJ, started slipping in disco. I didn't want any part of disco. I hated it. So Chuck E. ended up going off to the Sugar Shack to do the disco thing. I didn't want to hear Donna Summer and "Rock the Boat."

TRUDIE ARGUELLES: Sometime after Rodney's closed I remember Hellin saying we're going to this place, the Sugar Shack in North Hollywood, which is only for underage kids because they didn't serve alcohol. Of course there were all these big bouncer guys at the door. Upstairs there were guys tottering around on platforms fucked up on Quaaludes getting it on with each other. Nobody had told them that glitter was over, I guess. There was this one guy we used to hang out with who looked exactly like Ziggy Stardust.

HELLIN KILLER: After Rodney's there were these weird gay discos where all the glitter kids hung out for about a year . . . there was nowhere else to go.

CHUCK E. STARR: The Sugar Shack became the new hot place for the underage crowd to go. The Sugar Shack had been a stripper/biker club. Before that it had been a gay bar called the Outer Limits. It had an upstairs with a big round fireplace. "More More More" and "Love to Love You Baby" always packed the floor. We also played a rock-and-roll set. We started playing "The Time Warp" from *The Rocky Horror Picture Show* there . . . the actual formation dance was born at the Shack. This DJ named Michael Angelo, who's now dead, who worked there with me actually got kids to do lineups to "The Time Warp," "Suffragette City," and "Ballroom Blitz." The major songs from Rodney's became a set that we'd play twice a night.

HELLIN KILLER: We went there 'cause Chuck E. Starr, the DJ from Rodney's, played there, and we sort of followed him there. Most of the people who'd gone to Rodney's old disco went there, even Rodney himself, of course . . . and then there was a short while where there wasn't anything going on.

CHUCK E. STARR: The Shack didn't have any alcohol and it was open till five in the morning. Everybody went there. It wasn't gay or straight, it was a good mix. Then the Shack started to produce its own scene, its own little star system. And of course Kim Fowley and Rodney drifted over to the Sugar 'cause the Shack was where the white teenage thing was happening.

MARY RAT: We all thought Kim Fowley was kind of weird. Kind of an old man. But when you're fifteen, you don't think too much about stuff like that.

TRUDIE ARGUELLES: Kim would call my house and talk to my mom for hours! He talked to everyone he just wanted to know what everyone thinks about everyone. One night we had a party and we were like, "Let's invite Kim Fowley and Rodney." They came all the way out to the South Bay. Kim Fowley would hit all these high school parties. We thought he was just this famous guy because he did that song, "They're Coming to Take Me Away," which we'd heard on Dr. Demento's radio show. So he'd come out and he'd hold court and everybody would be sitting around and he'd be spouting, "I know what you're like. And I know what you do." And if he pointed at you it was kind of scary, so you'd try to hide. He was trying to intimidate everyone and make everyone think he was brilliant.

KID CONGO POWERS: In 1975 I was still in high school. There was a network of weekend suburbanites going to town and people in Hollywood welcoming the suburbanites. In the days before e-mail and the Internet we'd handwrite letters to each other about what was happening and what shows were going on. Me and Trudie used to write to each other all the time. It was about a lust for music and what was going on and not wanting to miss out on anything. We were spread out all over L.A. County and we'd meet up and get drunk at parties and see bands and it was really very underground.

CHERIE CURRIE: I'd seen the *Diamond Dogs* concert at the Universal Amphitheater back in '74 and realized that's what I wanted to do. I wanted to be onstage. I wanted to perform. I cut my hair Bowie style and went from surfer girl to glam queen overnight. My twin sister, Marie, painted a lightning bolt across my face. I went to school that way. People began throwing food at me and calling me names. After only a few months the hip crowd started painting lightning bolts on their cheeks, too, and gradually my whole school turned into this makeup freak fest.

PAT SMEAR: I was into rock and roll, the New York Dolls, the Stooges, the *Ziggy Stardust* album, and Alice Cooper's *School's Out*. Paul was only into oldies, '50s rock and roll. He hated Bowie at first. His sister had a Mexican lowrider boyfriend, who was into lowrider music, and lowriders only like '50s doo-wop. Paul originally thought Bowie and hard rock were crap. He said it was all screaming and noise, but when I came back to L.A. [after an absence of a year] he was into Bowie big-time. He said he liked the lyrics.

GERBER (AKA MICHELLE BELL): I was a surfer chick and a drug addict already. I had run away from home in Manhattan Beach and was heading for Hollywood. I was in this Taco Bell in Westwood and there was this guy with a red Bowie haircut with like a Bowie T-shirt, a Bowie belt buckle—basically it looked like he thought he was Bowie, except it was like a couple of years too late or something. So this Bowie guy was sitting at a table eating tacos. I walked up to him and said, "So I take it you're into Bowie." He told me to fuck off and started cussing at me. I told him to fuck off, too, picked up my tacos, and went and sat down at his table. Shortly afterward we were taking LSD in his mom's bedroom.

PAUL ROESSLER: Paul would wear a tuxedo jacket with reflective laser paper on the lapels and no shirt underneath and his hair was cut like nowadays we'd call it a mullet but at the time it was a Bowie haircut.

PAT SMEAR: We went to used-record stores and went for weird album covers like the *Witchcraft Coven*, the totally Satanic one with the nude girl being sacrificed in the gatefold and a black mass on side two. There's no way that record could come out today. We were little kids listening to the black mass in the dark. We tried to stay awake for a whole week once. I lasted a couple of days, but Paul did it, we did weird stuff like that all the time on a dare.

PAUL ROESSLER: Paul and George were on acid most of the time and always had this demented look on their faces.

PAUL BEAHM (AKA BOBBY PYN, AKA DARBY CRASH): You know what's fun? You take like 10 hits of acid and drink a six-pack of beer and you go down to Santa Monica Pier, there's a bridge that goes to nowhere 'cause they're supposed to lower it for boats and you go out to the end and jump off right, and you can swim and it's so great 'cause it's dark you know and you can just swim and it doesn't matter if you live or die or anything just swim and swim and you can feel the fish nibbling at your feet.

GERBER: Paul called me on the phone and said, "I got this purple microdot and you should come over." During one of our many acid trips in his bedroom we tried to fuck. It was a pretty heavy acid trip, and I think during the peak of that acid trip we decided that we were both gay.

PLEASANT GEHMAN: I first met Paul [Beahm] and George [Ruthenberg] at a Tubes concert at Santa Monica Civic in the spring of 1975, the *White Punks on Dope* tour. George was wearing a black cape, low hip-hugger pants with no shirt, and Alice Cooper makeup, and Paul had the *Ziggy Stardust* rooster cut and a perfect *Aladdin Sane* lightning bolt painted on his face. I gave them my number and they called me the next day and we started calling each other. We all lived at home and we'd be on the phone with each other for hours.

HELLIN KILLER: Paul's mom was intense, she was a scary lady. She was the screaming voice from the other room, the disembodied voice of Faith Baker . . . she worked nights cleaning up planes between flights and so she was usually asleep all day, and if you made noise, she'd scream from the other room, "Shut up!" I think she thought I was Paul's girlfriend, and in a way, I was.

GERBER: Paul Beahm's mom was a very scary woman and I was traumatized by her when I was tripping out on LSD in his room. I was like blazing, frying out of my body . . . and naked. We were playing that chicken game, where you throw the knife between your fingers. He was always trying to get me naked to play this chicken game on acid. Every so often his mother, who was very fucking scary—she was kind of Divine-like when you're on acid—would just barge in. His room had all these black-light posters and lots of Frampton stuff and Bowie stuff, too. His mother would roar at me in this big authoritarian voice, "Do you want some potato chips?" and she'd be clutching this big bowl of chips and stuff while I'm like blazing out on acid. "No, I don't think so." She was trying to be friendly, but like while on acid, naked with her son, discovering we were both gay, you know, it all seemed just too weird. There were times when he was naked and there were also a lot of times when I was naked and he was not, or there were times when he was naked and I was not. We were trying to figure out sexually if we were actually human beings. We'd look at ourselves naked in this full-length mirror with Bowie lyrics cut out and glued on it. On acid it was as if I didn't believe I was a human being.

PAUL ROESSLER: It was a two-bedroom apartment. It was dark, there were boxes stacked to the ceiling everywhere. Boxes of who knows . . . magazines or junk. Some seriously depressing things had happened to that family. Paul was not a person who would ever talk about it, but his whole vibe when you were around him was "I know something you don't know." One of the things he knew, even from the time he was eighteen, was "I'm gonna kill myself." When you have all this knowledge it really sets you aside. You know? He said, "You guys are all just little kids starting off your life, but I'm going to be dead in two or three years." When a person has those kind of thoughts, they are different. Plus, he had a 180 IQ.

PLEASANT GEHMAN: George and Paul went to IPS, this special school program at University High School, where they'd have classes on the lawn with people sitting in a circle, giving each other back rubs, playing guitar. Louise Goffin, Carole King's daughter, went there. Some other people, like Alby the magician, went there. I started dating George but he'd always get mad 'cause I'd make out with Paul. I went to Beverly High and they went to Uni High. I used to cut my school and take the bus to their school. I used to go around with them. They were always trying to see what you could make people believe or not believe.

HELLIN KILLER: Paul would call himself Astrid and write these letters about this Bowie-like character and put them up at school. He'd say he was a child from the stars, he tried to convince everyone of that.

PLEASANT GEHMAN: Paul had green hair and he'd tell people he was Dean Stockwell's son. Dean Stockwell was in that movie *The Boy with Green Hair.*

PAUL BEAHM (AKA BOBBY PYN, AKA DARBY CRASH): We went to IPS, the school they threw us out of for having our own religion. We called it interplanetary school. Everyone wore CERTIFIED SPACE CASE silver stickers. We convinced about half our school that I was God and George was Jesus, this one girl almost had a nervous breakdown 'cause I sat there for like half an hour telling her I was God and she started screaming and there were all these Bibles in the class and she started throwing them at us, she didn't come back to school for a week. They used to hassle me for having green hair, and [George would] walk around with ice creams in his coat without the wrappers.

PAUL ROESSLER: They were the kids where everybody says, "Don't talk to them, they'll brainwash you. They'll turn you into a follower." I just went, "Wow, I've never even heard of a seventeen-year-old kid that came with warnings like that, you know?" Most high schools don't have fledgling Charles Mansons.

PAT SMEAR: We carried around copies of *Helter Skelter* like it was a Bible, and told everyone I was Jesus and Paul was God. We had our little group of LSD friends, and Paul and I started convincing them that the teachers weren't right, and we got all these followers that rebelled. One of them was the head of the school's son. The student council kicked us out of the program. Paul's deal was that he'd get his diploma if he never came back to school; mine was to go to continuation school off campus.

GERBER: I believe they kicked Paul out of IPS—they offered him an honorary discharge, but he wasn't going for that. He took the attitude of "I'm taking it all down."

PAUL ROESSLER: Paul read the *Encyclopedia of Philosophy* and he had studied Scientology. One time we all went down and took tests at the Scientology place. They gave out free personality tests and they'd tell you, "Well, you did good here but you need work here. We can help you if you take this course." I scored normally—good in this area, but in that area I really need help or whatever. But Paul scored perfect on everything! And they said, "Well, we've never seen anything like this before. Would you like to come teach at our center?" And George scored zero. Absolute zero all across. And they said, "You're a dangerous person and you should be locked up."

PAT SMEAR: IPS was a combination of Scientology and EST therapy. The first day was called basic training, where they yelled at you and said you were assholes for eight hours, and you had to bring a parent with you. If you survived, you got to go to this special school. The big thing in IPS was that the teachers were always right, you were never supposed to question anything that they said or told you to do—which, of course, is exactly what we did.

KIM FOWLEY: Uni High, my old high school, was all rich kids, movie star kids, and TV actor kids during the '50s, when I went there. It was James Dean, repressed high school, just like in *Rebel Without a Cause*. It was: "Thou shalt not fuck, thou shalt not come, thou shalt not get drunk or high or have any fun. Thou shalt go to college. Thou shalt be a credit to our parents—we'll make them proud. We'll all be doctors, we'll all be lawyers, and we'll all be castrated, Episcopalian puppets. And we'll stand there and we'll be like Ozzie and Harriet's children"—because that's what everybody wanted their kids to be like at the time. By the time Pat Smear and Bobby Pyn were at Uni, it was "You better not smoke dope, you better not go to Hollywood on weekends, you better not suck cock, you better not eat pussy, you better not have a black girlfriend. Ooh, you better not start a band. Ooh, you better not shoot up. Ooh, you better not drop or smoke. You won't be a credit to this family." But of course, everybody's families by the '70s were like single-parent, dysfunctional families.

chapter 5

"Hello, Daddy! Hello, Mom!" Kim Fowley and the Runaways' Cherie Currie, 1975.
Photo Credit: Jenny Lens

KIM FOWLEY: The loneliness of a visionary is that you might be the only one in the universe at that time who recognizes magic. I'm a magical person, and so I recognize other magical people. It takes one to know one.

HARVEY KUBERNIK: When Charlie Manson was on trial in 1970, Kim and Rodney drove out to Spahn Ranch . . . there were still people living up there, the family girls. When they pulled up, Kim leans out the window and shouts, "I'm your new leader!" He was just too weird. Also, if you were at a party and talking to a girl, he'd literally push you out of the way and say, "I'm Kim Fowley, I have a hundred gold and platinum records. This guy doesn't."

KIM FOWLEY: It's a man's world, says James Brown, and he's right. When you get women doing traditional male things, you're gonna have combustion and controversy. The Runaways was my idea, and I went to find people to be the group, and through a series of confusion, luck, and design, five girls were selected.

JOAN JETT: I told Kim Fowley I played rhythm guitar and about my idea of forming an all-girl band. I just thought people would freak out over an all-girl teenage rock-and-roll band. Before I met Kim I had met Kari Krome at Rodney's, I believe, and I knew she wrote songs and that Kim was her publisher. I thought she played guitar or something, too, and I told her we should form an all-girl band. She said she didn't play, just wrote, but I should talk to Kim about it.

RODNEY BINGENHEIMER: Joan Jett was a regular at the English Disco. She had blond hair then. She was fashioning herself after Suzi Quatro. She stole the big Suzi Quatro poster from my club.

TOBY MAMIS: I had known Joan when she was a stone Suzi Quatro fan who dressed like Suzi and sat in the Hyatt lobby when Suzi was playing at the Roxy in March of '74. I'd see her just sitting there silently, not even daring to speak to Suzi when she'd finally walk past. She was first in line at the Roxy to get in the door so she could be right in front of the stage. That same night I saw her back in her chair in the hotel lobby with some guy and I told them they might as well go home because Suzi had gone to sleep and wouldn't be back in the lobby until 10 A.M. or whatever the next morning.

JOAN JETT: I wanted to be a rock star, not to be chasing rock stars for autographs or waiting around hotel lobbies for them.

KARI KROME: I met Kim a coupla times at Rodney's, then more formally at Alice Cooper's birthday bash at the Hollywood Palladium, where he picked my brain about songs and a contract came out of it. I met and became instant friends with Joan not long afterward. I told Kim about wanting my own band to create and write songs for, even if I wasn't a performing member of this band.

TOBY MAMIS: Kari Krome really played a key role in focusing both Kim and Joan on the goal line.

KARI KROME: Kim was one of those odd birds, brilliant at the art of the hustle. A master puppeteer, zeroing in on his prey with a wicked smile and a constant stream of dazzling bullshit it was hard not to get caught up in, at least in the spectacle of it. And if you didn't respond with the appropriate behavior, he could turn that skill to verbal venom and devastate you, anyone, flat with embarrassment. No subject was sacred: who you were secretly in love with (who may even be there in the same room), your drug habits, sexual rituals (gay, straight, or bi), what kind of geeky, uncool music you listened to alone in your room.

KIM FOWLEY: When I first knew Kari Krome she was a real poetry person who was much more interested in Jack Kerouac than Chuck Berry. She didn't have rock star potential. She was a pleasant-looking girl, but you gotta be Steven Tyler or Mick Jagger or Iggy Pop. Kari Krome wasn't Patti Smith. Patti was interested in all the same things Kari was interested in but one of them was a performer and the other wrote lyrics for people to perform.

JOAN JETT: When I first hooked up with Kim he said to send him a demo tape. A couple days later Sandy West met Kim in the Rainbow parking lot and told him she was a rock drummer. Kim gave Sandy my phone number and she called me the next day and I took four buses all the way to her parents' house in Huntington Beach so we could jam. We got along well. Then we decided to start looking for other people.

SANDY WEST: One night in the summer of '75 I saw this guy in this weird orange suit in the Rainbow parking lot at closing time, and my girlfriend said, "That's Kim Fowley. He's made records with Alice Cooper." So I walked up to him and said, "My name's Sandy West, and I'm a drummer." And his eyes lit up and he said, "Oh, really? Well, I know this girl who knows some girl in the Valley who plays electric guitar." And I said, "Really?" I'd been playing with guys all my life. A chick that can play guitar? I wonder how good she is. Kim called me the next day to give me Joan's number. She took about three buses down here . . . took her like four hours to get from Canoga Park to Huntington Beach. She had a little Sears guitar and I had my drums, a Marshall amp, and a piano set up above this three-car garage at my parents' house. Joan walked in, and I said, "Here's a fuckin' Marshall stack, what do you know how to play?" And she said, "The only thing I know is Suzi Quatro . . . that's how I learned how to play guitar." So I said, "Well, that's cool." We jammed on some song by Suzi and she had perfect rhythm. I was like, "God, this is so right on the money." I told Kim, "This girl's got perfect timing." And his eyes just exploded out of his head. A fifteen-year-old girl with perfect timing? He said, "If there's two of you who can play well together, there's gotta be more." Joan would come down to my parents' house on the weekends and we'd work on song ideas. Eventually we'd go to Kim's apartment in Hollywood every weekend . . . writing and auditioning and talking to people. Kim relied on me as a musician to check the girls out.

RON ASHETON: Kim Fowley said to me, "I need a place to audition women." So I hooked him up with this guy who'd been the conductor of the NBC orchestra for twenty-five years who had this little practice studio out in the Valley. I'd come by every once in a while and peep in on some of Kim's latest finds. It was really hilarious. It was hard to keep a straight face with some of the people who showed up for auditions.

KIM FOWLEY: Why couldn't there be a girl Elvis, or a girl Beatles, or a female Little Richard, or a girl Bo Diddley? There's always been that female version of everything in music, but nobody ever recruited five girls and said, "These five girls are magical, and if they sing songs and look a certain way, the public will buy it." It was like casting a movie.

SANDY WEST: I remember checking out some girl from New York or Cleveland. I don't remember how we found Micki Steele. I think Kim started putting out ads all over the place and we checked her out and she could play.

DON WALLER: Just about everybody from the *Back Door Man* staff and the Torrance/Carson contingent of old glam rockers and earth dogs were present when the Runaways played their first gig in Phast Phreddie's parents' living room in Torrance. There was a lot of beer and reefer and amphetamines.

PHAST PHREDDIE: The first Runaways gig was in my parents' living room. I don't remember a lot about it because I was so drunk.

JOAN JETT: I remember our first show at Phast Phreddie's house. Everybody was standing so close. Or that's what it felt like.

SANDY WEST: One day Lita Ford tried out as bass player to replace Micki Steele, who quit. I think she had stage fright. She used to freak out before we played.

MICKI (MICHAEL) STEELE: The official story [why I didn't stay in the band] was that ideologically I wasn't in line with the others . . . but early on this thing started with Kim, this sordid personal angle. He was enamoured of me in a way that I found very uncomfortable. I'd been raised in a sheltered manner . . . and wasn't savvy enough to know I could say, "C'mon Kim, fuck off." I got it in my head that he would throw me out of the band. But I didn't want to say yes because I definitely wasn't into it. I dealt with it by trying to stay neutral, but the pressure started building and building. My performance went down the tubes. I—I started going kind of nuts from it.

SANDY WEST: Lita and I started jamming on Deep Purple songs, and not just "Smoke on the Water," either. I was blown away. I was like, "You gotta be the lead guitarist." I told Kim, "This is the lead guitarist. She's fuckin' hot." Everything was moving real fast. Me, Joan, and Kim were always together.

LITA FORD: Kim was pretty scary when you're sixteen years old. I didn't grow up in Hollywood. I had a pretty normal upbringing. I didn't grow up around people that were eccentric. When I first met Kim, I thought, "Oh, this guy's a fucking piece of shit. I don't like him and I don't want to be around him." I packed up and left after three days.

MICKI (MICHAEL) STEELE: When Kim finally got rid of me, he was out for blood. He'd realized I wasn't into it, and I guess he resented my inability to simply tell him to knock it off. But I was just too intimidated. When he pulled the plug he went a little over the top. He said, "You have no megalo, you have no magic. This is the only chance you'll ever have to be a rock star and you've blown it." Perhaps my musical thing didn't lend itself to his slutty jailbait design, but the way Kim treated me made me depressed for a long time. Then I got angry, and I decided I was gonna show him. So it was a harsh experience, but it firmed my resolve. It's especially nice to know that he was wrong about the rock star thing.

HARVEY KUBERNIK: In the '80s, Micki Steele, or Michael Steele, went on to play in the Bangles, who achieved the platinum sales the Runaways never had.

SANDY WEST: We played the Whisky that September ['75] as a three-piece opening for Kim's other band, the Hollywood Stars, and tons of record company people came. I think Kim billed us as "Heavy Metal Schoolgirls."

JACKIE FOX: After Micki left, I had just got in as bass player of the Runaways. I remember the floor of Kim's place was covered with loose change and lyric sheets, and every available surface was covered with prescription medicine bottles. I thought, "Oh my God, who is this nut?" Kim called his apartment the Dog Palace. He looked me up and down and said, "Okay, whenever we go anywhere, the rest of the band will wear high heels and you won't so you'll all be the same height. And there'll be a battle between you and the drummer over who's going to be leader of the band." He had me terrified of Sandy before I'd even met her. I thought she was gonna beat the crap out of me.

LITA FORD: A few months later one of the girls called and said, "We can't find anybody to fit your place in this band as a guitarist. Will you please come back?" And I said, "Fuck, yeah. I'm on my way." I got my shit and threw it in my car and I drove back up to Hollywood as fast as I could. I don't know where they found Cherie. She was chosen because she was the youngest one, she had that blond foofy hairdo, she was thin, with blue eyes, and very, very cute. None of us really had that to front the band with. Cherie was totally clueless, pretty much as we all were. She got thrown in the middle of all kinds of crap. She had to hold a lot more weight on her shoulders than the rest of us. Kim liked her. She was cute, she had potential to sing, and it seemed like she'd do anything that you asked her to.

CHERIE CURRIE: One night there was this big buzz going on at the Sugar Shack that Joan Jett was there. I'd heard about the Runaways through the club grapevine. Her manager, Kim Fowley, approached me and said he liked the way I looked. He asked if I could sing or play an instrument, and I said that I could sing. And then Joan came up and we talked. Kim asked me if I wanted to try out for the Runaways. Kim and Joan wrote "Cherry Bomb" on the spot specially for me at the audition.

JOAN JETT: "Cherry Bomb" was written for Cherie so she could strut her stage stuff with the mic, and of course, the song was meant to be defiant . . . it pushed the limits of what people's idea of young girls' sexuality could be.

CHERIE CURRIE: Kim told my mother that I was going to be a rock star. That I was going to be the next Bowie, the next this and that. How could you refuse? Within two weeks he had a deal with Mercury Records . . . two weeks after my fifteenth birthday.

JOAN JETT: Kim always used strong language, and I wasn't around for the other girls' interaction with him. He knew if he'd picked on me, I would've quit to start another band. "The dogmeat thing" was his endearing nickname for us. After a while, I'm sure it wore thin with all of us. Kim was always calling us names, it was par for the course, but for some reason, I didn't feel threatened or pissed off.

LITA FORD: Kim just took a little bit of understanding . . . he was weird, but pretty harmless. By calling us names and stuff, it was just his weird way of trying to create something. He didn't physically abuse me or hurt me, and after a while his name calling actually became pretty funny. He completely has his own language.

KARI KROME: He'd yell like a madman: "Staying up all night eating pussy, chewing Quaaludes and listening to the New York Dolls and the Stooges with each other is fine, but not until you get this fuckin' song down! All right? Okay . . . Dog shit! One! Two! Three!" He would point his long skinny finger, snap it to command, and the girls would kick in again, over and over, until their fingers bled, while Kim stood in this dirty long-sleeved T-shirt, one sleeve down, doing an obscene derelict dance around the room. Six foot something, about 120 pounds, with a face like Frankenstein that never seems to age in all the years I've known him. He used to claim: "I am the Dorian Gray of rock and roll." What a nut.

JOAN JETT: Kim was fun to watch sometimes when he'd go off.

CHERIE CURRIE: Kim was verbally abusive. We were "dog piss," "dog cunts." We were lower than dirt, that's how he made us feel. That's how he kept control over us.

KARI KROME: Another day at the rehearsal asylum Kim was going through a stack of songs I'd given him. I was trying to get away from the typical approach to writing lyrics for rock and roll. He grunted and threw one up in the air. "This is a Springsteen rip-off!" "Springsteen? I hate that shit. Fuck you!" I said. He flipped through a couple more. "Dog shit! Dog shit, dog shit, dog shit!" I said, "Since you like dog shit so much, why don't you try this one? Here!" And I handed him some crumpled piece of paper I'd written on in a drunken stupor titled "Dog Eat Dog." Kim's eyes rapidly scanned the page, he grinned like a carnival barker, and declared loudly, "Teenage! Teen-fuckin'-age!"

DON WALLER: It was hilarious to listen to Kim Fowley working the phones, tailoring his raps to whoever he was talking to. He was always telling stories about some girl who wanted to be fucked on a hot stove or another who had everted labia—"turkey cunt," I believe he called it. He went off on a tirade when Joan Jett was living in his apartment: "She's eating pussy in my house!" He made up half the street slang in Hollywood: "Hustle." "Do the dog." "Failure cock."

JACKIE FOX: He didn't dare call us "dog cunts" in front of our parents.

KARI KROME: Here's a brief glossary of Fowleyisms . . .

Failure cocks (losers)

Urine-stained (decrepit, fucked-up)

Pig stink (bullshit)

Dirty/filthy pussy (all females)

Doing the dog (working hard)

Doing the death dance (taking big risks, sticking your neck out)

The Dog Palace (name for Kim's current abode, wherever that was at the time)

Dog meat (member of the Runaways)

KIM FOWLEY: The Runaways were told by me what was good and bad. It was a tight ship, and they rebelled. They were girls, they weren't women, they were actually as young as we advertised them to be. They were like all sixteen years old, girls in high school . . . there was hysterical squabbling over issues like "You wore the same color jumper as I did and now I'm gonna fight you over it." Or else it was "Don't talk to my boyfriend, or I'll scratch your eyes out, bitch."

JACKIE FOX: There were rumors that some of the Runaways were lesbians, and Kim got all these pictures of us taken with rock stars and tried to have them published everywhere to dispel those rumors. There was a very early series of pictures with Robert Plant and Jimmy Page, and I'm not in any of them 'cause there weren't any rumors about me.

LITA FORD: I think some of the band were having affairs with each other. I never knew gay existed until I joined the Runaways. One day somebody said something and all of a sudden I figured it out. I was like, "Oh my God, you mean you like girls? For real? Holy shit!" I didn't know what to think or say! I freaked out. I thought, "I can't believe this. This is something I never dreamed could ever exist in real life, you know?" I sat down outside and thought, "Ah, big deal. They're not hurting me. They're my friends. We're all bandmates together, it's okay. Get over it."

JACKIE FOX: The songs were extremely simplistic, and most of the lyrics were really very silly, although there were a few that I really liked. Kim claimed to have fed in every set of Beatles lyrics into a computer and had it spit out the words that were most commonly used and then he wrote a song using those words. It was the worst song we ever did.

SANDY WEST: I wasn't aware of our image at first, or how Kim was promoting us. I just loved playing my instrument. I didn't give a shit. I'm not a feminist, but I still didn't like the group being called "sex kittens" or "teenage jailbait" by Kim.

CHERIE CURRIE: We made the first album in a matter of days and started doing interviews right away. It was a blur. I was going to school but was released on a furlough to get the recording done.

JACKIE FOX: Patti Smith didn't have to worry about being marketed as a sex kitten. And she wasn't sixteen years old, either.

JOAN JETT: We went to see Patti Smith in Huntington Beach 'cause we'd heard a lot about her. Lenny Kaye had seen us at the Starwood and he really liked us, so we were backstage talking to him and then we went back to meet Patti, and the second we got to the dressing room (I was second to last, so I didn't even make it in) she goes: "Get those bitches out of here." Ivan her guitarist was wearing a Runaways T-shirt onstage. She was being real rude to us for no reason. We were trying hard to be nice and she just walked on by. Lenny said that Patti was only into her own trip and we just weren't in her world. We were getting in her way. I guess she was seeing us as female competition. She couldn't even say "Would you please leave?" She just threw us out. We were real hurt.

JACKIE FOX: Our first tour was just trying to survive. Kim had passed tour management over to Scott Anderson, and Scott was dating Cherie. He had all the money and he and Cherie would just disappear and the rest of us would be left in the middle of nowhere with no money trying to figure out how to eat. We were completely unsupervised. We were living like runaways!

CHERIE CURRIE: Joan and I were inseparable. They used to call us Salt and Pepper. Lita was very hard. Very intimidating. She seemed angry all the time, and she scared me. I wanted to be her friend terribly, but she was just so tough. I was uncomfortable around her. Jackie was just a whiner. She just whined about everything. And she would get on everybody's nerves. She also knew we were getting ripped off and she was trying to open our eyes to all this, but we were too afraid to rock the boat.

DON WALLER: Punk Rock really started when the Ramones and the Runaways went over to England to tour their respective debut records in 1976. They took it to the English kids and from there you get your Sex Pistols and your Clashes and all your great English punk singles bands.

GARY STEWART: The Runaways were truly pioneers, yet they're so under-appreciated. The sad part was that the things about them that didn't work were used to dismiss the things that did . . . but even the stuff that didn't work was done as a reaction to the empty spectacle that rock had become. They don't have a legacy like the Ramones in terms of great songs or records and people acknowledging them as an influence, but they made more of a difference at the time than they'll ever get credit for. They came along when they were needed.

ROBERT LOPEZ: I'd start to read about the New York bands in rock mags like *Rock Scene* and *Circus*. When glitter turned into punk rock, I'd start to hear hype about bands like the Ramones and Richard Hell and Television and Patti Smith and I'd have to imagine what they sounded like.

GEZA X: You'd hear people talking about, "Yeah, there's this band the Ramones, and they're all brothers. You should check them out."

CHERIE CURRIE: I didn't really know what was going on with the CBGB scene, but we got to hang out with the Ramones from there. I personally didn't like their music. It was too heavy for me. But I liked the guys. I thought they were great. But I've always been more into power ballads.

BLACK RANDY: I worked in New York doing these corporate training video films and some friends who were in underground theater— Warhol-type people—knew the Ramones from when they first started, like their very first show. I videotaped the Ramones' third show and became really good friends with them, and I hung around with Dee Dee, so when I came back to the West Coast later in 1974 I already had a nihilistic philosophy, actually more ironic than truly nihilistic. I already felt that something was going to take place at the end of the decade. Like everybody else in the mid-'70s, I was wishing that something would happen that would shake us free of the legacy of the hippies, and that there would be something new and there would be excitement again instead of disillusionment and total apathy. The Ramones felt they were reviving the sound of the Hollies. That's what they were seriously trying to do. They didn't think of it as glitter or punk at all . . . they weren't like the New York Dolls at all, and they were awkward, ugly, creepy-looking guys, and their idea was also to play the music real fast. The themes of the songs were, uh, "beat on the brat with a baseball bat," and "I don't care," and all that stuff that everybody else did to death afterward . . . it was all there in their first ten songs on the Ramones' first album.

RODNEY BINGENHEIMER: I heard about the Ramones as early as 1975, when my club was still going. People would come into the club and say, "Hey, I was in New York at Max's Kansas City and everyone's talking about the Ramones." But they didn't have anything out yet. Then they released their first album and went over to England to support it and it just exploded.

JACKIE FOX: In England the Runaways got lumped in with the punk scene. The crowds over there were almost all male, who were really there to ogle. When we played in Liverpool the crowd broke through the safety barrier and I remember being rushed offstage. I remember looking out on the crowd at Leeds University and not seeing one female face, just these really pimply wound-up young males pressing up against the stage, and I remember praying there was enough security. The Japanese crowds were a lot nicer and the support was more genuine and a little less lecherous. Japan was a lot of fun. England was scary. The record company threw a party for us and the Sex Pistols crashed it and set it on fire.

SANDY WEST: Punk was amazing. During that first tour in England they were spitting at us onstage and so we started spitting back.

LITA FORD: The more spit you got, the better you were. Oh, fuck, yeah. We had loogies hanging over us by the end of each set. It was great. Now I'd run for the antibacterial wipes, but back then it was awesome. "Man, look at that loogie on your neck, that's cool!" We just got spat on left and right. In Europe the whole audience was just a sea of leather and denim, bad to the bone. Everybody was drunk off their ass, especially me.

CHERIE CURRIE: What started out as six weeks turned into a three-month tour. I stayed sane through my family. I did the best I could to send gifts and talk to them, but after three months away when you're that young, you don't think you're ever gonna see your family again.

JOAN JETT: We'd gotten back from the tour and had started work on our second album when Paul Beahm and George Ruthenberg—who became Darby Crash and Pat Smear—showed up at the studio one day to say they were gonna start a band.

KIM FOWLEY: I had seen Paul and George before. They were male groupies lurking for the Runaways. More like baby brothers, but there was some male groupie veneer beneath their shtick.

JOAN JETT: They'd see us play gigs in Hollywood and they got inspired. Darby liked the tough girl thing. The rebel aspect. He got a real kick out of that. We were really flattered.

SANDY WEST: The Germs were really sweet people who told everybody that we influenced them. That's cool. I liked them. They were fun to be around. Me and Joan were the kind of people whose vibe was always "Come on over to my apartment and hang out." Her parties were pretty notorious.

CHERIE CURRIE: We were rebels, all of us were. And a lot of people looked up to us. It helped a lot of kids who had very mediocre, uneventful, unhappy lives. It gave them something to hold onto.

PAT SMEAR: We thought the Ramones were a throwback to the long-haired denim '70s thing. Paul and I were much more into the Runaways. We thought if they could do it there was no reason why we couldn't do it, too.

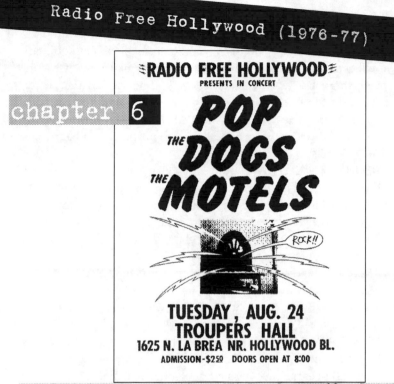

Radio Free Hollywood promotional flyer, 1976. Flyer: Courtesy of Gene Sculatti.

DARRELL WAYNE: Around '76, KROQ went back on the air after a two-year absence, and most of the jocks were still hippies. Our standard playlist included the Steve Miller Band, the Grateful Dead, Little Feat, Elvin Bishop, and the Outlaws. When the station's owner Gary Bookasta hired Rodney, that year was a turning point for us. Rodney sounded nothing like a radio announcer. Most radio announcers talk very quickly. Rodney didn't care. He drew out his delivery. "Allllriiiight."

RODNEY BINGENHEIMER: After the English Disco closed, there was a year where I didn't do anything. Gary Bookasta at KROQ knew what had been going on at the club and in 1976 he or somebody at the station had the idea to put me on the radio. The idea was to get famous people that came to my club to be on-the-air guests.

JED THE FISH: Gary Bookasta was one of these people who could talk anybody into anything. He was a scary character, with his dark glasses and vampire countenance. Because of his extraordinary intelligence and persuasive powers, he insinuated his way into ownership of KROQ. He somehow got his grandfather listed among the fourteen licensees. Mysteriously the other thirteen disappeared. His grandfather at one time was the only surviving licensee of KROQ. One wonders whether the thirteen other people even existed.

RODNEY BINGENHEIMER: Gary wanted me to play glam rock, but as soon as I went on the air, from the first show on, in August of '76, I went right into punk. The first thing I played was the Ramones. I could play whatever I wanted. As far as L.A. bands, I played the Berlin Brats, who had one foot in glam, the Dils, and the Motels, who were more new wave.

JOEY RAMONE: The Eagles and the Captain and Tennille ruled the airwaves, and we were the answer to it.

RODNEY BINGENHEIMER: By early '77 bands were handing me demos, and sometimes I'd play those, too.

HARVEY KUBERNIK: After Rodney went on the air, it went from, "Who's that little glitter runt in high heels you hang around with?" to "How can I get in touch with Rodney Bingenheimer?" KROQ was blasting out on AM and FM simultaneously, the only station in town with the twin setup.

RODNEY BINGENHEIMER: We broadcast out of the Pasadena Hilton Hotel on AM and FM simultaneously so everyone in Los Angeles County could hear it.

JED THE FISH: There weren't many others in America apart from Rodney playing punk rock on commercial radio at the time. Apart from KROQ, there was WLIR in New York that used to play punk. There was WHFS, which served Washington, D.C. There was KSAN in San Francisco that Tom Donahue started, and there was a station right before KSAN. To what extent they played punk rock, I don't know, but Rodney was the sole lightning rod and focus for punk at KROQ.

HARVEY KUBERNIK: Whatever it was, KROQ was a station that didn't play the Eagles, didn't play Jackson Browne. There was the Young

Marquis and Stanley, also the Insane Darrell Wayne. There was the Hollywood Night Shift. Phil Proctor of the Firesign Theater and Michael C. Guinn, a great actor. There was free-form improv comedy for an hour a day, none of that godawful Loveline going on there. Spoken word on the radio. Radical comedy. Dusty Street was there, too. No country rock, no prog, and no disco. You could also get a DJ on the phone then. You'd give requests, you'd suggest the set list for an hour. It didn't have the clout of MTV's *Total Request Live* that it's since become.

DARRELL WAYNE: The industry wasn't paying attention to Rodney at that point, but he developed a great audience and a wonderful following with local musicians because he was the only one really listening. If he liked their tapes, he'd play them on the radio.

STEVEN HUFSTETER: If you went backstage at a cool show in the early '70s, there'd be these guys in these carefully dandified suits and shag haircuts and bangs and they'd have little buttons on their suits . . . they were called the Pop. Those were the people who really struggled, the Radio Free Hollywood people like the Pop, the Dogs, Max Laser, and the Motels. They were a little older, but God, I have to hand it to them.

MARTHA DAVIS: I moved down to L.A. with the original Motels in '75. Before that we were the Warfield Foxes. We came here with the notion that we were gonna be signed overnight, like every band who comes to L.A. believes, but local FM radio was dominated by that slick California sound and there was no place for anyone to play. The only way you could get booked was if you had a record deal. I'd moved here with my kids and I was like, "Oh my God. We can't even play. How are we supposed to get signed if nobody can even hear us?" We didn't have any money for showcases. Then we met up with other bands like the Pop and the Dogs. We bonded as a sort of grassroots movement who stood up to say, "Fuck this shit, we've got to play somehow."

GENE SCULATTI: In the summer of '76 Dean Chamberlin, the guitar player in the original Motels, told me about a show his band and a bunch of other bands, the Dogs and the Pop, were promoting themselves. I suggested they call it Radio Free Hollywood, and Dean loved the name—so, apparently, did the others. I also pro-

posed to KROQ that they broadcast it as a regular live radio show, but never heard back. The show was promoted by flyers and a newsletter.

MARTHA DAVIS: We pooled all our money to rent a place called Troupers Hall, which used to be on La Brea Avenue, and we bought kegs of beer and hired a security guard, I think the whole thing cost eight or nine hundred dollars, which was all we had. The hall was packed. We only lost like ninety dollars, which was good considering how many free passes we gave away. Troupers Hall was a turning point. Some of those guys showed up and we started getting a little action, we started getting played on KROQ. A few weeks after that, clubs like the Starwood and Whisky started calling us.

MARY KAY: As soon as Radio Free Hollywood began to take off, Kim Fowley came around acting buddy-buddy with us and the other bands that he wouldn't even give the time of day to a few months ago. But Kim openly hated the idea of strong women, especially the likes of a self-powered Martha Davis. That was anathema to him. He preferred naive teenage girls that he could easily control. He told me so to my face. Now he wanted us to put the Runaways on the bill at one of our shows and we refused . . . what gall.

RICK WILDER: I always thought Kim Fowley was Mr. Johnny-Come-Lately. We're already there. We're already doing stuff. We're already putting on our own shows . . . all of a sudden he shows up with the Runaways and wants to get credit for starting everything.

HARVEY KUBERNIK: Fowley was on the heels of Radio Free Hollywood, but he was an older guy who had better access to the media.

MARTHA DAVIS: After punk hit, Kim announced that he was starting Venus and the Razorblades, a punk rock band, and he called to see if I wanted to be in it. I said, "Well, I'm really serious about my music." And he said, "Oh, okay." And he hung up. That says it all about Kim.

MARY KAY: Before Radio Free Hollywood, Rodney and Kim had this town sewn up if you were an unsigned band. Without their endorsement you were cut out from airplay on KROQ and from playing the Whisky. You couldn't even get written up in certain rock magazines. The Whisky and the Roxy, whose owners always claim what big supporters of the local rock scene they were, never did for a minute during those times until the time came to cash in on the new scene created by other people. The local prepunk "street band" scene didn't count, it didn't even exist unless you went through Kim and Rodney. When punk started to happen, Kim put out the word that he was looking for a new, more extreme punk rock version of the Runaways to capitalize on the new thing, and Dyan Diamond, a fourteen-year-old girl from Huntington Beach, was made lead singer.

HARVEY KUBERNIK: KROQ started to promote punk shows. The first big one was at the Bel Air Sands Hotel, also that August, with Venus and the Razorblades, and the Quick . . . another one from Kim's stable.

DARRELL WAYNE: After Radio Free Hollywood, KROQ started promoting shows with local street bands. They called it the KROQ Cabaret. They were usually held at fairly seedy halls but people would come. It generated cash at the door, which was great 'cause it helped to make payroll.

STEVEN HUFSTETER: The Bel Air Sands Hotel was a strange situation where we got a call in the afternoon saying KROQ was doing a free show there. The Quick went down and there were three thousand people there. It was insanely crowded. I think that was when many people first realized, "Wow, there really could be a new thing here." Something that could be exploited. There was also a definite connection between that night and the new wave thing and the point where KROQ became the model for radio music all across the country.

LISA FANCHER: The Quick was Steven Hufsteter, Danny Benair, Ian Ainsworth, Billy Bizeau, and Danny Wilde. Great songs, great live band. Whether it was my age or my hormones, I loved them to death, but their sense of humor and arrogance rubbed some the wrong way. They just carved their own path, using other great rockin' bands like the Who and Idle Race as mentors. They appealed to the girl and the record collector in me. Others on the scene would rather have their eyes gouged out than hear a note of them.

STEVEN HUFSTETER: The Runaways were getting a lot of attention, so Kim Fowley had the juice to pitch Denny Rosencrantz at Mercury on a boy band, a teen boy band with original songs. I already knew how impossible it was to get a record deal, since we were neither country rockers or a disco band, and so the concept seemed appealing. At that point you had your Shaun Cassidys and your Leif Garretts, but all those people were from TV shows . . . and so their whole concepts were doomed to failure from the beginning.

LISA FANCHER: When Steve Hufsteter made it clear he wasn't a Kim puppet (much like the Runaways), Kim moved on rather quickly. When Mercury dropped the Quick, they made those demos for Elektra with David Campbell, whose six-year-old son, Beck Hansen, ran around the studio making us nutty.

BIBBE HANSEN: Beck loved the Quick.

LISA FANCHER: Those demos are amazing—I hope they get released someday. Every A&R guy checked them out, but somehow it just didn't happen.

STEVEN HUFSTETER: Unfortunately, Kim, who was managing us, was not interested in the follow-through. He's great at getting you a record deal, but as soon as he gets the cash from getting you signed, he immediately goes on to his next thing. As he'd put it, "What's the next urine-stained piece of rock-and-roll street trash that I can get signed to a label?" Unfortunately there was nobody else at the time to pick up the ball. The shame about the first Quick record was that within six months to a year later, we really became the band we were supposed to be, but the record catches us at the time when I really wanted to sound like Sparks.

RUSSELL MAEL: I really didn't have any sympathy for any of the Sparks rip-off groups. I don't like groups who borrow some of the eccentricities of what we do but smooth off the edges so it will be more palatable for A&R men and the public.

STEVEN HUFSTETER: It was so stupid of me . . . of all bands to copy. If I'd decided to copy Led Zeppelin, we would have been huge, but I was such a huge fan of Sparks . . . and Sparks' most recent albums had changed . . . and I just didn't like where their music was going anymore . . . and I badly wanted to do something that brought the sound of their first few records back . . . it was just a misunderstood carried-away fan thing.

chapter 7

The Weirdos at Larchmont Hall, 1977. Photo Credit: Jenny Lens

PHIL S. TEEN (AKA PHIL MILLER): The Screamers began life in Seattle as the Tupperwares with Tomata du Plenty, Tommy Gear, and Rio de Janeiro all fronting the band with a fifteen-year-old drummer named Eldon Hoake, who'd go on to notoriety as El Duce of the Mentors, the X-rated king of porno metal.

FAYETTE HAUSER: After a spell with the Cockettes Troupe in San Francisco, a bunch John Waters called "the first drag queens to make transvestism and transsexuality hip on the street," Tomata du Plenty became a wheel in an early-'70s Seattle-based cabaret act known as Ze Whiz Kids who performed regular gigs at the Exotic Paradise Room in the basement of the Smith Tower in Seattle.

PHIL S. TEEN (AKA PHIL MILLER): The Exotic Room was in the basement of this fabulous old building from the '30s. Nobody was using it so we would have events there. That was the first place I ever saw Tommy Gear. He wasn't Tommy Gear yet, of course. He was Melba Toast. He was wearing a Mylar suit and his hair was standing up off his head about three inches, but it wasn't punk rock. It was just frizz.

PENELOPE HOUSTON: In Seattle I was hanging out with the Screamers when they were the Tupperwares. It was really a tiny, just-forming scene. Guys with skirts, beards, and glitter eye makeup. Kind of a post-glam, Whiz Kids/Angels of Lights gay scene, but there were also these garage rock bands forming around the same time, bands like the Telepaths, the Meyce, and the two scenes kind of converged. It was really quite a bizarre conglomeration in Seattle at the time. Before they formed the Tupperwares, Tomata and Tommy were in Ze Whiz Kids. They put on plays and musicals. Wacky gay theater. There were real women in Ze Whiz Kids as well. It was performance art, theater, and music all rolled into one . . . and they lived it as well. There were three of them sort of fronting the band, Tommy, Tomata, and another guy named Rio de Janeiro. They were backed up by musicians on loan from the Telepaths. Their personas in the Tupperwares were already similar to what they'd become in the Screamers, except maybe they were a little more new wave and not quite so intense.

TOMATA DU PLENTY: I wound up in Seattle after I left New York in 1975. And I got involved in doing the Tupperwares. It was a lark. At the time there were only three bands in the whole town. Three bands that you wanted to listen to. One of them was Heart! The Tupperwares were like a bubblegum band. We did these really silly songs like "Going Steady with Twiggy." These cute, little bubblegum rhymes. Later we turned some of them into Screamers songs. In the Tupperwares version, I said "Dear Twiggy, I look at your picture every day. I love you." When we turned it into a Screamers song it became, "I look at your picture every day, Twiggy! I want to stab it!" Once we became the Screamers, Tommy Gear said, "Let's go to L.A. and see how far we can take this." You know, so we took it . . . somewhere.

TOMMY GEAR: Seattle was generally a pretty boring place. There wasn't much happening and we were trying to amuse ourselves and everyone else. Finally it wasn't enough to stay in Seattle to do these quirky performances. We wanted to challenge ourselves. We also thought if we could be successful [in Seattle] maybe we should take it a step further and see what happens somewhere else. We had nothing to lose.

PENELOPE HOUSTON: Tommy and Tomata relocated to L.A. without Rio, who wanted to stay in Seattle, and the make-over into the Screamers came together pretty quickly as soon as they hooked David Brown and K.K. into it.

BLACK RANDY: Somebody I knew went to England in 1976 and brought back a Sunday *Times* that showed the punks in London. I took a copy of that article to my friends in the Screamers, who were one of the first punk bands around town. I said, "This is going to be what happens next."

TOMATA DU PLENTY: I knew this girl in England who kept sending me fanzines about the Sex Pistols. Before that, I had a bowl haircut. I looked like Peter Noone from Herman's Hermits.

TOMMY GEAR: When the Screamers came to Los Angeles from Seattle, the punk thing was happening in England, and we decided in a conscientious way to have a sense of solidarity with it.

BRENDAN MULLEN: On December 6, the *Los Angeles Times* London correspondent, Tom Lambert, published a piece that focused on the antics of the Sex Pistols, who'd recently cussed out U.K. talk show host Bill Grundy with a string of obscenities on live prime-time national TV after he egged them on to "say something outrageous."

RODNEY BINGENHEIMER: When the Sex Pistols really made it big after cursing on that TV show, it was all over for the Quick. It was impossible to compete. They were front-page news.

HAL NEGRO: It was the big bang. And we felt it here.

TOM LAMBERT (*L.A. TIMES*, DECEMBER 6, 1976): The reaction was instantaneous. Viewers screamed in protest. Some threatened to boycott advertisers. The *Daily Mirror* said it was "the filthiest language ever used on British television." This alleged form of music played by the Sex Pistols . . . and other groups around London with names like The Damned, The Clash and The Vibrators . . . is being attacked by detractors as "violent, obscene, anarchic and insolent." Punk has been labeled as "appalling" by musical experts. One said it is a "cynical, blatant progression in outrage." Critics began eyeing the "punk rock" outfits not as musicians but as social phe-nomena—when several of their appearances climaxed in screech-ing, chaotic brawls. Their pounding, generally rubbishy per-formances on conventional guitars and drums won few plaudits, but their [lyrical] themes—anti-love, anti-peace, contempt, defi-ance of everything—galvanized many of their young listeners into violent pandemonium. The "punk" rockers profess to despise any-one over 20. Their "performers" favor tight, paint-daubed jeans, swastika armbands, leather jackets, occasional rubber masks, and soiled T-shirts adorned with designs emphasizing sex. The musi-cians chop their hair short, tint swathes of it green, pink or purple, sometimes all three, and spike it upright with oil. Some of them wear safety pins through their faces. Sex Pistoleer [*sic*] Johnny Rotten fastens two through his right ear lobe.

BLACK RANDY: At that time, the Screamers were trying to imitate Bryan Ferry and Roxy Music, doing some sort of elegant synthesizer thing. As soon as they read that article, the first thing they did was to shred their clothes and chop their hair.

JANE WIEDLIN: After punk got really big, it was all about taking speed and staying up all night and talking about the great band you were gonna have, then never doing it.

HAL NEGRO: You also had to have a punk name, like Johnny Rotten. You couldn't just be John whatever. John Lydon. It had to be the perfect punk name.

KID CONGO POWERS: Hellin Killer has the best punk name ever.

PLEASANT GEHMAN: As I remember it, my mom named Hellin Killer. And she named Cliff Hanger.

HELLIN KILLER: I changed my name to Hellin Killer when we came back from New York in 1976. I was always the hitting-everyone type. The punch-you-in-the-arm tough guy. A friend used to always call me Killer, and that's where it came from.

HAL NEGRO: I don't know when Paul Beahm became Bobby Pyn. I'm sure it was sometime in early '77 when everyone started changing their names. Bobby Pyn, it's very British.

GERBER: One day I went over to school and I bumped into Paul Beahm and he'd had his hair permed like Peter Frampton, it was real long. And it was blue! He had safety-pinned cigarette butts all over his jeans and he told me, "Glitter is fuckin' over and punk rock is what's happening." I said, "Wow, you finally noticed." He told me that he and George were starting a band. I know they were fucking around in George's garage, but a lot of that was just all of us getting really drunk, and certainly Paul and I were doing drugs and then Lorna Doom got recruited . . . and then Donna Rhia.

BELINDA CARLISLE: Terri Ryan, who later renamed herself Lorna Doom, was my best friend in high school in Thousand Oaks, California. We didn't go to any of the glitter clubs, but we'd go to the Rainbow on weekends and say we fucked Ted Nugent. Lorna and I met Darby and Pat at the Beverly Hilton, waiting for Queen. We were all trying to get Freddie Mercury's autograph. We actually knocked on his door, which was really obnoxious. A no-no. It's the most annoying thing when a fan knocks on the door, and there were four of us knocking on Freddie's door. But he never came out. Darby and Pat thought we were bizarre. These two girls with little hairdos from Thousand Oaks, California, who smoked colored Shermans.

PAT SMEAR: Queen was staying at the Beverly Hilton, and we'd met them in the lobby the day before. The next day we went back and we were hanging around the pool watching Freddie on his balcony. We met these two girls from the Valley, total twins, with matching poodle haircuts. We snuck into the room below Freddie's and [Darby] tried to climb the balcony to get into his room, but couldn't. They gave us a ride home, we didn't exchange numbers or anything, and we thought we'd never see them again. We put up flyers looking to form a band with "two untalented girls." We put one up at Licorice Pizza and they called and asked: "Are you those Queen guys?" That's when we started hanging out and we formed the band. We made T-shirts with iron-on letters that said THE GERMS in the front, and AFTER YOU on the back. We were a band long before Lorna even had a bass. We'd make posters and put them around town, not for gigs, just to advertise the band.

CHRIS ASHFORD: When the Germs first started they had a sense of humor to it that made it fun. They were huge Bowie and Iggy fans who first started in the garage with the name Sophistifuck and the Revlon Spam Queens. You couldn't get much more vulgar glam than that. They were the Revlon Spam Queens for at least four or five months during late '76, early '77. They were still in school, and originally they didn't play at all, they just had matching T-shirts.

BELINDA CARLISLE: I was the original drummer for the Germs. The drummer that never played because I came down with mononucleosis.

PAT SMEAR: Belinda wanted to be responsible when she quit. When we said we wanted to buy our own instruments she brought in her friend Becky to replace her.

GUS HUDSON: Becky Thatcher, who was sometimes also known as Becky Barton, became Donna Rhia. She was a theater arts student I was dating who told me she was getting involved with this band and asked me to help her come up with a name for it. They were already called Sophistifuck and the Revlon Spam Queens and they wanted a shorter name. They were practicing a lot. Becky and I went to Bobby Pyn's mom's house in West L.A. He had Bowie memorabilia all over the wall. Pleasant was in the room and they were sitting in front of a turntable listening to a Sex Pistols seven-inch. Bobby treated me like crap 'cause I was already over the hill. I was twenty-one. It was like, "You're not one of us." He had contempt for people. I never had a conversation with him besides "Oh, can you do this for me." Bobby and Pat were using Becky to get access to things 'cause she had a credit card. She could rent all the equipment they needed. I'd drive them out to Pasadena to rent everything and we'd crate it into Hollywood. Becky was willing 'cause she so badly wanted to be part of it. Becky could barely keep a beat. They knew she was terrible but I think they sort of liked that.

PAT SMEAR: When we came up with the name the Germs the girls were disappointed. They said they thought we were more creative. It was supposed to be like the germ of an idea, so you'd know we were there at the start.

PETER CASE: Back in '75, I was a street busker in San Francisco and I was thinking, "Where the fuck is my generation? Where the fuck is everybody?" I was playing on the street every night from 1973, '74, '75, on the corner of Broadway and Columbus. I met up with Jack Lee and we put a band together and we played *Animal House*–style frat parties where people were going, "Kill the band. Kill the band." We finally got really pissed off with San Francisco.

We bought an L.A. newspaper and thought maybe something was going on. Even hell would be better than the rock scene in the Bay Area at that time, so in '76 we loaded up our shit and drove down and moved into the Vine Lodge, this skeezy whorehouse on Vine Street. I went to the Whisky the second night I was in town and Van Halen was playing there for fifty people and I was like, "This dinosaur shit is still going on? It's so stupid. I thought this was L.A." We wanted to play the Whisky, too, but when we called their attitude was like "Fuck you." We couldn't get a gig anywhere. We gave our self-produced single to Peter Leeds, the guy who managed Blondie, and he told us it was the worst shit he'd ever heard. The Nerves became so desperate, we were getting into some shaky business shit, always bad news, but when I got down here, I was like, "I don't wanna do that shit. I wanna be a musician. I wanna play my music outside some concrete bunker." We had the last of the loot from some smart money deal. So we said, "We're gonna take this money and rent out some hall and we'll put on any bands we can find. Punk rock's happening, we'll call it the Hollywood Punk Palace." But we couldn't find any bands.

TONY KINMAN: The Nerves weren't punk rock, but my brother Chip and I had read about them in *Rock Scene* magazine, they'd already put out that first EP, which had some really neat songs on it, Beatle-y poppy stuff. Word got around fast that they were doing this independent promotion thing.

PETER CASE: First we worked the Screamers, who lived next door . . . we tried to talk them into playing a gig that we'd promote, but they were too overcontrolled about everything. We didn't know anybody else. One day we were out on our daily punk hunt and we were driving by Denny's on Sunset and we're like, "Hey, there's Kim Fowley with that little short guy—what's his name?—out front." We jumped out of the car and told 'em, "We're having these punk rock shows, man." The first show in the basement of the Columbia lot was with Zolar X, this crack-up band in space suits . . . leftovers from glitter . . . but they were the only band we could get who were that desperate for a gig they'd do anything, even our show. We easily got them to take part in the Nerves' big punk rock cash-in scam to cover our hotel rooms and make a little! They were hilarious, but we wanted to meet some real punk rock bands. Then we finally met the real deal: the Weirdos. But they didn't have a drummer, so at first they were saying, "We can't do it." Then we said, "Fuck it, man, just go play and you'll get a drummer. You don't need a fucking drummer. Just show up, you guys are like the greatest group in the world." The Weirdos were fucking great. Those songs like "Life of Crime," "Idle Life," "Hitman"—those are still great tunes.

JOHN DENNEY: The Weirdos formed in February 1977. We were rehearsing at this cheap hole-in-the-wall rehearsal space called the Dress Revue at Hollywood and Western. We were students from Cal Arts [California Institute for the Arts]. The band was for our own amusement really, sort of like some fantasy group for fun with a bit of art damage thrown in, at least that was my take on it. One day this guy Peter Case, who had a band called the Nerves that we'd vaguely heard of, came into our room and asked us if we'd play a gig with his band at some space they were renting in the basement of the old Columbia lot. We said we were stoked to be asked but we really weren't ready to play in public yet; specifically, we didn't even have a drummer. But Peter was such a convincing talker, backed up by the other two, that they talked us into doing it.

PETER CASE: The second show the Nerves promoted was called Punk Rock Invasion, a much better name. We had the Weirdos, the Dils, the Zippers, and this band called Short Ice from New York. We didn't have any place to put it on, so I called SIR Studios and rented one of those huge rooms with a soundstage. We took the rest of our dough and put up posters. The show was a big bust. The Dils came out and they were really too weird. They were way out there. This guy Jeff Scott was the spazziest lead singer in the world. On the first song he freaked out and hit himself in the face with a mic, hurt himself and broke the mic.

TONY KINMAN: I really didn't like the whole hippie thing, the whole long-haired rock thing. That rubbed me the wrong way.

RODNEY BINGENHEIMER: The Dils had really long hair before punk came in.

JOHN DENNEY: We thought the Dils were playing old-fashioned rock like Led Zeppelin, with a slight Ramones touch to it to make it seem contemporary.

PETER CASE: Equipment was wrecked, shit disappeared, people puked all over the gear. Afterward we called up the Whisky again and said, "Are you ever gonna fucking book this music?" And the owner Elmer Valentine said, "Fuck, no." And so we said, "Fuck you, then, we're gonna play at the Orpheum, right across the street." We got in the Orpheum with the very fucking last of our cash.

JOHN DENNEY: Peter Case discovered the Weirdos. Who knows, maybe we would have stayed in our own private little world if he hadn't been so aggressive in talking us into playing out before we even had a completed lineup. We had a blast—we loved playing the gig so much they asked us to play another a week or so later. I think we did two or three of these shows with the Nerves, and then Cliff took over when it was obvious people were coming to see us rather than the Nerves.

HAL NEGRO: By the second Orpheum show the Nerves had given up on promoting gigs, they weren't being paid attention to. They had matching suits like the Beatles and they were a continuation of music that was familiar, with cutesy vocal harmonies and all that, whereas the Weirdos were something phenomenally new. It felt different. It looked different. It smelled different. Your body moved to it differently. Even without a drummer, I couldn't stand still when they were playing.

PETER CASE: Right before the Nerves broke up, we got these really stupid matching suits. I was drunk out of my mind and we got into a big fight in the dressing room at the Masque and we just told each other to fuck off and basically that was it for the Nerves.

K.K. BARRETT: The Screamers had already begun buckling down to serious practicing when the Orpheum shows with the Weirdos were happening. Everybody already knew who the Screamers were 'cause we were always out at any show that had any relation to new music. We made the scene and hung out. We saw the Nerves at the Orpheum and thought, "Oh, this is music of the past." But we thought the Weirdos were genius . . . guitar, guitar, voice, and bass. No drums—that was genius.

GREG SHAW: To me, the Weirdos were the most significant band of the early L.A. scene. This, following the theory that if New York punk was about art, and London punk about politics, L.A. punk was about pop culture, TV, and absurdity. The Weirdos had great songs, a great image, and a very good singer. The look was the most extreme of any band around.

JOHN DENNEY: We crashed the Damned's in-store at Bomp Records, Greg Shaw's record outlet in North Hollywood to try and call some attention to ourselves and this gig the Weirdos were promoting at the Orpheum.

DAVE VANIAN: It was the Damned's very first trip to L.A. I remember getting out of the car, standing on the sidewalk, and seeing the stars on Hollywood Boulevard. It was evening and still warm compared with the chill of Britain. It all seemed very exotic riding in a car with Debbie Harry sitting on my knee on the way to a radio station to do interviews with the Damned and Blondie. "Hotel California" by the Eagles was on the radio every five minutes whether you wanted to hear it or not. I was in awe that I was in Hollywood and was thinking: "This is where James Dean revved up his motorcycle outside the church at Pier Angeli's wedding." I remember seeing Bela Lugosi's chateaulike home off the Strip. Music had very little to do with my first impressions. I was a twenty-year-old English kid who had a passion for the Golden Age of Hollywood and its history. The Bomp shop had cool '60s American garage band records by the Shadows of Night and the Seeds that I had listened to on pirate radio stations in England. Bands like that were unknown in the U.K.

NICKEY BEAT: There were all these unruly little punky kids at the Damned in-store. It was Darby, who was still Bobby Pyn, and Pat Smear and Lorna Doom and Donna Rhia.

PLEASANT GEHMAN: I convinced the Germs that they should be ready to play when we were at Bomp Records for the Damned, which is also the first time I saw Angelyne. She was in a baby blue corset with blue maribou trim. She was at least in her mid-to-late thirties then. She was like *Whatever Happened to Baby Jane* in the sunlight.

BOBBY PYN: When we first started, we couldn't really play and neither could anybody else so you have to do something to draw more attention to your band . . . so that was an easy way.

BELINDA CARLISLE: After I recovered from my mono condition, I became Bobby Pyn's prop girl. I'd hand him salad dressing and peanut butter when he was on stage.

PAT SMEAR: We went to Bomp Records where the Damned were doing an in-store. We were drunk out of our minds causing trouble. We kept bragging about how we were a band, and someone said if we were a band, why didn't we play at the Weirdos' show tonight? We had no songs or anything. It was a dare.

JOHN DENNEY: Bobby Pyn and Pat were at the Damned in-store when Bobby came up to us and said in quite a timid small-boy's voice, "We have a band. Can we play?" We thought it was the perfect setup for us. A band of young kids who could barely play at all wouldn't threaten us because we'd been gigging without a drummer.

PLEASANT GEHMAN: On the way to the Orpheum, we were fucking gone, we had bottles and bottles of cold duck and we were screaming out the window at people.

GUS HUDSON: I was Becky's [Donna Rhia's] date. When we were driving to the show, Bobby was sticking his head out the window screaming randomly, "You fucking fag! You fucking fag!" He wanted to make a scene.

PAT SMEAR: Lorna wore her pants inside out, and Darby covered himself in red licorice that melted into a sticky goo.

ROBERT LOPEZ: It was cool to be sixteen and playing on Sunset Boulevard. The crowd was really into it. There were a lot of people with longish hair, jeans, and T-shirts. Nobody was as fashionable as you might think. Except the Weirdos. They were from art school, so they all had spray-painted pants and plastic wrappers wrapped around their legs. Shirts made of trash bags. The Germs were wearing tight jeans and homemade white T-shirts that were stenciled with THE GERMS in front and stuff like COMIN' AT YOU! on the back. Kind of like a Kim Fowley–esque, rock-and-roll Runaways kind of thing

JOHN DENNEY: When the Germs went on, it was obvious very fast they had no music at all. They were just kids literally playing feedback and banging around and smearing mayonnaise and peanut butter all over themselves and the PA. It was very amusing and really entertaining, but the gag wore out fast . . . it became tedious and unfunny after about ten or fifteen minutes. I hate to bust a few myths, but what really happened was that Dave Trout, Cliff and Hal Negro, our roadie, and myself looked at each other and we all agreed it was time to move on with the next band. They'd made their statement and we thought it very cool and gutsy. We escorted them offstage; the truth was it was a lot more low-key than the folkloric version, which has them being pelted and forcefully dragged off.

PAT SMEAR: We made noise. Darby stuck the mic in a jar of peanut butter. We made noise for five minutes until they threw us off.

NICKEY BEAT: The Germs were absolutely fucking terrible! They came onstage, tuned up for ten or fifteen minutes, then got through maybe one-third of their first song and stopped and started over again. Bobby Pyn was inciting people to throw shit. Bobby took the mic and stuck it in a jar of peanut butter. The sound man screamed, "That's fucking it!" and pulled the plug on them. Shut down the electricity. The roadies went onstage and threw them off. When I say threw them offstage, I mean picking up the bass drum with the foot pedal and tom-tom attached and throwing it eight feet into the corner. The Germs weren't to be taken seriously after that night . . . for a while.

RODNEY BINGENHEIMER: Yeah, the peanut butter was a big tribute to Iggy, but he turned it into something different.

PAT SMEAR: We'd read the stories about Iggy and the peanut butter and cutting himself up and stuff, putting cigarettes out on himself. Darby said: "Oh, I'm gonna take that to the extreme." There's the real version of what Iggy may have been doing and there's the teenage exaggerated version, and Darby was going for that one.

GUS HUDSON: After the Orpheum, all you heard about was peanut butter this and Iggy Pop that. Really, Bobby only did the peanut butter thing one time, yet people talked about it for the next couple of years. They still talk about it!

GREG SHAW: The Zeros went on next. They were probably the most sincere band on the scene. They were real midteens from near San Diego who worshiped the Ramones and the New York Dolls.

ROBERT LOPEZ: Right after our gig at the Orpheum, Greg Shaw of Bomp offered to do the Zeros' first single. It was pretty magical for a sixteen-year-old San Diego kid to have someone say, "You guys were great. I want to put out your first record."

HAL NEGRO: The Weirdos went on last. Once they got Nickey Beat, it elevated two more steps up. What had been great now just became unbelievable.

JOHN DENNEY: We knew the Damned were in town, and we called over to the Screamers' house, where they were crashing on the floor because Tom Verlaine from Television had kicked them off the bill at the Whisky. So we were really stoked when their bass player, Captain Sensible, showed up and jammed with us. I think we did a trashed-out version of the Seeds' "Pushin' Too Hard" or something like that . . . it was fun.

ROBERT LOPEZ: We didn't know it at the time, because we were from San Diego, but it was one of the key shows that gelled the scene.

ALICE BAG: The first local punk show I saw was the Weirdos, the Zeros, and the Germs at the Orpheum. When I saw the Germs, I was surprised and outraged and excited all at once. I didn't think very much of what they were doing, but I thought, "Wow, if they can do that, surely I can do something better."

PLEASANT GEHMAN: The Germs had four practices or less by the time they played. The Germs and the Zeros were probably the first teen bands to bypass the whole Kim Fowley thing by creating themselves. I don't think Kim liked it very much that the Germs and the other new bands were already well beyond his control.

CHRIS ASHFORD: The Germs and the Zeros and F-Word were the first teen groups that broke away, that weren't casted and controlled by Kim. They'd invented themselves.

KIM FOWLEY: You get a donkey and you get a baboon and you feed 'em a diet of chili and custard for thirty days and then you get 'em to fuck. Their children would be the Germs.

DAVE VANIAN: Television's Tom Verlaine, on hearing accounts of the Damned's other shows across the U.S., decided he didn't want us playing on the same bill at the Whisky. This is how we ended up enjoying the hospitality of Tomata du Plenty and the Screamers in Hollywood, who put us up at their house, the Wilton Hilton. We slept on their floor because we were so broke after spending all our money on the flights to Hollywood for the Television shows. Without any money from playing any shows, we were seriously stranded.

X-8: Jerking the Damned from the Whisky gig earned the stuffy old New York new wavers a bad street rap as these prissy old literary wimps—they seemed like tired people from another era.

HAL NEGRO: Stan Lee of the Dickies got the Damned a last-minute booking at the Starwood. Indirectly, this gig made them the first bona fide U.K. punk rock band to play Los Angeles, and I can tell you, there was mutual awe all around.

LEONARD PHILLIPS: The Damned played for twenty minutes and by the time they were done, I had tears in my eyes from laughing so hard. I was so used to seeing bands play for an hour and judging them by those boring old '70s standards. Like, "Wow, that guy did a great solo . . . or gee, I wish I had his equipment." Instead, a fight broke out, the drummer had more attitude than the singer—the Dracula guy—and the bass player took off all his clothes. The club manager was threatening to call the cops on them. They were fabulous.

DAVE VANIAN: At the Starwood I remember people who seemed left over from the '50s and '60s whoopin' around in the front row. They'd come just to see what the hubbub was all about. We were well received. We asked the crowd from the stage to throw money so we could get home, and many of them obliged.

SANDY WEST: We were backstage at the Starwood in L.A. and Rat Scabies from the Damned was yelling at Joan Jett and wanting to punch her and shit, so I moved in fast and smacked him one upside the head. Hard. Cold-cocked him. Calmed that motherfucker's ass right down. I had to do the same thing in England with that drummer for 999. He was bugging me at my hotel door and I was like, "Dude, I'm going to sleep," but he kept getting pushy with the door, and I was like, "I don't think so." So I hit him. Knocked him out. The next day at breakfast, they were all applauding. I'm a real sweet, nice gal, y'know, but you don't let people take advantage of you. The Runaways called me the Rock, 'cause I looked after everybody . . . and I was steady, always ready.

ROBERT LOPEZ: After the Orpheum shows and the Damned at the Starwood it seemed like everybody in the audience started their own band.

PLEASANT GEHMAN: The Damned was the first night that I stayed out all night and said, "Fuck it, I'm not going home." That was my turning point.

chapter 8

Slash magazine's chief scribe Claude Bessy, aka Kickboy Face, 1977.
Photo Credit: Jenny Lens

JUDITH BELL: I already knew Claude Bessy from Venice Beach when he was a short-order chef at the Feed Bag. I went there with this gay guy and we both fell for Claude and we were fighting over him. We sent Claude a card behind the counter where he was chopping veggies. We invited him to our house. We decorated, we got some opium, we bought flowers, we set the house up, all so that Claude would pick which one of us he was gonna be with, but he never showed up, so we smoked the opium and we both fell asleep. Suddenly I woke up to this clanging noise and it was Claude riding his bicycle at four in the morning. He was a speed guy in those days. I had no idea he was a writer or anything till much later on.

STEPHEN RANDALL: Before *Slash*, Claude's notoriety derived mostly from being a terrible waiter at Al's Kitchen on Santa Monica Pier circa 1973, cigarette hanging from his lips, ashes flicking into your food. He was semivigilant, grabbing the empty plate in front of you, even though you were just taking the first bite of your burger. Of course, because it was Claude, it all seemed like great fun. That was the best thing about hanging out with Claude and Philomena—everything became great fun. He could turn any event—even having a cup of coffee at 3 A.M. at Zucky's—into some sort of picaresque adventure. He was never boring and he never got bored, which made it easier to overlook ash in your chow.

PHILOMENA WINSTANLEY: I would go down to the beach every day and eat in this little restaurant called Al's Kitchen, and Claude was the waiter. I met him when he came up to me and told me that he was reading the same book that I was. It was a book of scientific explanations for stories from the Bible, like the parting of the Red Sea. I went back to his flat and discovered that we had a lot of records in common. A lot of reggae.

JUDITH BELL: Claude, Philomena, and I coattailed a birthday party for some TV casting heavyweight. It was all Brooks Brothers guys, faux Marlboro Men in long western dusters with two-thousand-dollar Tony Lama cowboy boots, and beige linen Armani dudes from William Morris cruising for new SAG whores. When the candles were lit on the cake and everybody sang "Happy Birthday," somebody handed an uncorked bottle of '65 DP to the birthday boy. Claude walked over, grabbed it right out of the guy's hand, and started chugging on it nonstop like a baby that was late for its feeding—he snoggled away on it until the entire bottle was empty. The room went dead, and we ran for it and went off to see the Germs, laughing all the way. Come Monday morning, birthday boy and his partner at William Morris wanted to do lunch with Claude. With verbal assurance there would be no violence, Claude went to read for a part in some remake of *The Hardy Boys*. With no previous acting experience whatsoever, Claude got a contract for six episodes and a SAG card to play Frenchy, a transient bohemian rock star. The agents just loved the whole bad-boy thing, his inimitable dark dangerous beauty, his catlike grace, and of course the lurid cussing in that heavy accent.

TOMATA DU PLENTY: Philly was sweet, demure, and considerate, everything that Claude wasn't. They were the perfect match. Kickboy was loud, rude, and bombastic, French accent included, and I wouldn't have wanted him any other way. The late '70s were drowning in a sea of mellowness and complacency. Claude was the voice of beautiful rage crying out of the wilderness.

PHILOMENA WINSTANLEY: Claude was doing this little reggae fanzine called *Angeleno Dread*, writing under the Kickboy Face. Then our friend Steve Samiof came back from England and said that we had to start a punk movement, that there were all these people there with spiky hair. We had seen the Screamers around Los Angeles, so it seemed like a smart idea. And Steve was kind of a professional. And Claude was a writer. And Melanie Nissen was a photographer. When we started *Slash*, I was the only nonprofessional, so I transcribed everything.

STEVE SAMIOF: In the spring of '77 Claude was working as a waiter in Venice when he began putting out *Angeleno Dread*, which was very likely the first ever reggae fanzine in L.A. County. *Angeleno Dread* was basically a few hand-stapled mimeographed sheets which featured reviews and features on Lee "Scratch" Perry, Burning Spear, U-Roy, Dillinger, Prince Far I. Also around this time I was working days doing pasteups for the *Watts Star-Review* and the *Herald Dispatch*. I had worked as a flower shop proprietor, a chef, a blues bar manager (Rick's Blues Bar in Venice), a fabric wholesaler, a graphic designer, a rug dealer, an Art Deco shop owner, a plumber's apprentice, a stage designer, a house painter, a purchasing agent, a warehouseman, an interior designer, an importer . . . basically a scam artist. I read an article in the *L.A. Times* in March '77 about the Sex Pistols throwing up on someone at Heathrow Airport, and that really appealed to me, because it was so absurd. I knew something was happening, and I wanted to write an article—not to be a writer, but as self-therapy. Since I had experience in pasteup I knew the basic mechanics of putting together a magazine, and I knew Claude was a writer. So we started *Slash*. We got advertising from the record companies and then we turned around and said, "Fuck you in the mouth" to them. Our primary goal was not to get co-opted by anybody—except by ourselves.

DON WALLER: *Slash* was successful 'cause it was a bunch of people writing about their friends and running their pictures in the zine. It was all about the new thing. *Back Door Man* was a little more ecumenical. Localism is always a sound political principle, isn't it?

BOB BIGGS: I had a studio loft on Pico near La Brea back in '76. Two guys moved in next to me; one of them, Steve Samiof, started *Slash* magazine with Philomena Winstanley and Claude Bessy. They would have people over with purple hair and shit. I had money, so I eventually gave them about a thousand dollars and I began to invest incrementally starting with like 10 percent, then I bought them out. Claude did most of the writing, and he was a total contrarian iconoclast. He was fiercely antimainstream.

CLAUDE BESSY: At *Slash* during the very very very beginning we were not very choosy about who we were going to put in the fucking magazine. Issue number one featured a band which had never even played live, the Screamers. We just liked their hairstyles!

TOMMY GEAR: We were seen as visual figures before anyone had heard us.

BOB BIGGS: We had a foundation at *Slash* in terms of what we were doing because we were older and came from the art scene rather than coming into it with any street rock-and-roll background. It made it easier. I didn't want the burden of knowing these people so closely that I was gonna have to change how I did things. And they wanted it that way, too. My stake in punk was always more financial.

MATT GROENING: *Slash* was the focus. It sort of pinned down the scene and made it real.

EXENE CERVENKA: *Slash* was so good that it legitimized the scene quite a bit. New York had the *New York Rocker* and great writers and great bands like the Velvet Underground . . . and the new band scene at CBGB was continuing that legacy there, whereas in L.A. we were starting from scratch, we had all these horrible bands like the Eagles, when all of a sudden this new scene seemed to come out of nowhere when it was actually a long time comin'. They said we didn't have the Velvets and the Ramones and like who did we think we were.

DAVID ALLEN: I got the first issue of *Slash* in May and thought Claude (Kickboy) Bessy's editorial "So This Is War?" was brilliant. I called the *Slash* office and offered my services, which the core collective Steve Samiof, Melanie Nissen, Claude Bessy, and Philomena Winstanley readily accepted. I designed abstracted typefaces, logos, and illustrations, and drove Samiof to the printers.

EDITORIAL, "SO THIS IS WAR, EH?" (*SLASH* MAGAZINE ISSUE 1, JULY '77): This decade's biggest musical fad has been the dreadful dripping sounds of disco music. Up to now. Because lately there've been rumors of strange goings-on on the fringes of the music world. Violence at concerts both on the part of the performers and of the audience, outraged editorials in daily newspapers, foul-mouthed interviews on live TV and frightened record companies dropping contracts faster than a chimp would a hot potato, oddball fashions of slashed clothing, repulsive make-up and bondage paraphernalia, and of course music, dirty primitive music that has little to do with the stuff music stations have been pouring in our ears for what seems to be an eternity. Today this madness is mostly an English phenomenon, but there are signs that it will not stop there. This publication was born out of curiosity and out of hope. Curiosity regarding what looks like a possible rebirth of true rebel music, hope in its eventual victory over the bland products professional pop stars have been feeding us. May the punks set this rat infested industry on fire. It sure could use a little brightness. So there will be no objective reviewing in these pages, and definitely no unnecessary dwelling upon the bastards who've been boring the living shit out of us for years with their concept albums, their cosmic discoveries and their pseudo philosophical inanities. Enough is enough, partner! About time we squeezed the pus out and sent the filthy rich old farts of rock 'n' roll to retirement homes in Florida where they belong. Let them play at Saturday night dances for the mink and Geritol crowd at the Sheraton hotels, let them remember the old days when they'd rather die than be seen with socialite

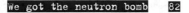

creeps and being heard talking trash and let them shit in their pants with envy. As The Clash say, NO ELVIS, BEATLES OR ROLLING STONES IN 1977!

CHRIS D.: I was a teacher at the time *Slash* first came out. A lot of the kids had long hair and I'd just gotten my hair cut and a lot of the kids in my class were calling me "fag" 'cause I had short hair. I got fired 'cause I was too strict. I actually wasn't that strict. I just didn't like them to be rolling joints in class. I sent in a review of "I Got a Right" by Iggy and the Stooges and that was the first thing I got published in *Slash*. I went as Chris D. at first but then Claude had me write so many record reviews that I would use pseudonyms like Half-Cocked and Bob Clone and Mr. OK. Nobody was getting paid, but whatever records we reviewed we got to keep. It's pretty amazing that the issues came out on a fairly regular basis. Everybody was so drunk. There was a lot of time spent at clubs at night getting really fucked up and listening to music and partying afterwards, plus a lot of tumultuous interpersonal relationships. The deadlines were pretty loose but everybody pretty much met them.

MATT GROENING: Claude Bessy, aka Kickboy Face, was fantastic. He and Steve Samiof did a great service because of their humor and because they published Gary Panter, who was the best artist to come out of the punk scene, which originally had a great deal of wit and humor to it. That's where I met and became best friends with Gary.

GARY PANTER: I saw the first issue of *Slash* at the big newsstand on Cahuenga and I said, "Wow, either they're really scary people or they're gonna be friends." It looked really aggressive. An illustration agent I knew said, "They're not punks, they're just designers and artists." So I just called them up. My scratchy kind of crap cartoons were not hippie-themed, so I'd never sent them to any of the hippie mags. My stuff was really young and negative, and it came out of painting ideas, as did a lot of punk—out of the '60s art school thing. A lot of the early punks were well-educated art school people with a good sense of humor about it, like, "Let's scare everybody's mommy." I think I met Steve and Melanie first and Claude in turn. My picture of *Slash* is Claude at his desk with his head buried in piles of material, yelling, "Listen to thees!" Or

"Thees ees sheet." And he would steer me to certain stuff that he thought I'd like.

PLEASANT GEHMAN: I went to the *Slash* offices to meet the people behind this cool new magazine and was horrified that Steve Samiof had a beard. I thought Claude and Philly and Steve and Melanie were really nice but they were all really old! They were in their late twenties, early thirties. I kept trying to get Samiof to shave.

GARY PANTER: They were really well organized. Claude was a power-house, and Steve was dedicated to it. His art, as he describes it, is always about scams and business projects—he has a sarcastic facade—but he's a real solid, generous, wonderful person. He always had a big beard and an Alfred E. Neumann shirt. It was a time when everybody was trying to look mean and vicious, and there'd be Steve and Melanie Nissen with her big poufy hair jumping around . . . you realized there wasn't going to be some strict dress code.

JOHN DOE: If it wasn't for *Slash* and the other zines, or Kristine McKenna writing for the *L.A. Times,* the scene would never have become what it became. More people eventually came to the shows so you could get paid better, play bigger places. Gradually it created a local music scene because it was being publicized. It was being verified. Value was now being attached to it. If it's written about in the *L.A. Times,* then it's real. *Slash* was a music paper that predated the *L.A. Weekly.* A whole magazine about this under-ground thing. People saw it and said, "Shit, maybe I'm missing something." Later on it got a little gossipy, like high school, like "Who's on the cover?"

HAL NEGRO: *Bomp, Back Door Man, Slash, Flipside, Lobotomy, Generation X* were all different, they were all great sources of information, but I lived to read *Flipside* to see if I was mentioned. *Flipside* was like the Bible. You looked in it and it had the shows you missed—"Damn, why wasn't I there"—plus coverage of the shows you went to. Best were the record reviews. The style of turning on a tape recorder with a bunch of people talking about the record. *Flipside* had their finger on it. *Slash* was a real kind of magazine but it became very new wave and trendy, very arty, but *Flipside* was more folkish, more about the grassroots DIY side of punk. They covered the art-damaged bands less and championed the Germs as much as *Slash* did, if not more, but I think they hated X for some reason. The other mags were about other people looking at the scene. But *Flip-side* was the scene. They reported on the social side as well as the music . . . what Trixie and Trudie and Hellin and Gerber and Dix were doing was just as important as the music and the bands . . . it strengthened this sense of community, even if some of the more sophisto art punks dismissed it as trivial, like the trashy gossip of *Flipside* was beneath them.

X-8: I was going to Whittier High School from '74 till '77. People from Whittier that liked the New York Dolls started hanging out. We were all reading the same rock zines—*Creem, Rock Scene, Craw-daddy, Back Door Man, Bomp,* and *Circus*—and we formed a little union in suburbia. We used to ride the bus from Whittier to Hol-lywood. We'd pick up flyers from Licorice Pizza and Peaches and that's how we found out about the Germs. Al and Tory, Larry Lash and me. We used to hang out and get drunk on NyQuil together. I was editor of the school newspaper, so *Flipside* was a way to hone journalistic skills and write about stuff that I liked. For some of us it became a free ticket to get into clubs.

POOCH (PAT DI PUCCIO): Some of the early *Flipside*s were literally hand-written or typed on a manual typewriter. We were a group of Whittier High School students, an integrated group of blue-collar Hispanic and Euro-American kids from the South Bay. There was Al Kowalski, myself, Sam Diaz (X-8), Steve Schumacher (Larry Lash), and George Torrez. We were basically loner music geeks who couldn't get dates.

X-8: *Flipside* was about trying to share things we were experiencing, things we thought were important to youth and society and cul-ture, even on such a low level. *Flipside* was already well into its con-cept phase, but *Slash* made it to the newsstand first. They were twenty-five cents. Four Xerox sides initially. For the first issue we interviewed the Germs in Pat's parents' garage. Darby was talking about taking acid on the Santa Monica Pier. I couldn't help zeroing in on the Germs 'cause they were so nontraditional. Al was into Bowie and stuff. I was into more trashy types of rock. The Germs captured that expressionistic trash aesthetic well onstage. Musi-cally it was just "What the fuck?" Most of the early *Flipside*s were just transcriptions of us getting drunk in somebody's living room . . . we'd just tape ourselves saying what was crap and what we did and didn't like. We came across like a bunch of real snotty, adolescent brats.

PLEASANT GEHMAN: The *Lobotomy* zine was a lot of work. We'd go to every show and write reviews, we'd interview people and get them really fucked up. *Slash* interviews would have stuff about politics and art, but *Lobotomy*'s trademark was that the interviews would be about sex and drug experiences. I'd sell it at Licorice Pizza and Bomp and Peaches and Rhino or at gigs. We'd sell it to them on consignment, five or ten copies, then get our fifty cents or whatever and bring them more.

chapter 9

The Screamers (*left to right:* Tomata du Plenty, Tommy Gear, K.K. Barrett) make
their world debut at the original *Slash* offices in a storefront on Pico Boulevard, 1977.
Photo Credit: Jenny Lens

K.K. BARRETT: The Screamers were totally photo-op whores from the
very beginning. Before we'd even played, they ran this photo shoot
of us in *Slash*. Nobody had even heard us play, so everyone was like
"Who're the Screamers?" They had a coming-out party for *Slash*
and we were invited to play at this storefront loft space. We'd been
rehearsing pretty solidly for a few months, we'd also done a four-
track demo, and so we were pretty tight. The place was packed,
there's attention, there's desire, there's a hubbub going on. Nick
Lowe was there, Jake Riviera of Stiff Records was there, and everybody was drunk. That's when I met Trudie again. She had a target
shirt on that said KILL ME. She'd been to New York, where she'd
been called "L.A.'s favorite punk rocker" in a photo caption, and
she'd been drinking red wine, so the target was covered with red.

TRUDIE ARGUELLES: Pat Smear spilled it on me. Plus I had a big black eye from crashing Hellin's mom's Nova on my eighteenth birthday.

HELLIN KILLER: I was there on crutches.

TOMMY GEAR: We played for about 500 in a space meant for a lot fewer. The stage was about the size of a small dinner table. It was truly a crunch.

ANDY SEVEN: Before they went on I only saw two little keyboards and a small drum kit, and I thought, "Oh, I guess the band's not gonna play tonight, 'cause there's no amps, no guitars set up." Then they came on and it was like nothing I'd ever seen or heard before. In 1977, outside of Kraftwerk and maybe Suicide, you never saw a band with no guitars, and this one had just two small keyboards and a drummer backing up a lead singer. This was radical, it was completely new to everybody.

TOMATA DU PLENTY: When we started playing we just didn't think we needed a guitar. It wasn't a political thing, it just evolved that way. And then all the writers made something else out of it. That we were antiguitar because it was a phallic symbol, and absurd Freudian things like that. Or that we were the sons and daughters of Kraftwerk and all this bullshit.

K.K. BARRETT: That night the Screamers were kind of baptized, legitimized by the growing new punk scene makers of Bowie club kids barely out of high school and the older, mid-to-late twenties art swingers from Venice. We actually could play, so people gave us credence, and then the race was on. Now it was us and the Zeros and the Weirdos and the Germs.

GARY PANTER: The Screamers played the *Slash* party, and it pissed me off that Tommy Gear threw a music stand into the audience as a spear. But they looked fantastic! A really fantastic look, and they sounded great. When Tommy and Tomata entered a room, it was really electrifying. They just came in like exploding heads!

TOMATA DU PLENTY: I didn't know how to sing. I just yelled. I am tone-deaf. I took a voice lesson once and they threw me out!

K.K. BARRETT: Tommy was like Kim Fowley, the guy with the big master plan. The personal dynamic between Tommy and Tomata was good cop/bad cop. Tommy was the meanie to Tomata's likeable clown. It was this lighthearted thing and then this boot stomp at the same time; this pop sensibility and then this dramatic drill mentality. Tommy could be one of the funniest people you've ever met, then he could turn around and be the coldest. He wrote most of the songs. Tomata wrote the songs that are lighthearted. Tommy would write "Punish or Be Damned" and "Violent World," while Tomata would write "I'm Going Steady with Twiggy." If it was all Tomata's thing, we would have been much too light and wimpy, and if it was all Tommy's thing, we would have been . . . Rammstein. We were right down the center between the two of them.

TRUDIE ARGUELLES: I was scared of Tommy. He was very stern. When you got to know him, when you were partying with him, he'd get real goofy and start dancing around and be much more faggy and funny and laughing, then an hour later, he'd freeze and go back into this teeth-gnashing Nazi pose where he just wanted to be in charge of everything.

K.K. BARRETT: David Brown [also a Screamer] is a genius abstract piano player from the Berklee College of Music who invented the core Screamers sound, the wonderfully corrupted timbre of a Fender Rhodes electric piano fed through a distortion box. David just rammed it through a Big Muff distortion box.

GARY PANTER: I don't remember if the Screamers asked me to do their logo or if it was me who asked them. Every once in a while I'll see a version of it over the years. There have been tattoos of it. ACT UP, the AIDS organization, uses it as a giant banner, so I've seen it on CNN. On a tiny scale it's like "Keep on Truckin'," or the happy face, or the fish with feet . . . an image that just got away and took on its own life.

TOMATA DU PLENTY: Oh, they use it all the time. I see it used to advertise the Insult Line, the phone number you can call to be insulted. 976-INSULT. I once called it up and said, "That's a portrait of me, please stop using it." And the guy says "Oh, no, that's our boss Irving. That's Irving's picture." Irving!

K.K. BARRETT: In 1977 I moved into the Villa Elaine, this wonderfully run-down apartment building on Vine Street where Man Ray once lived. I didn't really have anything going on. I was a huge music fan, but there were no good shows. I'd go to Music Plus, and all that existed of English or New York punk music was one little box of 45's on the counter, and if you were lucky, you'd find a Buzzcocks or a Ramones single. We'd go to any show at the Starwood or Whisky that had some connection to the early '70s, the glam scene, John Cale, or whatever. We'd go to these shows and we'd start to find each other by dress or whatever. Tommy Gear and Tomata du Plenty were at this show at the Whisky. I think it was Johnny Cougar in a jumpsuit or something. They were both wearing black wraparound sunglasses that old ladies wear in Miami Beach and their hair was spiked up and I just decided I had to meet them. I said, "What are you doing?" and they said, "We've got this band." But it wasn't a band yet, they were kind of collecting people. David Brown was already in. They hadn't played and they hadn't rehearsed. I told them I'd played in bands in Oklahoma. We exchanged phone numbers. Tommy and Tomata lived at 1845 Wilton at Franklin, which got named the Wilton Hilton.

KID CONGO POWERS: I lived at the Wilton Hilton. I had a closet made into a room and I used to do the Screamers' fanzine newsletter on a manual typewriter. The Wilton Hilton was great. The interior was all black . . . they had parties all the time . . . they would listen to Nico all day, Kraftwerk and Neu! and Goblin. They knew all about Krautrock and gay underground art.

PHIL S. TEEN: Tommy would read *How to Win by Intimidation* religiously. He would read it every night. Maybe that's why all these other bands were desperate to play, but the Screamers didn't do very many shows. It made it more of a big event.

KITTRA ALLEN: K.K. played drums behind Tomata, Tommy Gear was on synthesizer, and David Brown played electric piano. Tomata had a uniquely shaped head with a beautiful high crown and with his cowlick hairdo he looked like a Gerber baby. Tomata walked back and forth with the microphone in his hand grinning from ear to ear looking like a mad little duck quacking around.

PHIL S. TEEN: Another thing that might have contributed to their early mystique is that Tommy is totally nearsighted. And the reason for all his attitude was that he couldn't see anybody. He couldn't tell who people were. He'd lose his contact lenses and couldn't replace them because he was very poor . . . but he wouldn't wear glasses.

GERALD CASALE: Devo loved the Screamers. We thought the Screamers and Tomata du Plenty were fucking unbelievable. You see a band that you're creatively and intellectually inspired by and envious of and we were like, "Why didn't we think of it?" They were so way ahead of their time. It was almost as if what they were thinking about, what they were after was like "Firestarter" by Prodigy, but this was the summer of '77. They were using rudimentary synths and sequencers but with punk energy and aggressive lyrics and theatrical staging with German expressionist lighting.

TOMATA DU PLENTY: I was so involved in the stage act. You know, every show was so much work. It was my only focus, the performance, it really was. I didn't do very much of the business, and I have to give credit to Tommy Gear. He did most of that work. I was free of that responsibility so that I could devote all of my time to going out there and making a total fool of myself, which was actually a lot of hard work.

chapter 10

Devo takes Los Angeles, 1979. Photo Credit: Jenny Lens

GERALD CASALE: The hardcore punkoisie never accepted Devo and always said we were transplants, but we transformed in a much more intense way by coming to L.A. We were pissed-off Spuds with a plan and had a lot to say, but L.A. really organized the way we could say it. It made us super-dedicated and committed to being the best Devo we could be. Our sense of how we connected with a culture and an audience completely came into being here. We were infants until we came to L.A., and this was our coming-of-age experience.

MATT GROENING: Devo was probably my favorite band at the time. They went way out of their way to have fun with it with films and costumes and their own language, and I thought it was a hoot.

JED THE FISH: I became obsessed by everything about this band.

MARK MOTHERSBAUGH: People were trying to figure out what the fuck Devo was, so they lumped us in with the punks. We enjoyed camaraderie with punks. Some people thought of us as an art band, but if the Tubes were considered an art band, I didn't want to be an art band. We had more things in common with the punks. We were angry with the system.

GERALD CASALE: Back home in Ohio, Devo were considered the biggest asshole losers 'cause none of us had long hair, none of us drove around in vans, none of us were managers of McDonald's. We had menial jobs and we spent our free time writing and recording in the basement of a rented house. We did the graphics and writings on the philosophy of deevolution and people were like, "Oh, these poor fucks. What losers. They're out of their minds."

MARK MOTHERSBAUGH: We'd lie to clubs and say we were a Top 40 band. It was rare if we got to play through the whole night. It incited people to want to get in fights with us. We'd go, "Here's another song by Foghat, it's called 'Mongoloid'!" These were people who just got off work at the tire factory and they're like, "I don't need this shit!" There'd be stuff flying at the stage, and these long-haired gnarlers coming at us going, "You callin' me a monkey? That what you're sayin'?"

JOHN DOE: People knew Devo for some reason, so that's what hicks would yell out of their pickups to slag you: "De-e-e-v-o!" or "F-a-a-g!" You could elicit that response just by wearing tight black jeans and a leather jacket with a regular haircut. Here we were in Hollywood, where you're supposed to be able to do anything and not faze people, and the general public was offended by this style. Everyone I knew just scratched their head, wondering what it was that pissed people off so much, but it gave you the feeling that you were fighting the good fight.

GERALD CASALE: Many punks have told me that they got sneered at, chased, or beaten up and called "Devo!" And Devo didn't even wear Ramones-style leather jackets and ripped jeans or any of the English safety-pin stuff. Onstage we had a distinct graphic presence of our own which had nothing to do with classic Brit punk style, and offstage we were typical anonymous-looking white lower-middle-class nerds from the Midwest. So it's really strange to us that anybody who dyed their hair or wore personalized clothing got screamed at and called "Devo" from passing trucks. Devo became synonymous with being different. We became this iconic new wave/punk identity the general public could grab on to that didn't have the faintest idea of what was going on, so everything got lumped under Devo if it was different or "weird."

MARK MOTHERSBAUGH: So many people got their asses kicked and called Devo for dressing punk. The lightning rod for hostility that we were in Ohio kind of continued on all our fans, even people who weren't fans. All they had to be was different from the norm and that became some kind of badge: Devo. It was accusatorial. And when they said it, they usually meant it as a condemnation. We were shocked by it, but we were like, "It happens to us, too. We understand."

X's Exene Cervenka, thrift store Queen, at the Masque, 1979.
Photo Credit: Frank Gargani

EXENE CERVENKA: I was living in Tallahassee and I wanted to get out of Florida 'cause I'd never lived in the big city. It was around August '76, and a friend who was moving to California asked me if I wanted to ride with them to share gas costs. My friend Fay already lived there in a one-room apartment in Santa Monica with four other people, so I became the fifth person. I slept in the kitchen. I was just glad to be out of Florida for the first time. It was exciting to be in a city. I didn't have any plans about what I was gonna do when I got there. I was just looking for fun, I guess.

JOHN DOE: The earliest stage of my relationship with Los Angeles was through books, writers like James M. Cain and Bukowski. I grew up in Baltimore. I wanted a big change. The New York punk scene was pretty set by the time I was ready to make a move. I saw a few bands there. I saw Talking Heads and Blondie, and the Heartbreakers. This was '75 or '76. From looking at the flyers and seeing those gigs it was pretty obviously locked down, and I didn't wanna try to weasel my way into something that was already set up. There was a community there, but I didn't know if I could fit in. I'd been writing my own songs for five or six years and I was looking for a change. Baltimore's a lot like New York in terms of architecture and overall vibe. It's East Coast. I left there on Halloween of '76.

BILLY ZOOM: I took up guitar in 1954, at the age of six, after studying piano, violin, and accordion, although my main instruments were sax and clarinet. My father was a jazz musician, and I was trained to be a musician almost from birth. I had years and years of lessons on sax, clarinet, and flute, as well as music theory and arranging on everything except guitar because my mother didn't consider it a legitimate instrument. My dad taught me the basic chords, and I took it from there. When Elvis came out, things got more interesting.

TOP JIMMY: I met Billy Zoom about thirty years ago. Around 1971. Thirty fuckin' years ago! He played a lot with a band called Art Wheeler and the Brothers Love. He was one of the Brothers Love. They'd play down on Slauson Avenue and Crenshaw Boulevard. It was a black group, and he was the token white boy guitar player. He had hair down to his ass and little Benjamin Franklin spectacles and drove a '53 Ford truck. We got friendly. He liked rock and roll and country. He was from the Midwest and stuff, so he was my type of people.

BILLY ZOOM: I started playing in surf/instrumental bands in the early '60s, went through the Beatle thing in the mid-'60s, and ended up touring with black R&B bands in the late '60s and early '70s. I played around Watts with groups like the Brothers Love and backed up everybody from Etta James to Johnny "Guitar" Watson while doing whatever session work I could find. For a while I played with a bar band called the Alligators. Some of their demos were released a while back on a CD called *Pre-X Zoom*. I had also finished electronics school and had a little amp repair shop just off Sunset and Vista.

TOP JIMMY: Billy met Kittra Allen not long after I did. I think he picked her up hitchhiking or something.

KITTRA ALLEN: I met Billy Zoom in 1971. I had already been living in Hollywood for a year in my own apartment.

TOP JIMMY: Billy had an apartment at Afton and Gower. He lived in the basement. Then he and Kittra lived in the truck for a while—they used to park outside my mom's apartment and she'd tell me to go down and get them and bring them up so they could take a shower and eat something 'cause she felt bad for 'em. She got Kittra a job where she worked, a coffee shop next to the Chinese Theater owned by Eddie Nash, the gangster's brother. Billy was doing the best he could. He actually tried working at the taco stand where I worked for a little while.

BILLY ZOOM: When R&B turned into funk, I lost interest and looked for something else to play. I couldn't stand Elton or Frampton, so in desperation I started doing rockabilly, which I had always been into. But rockabilly had gone nowhere, and I was looking for the next big thing that I could stand.

TOP JIMMY: Me and Billy went to see the Ramones and Van Halen in March of '77 out in Norwalk. I'd heard of punk rock, but the Ramones just seemed like a funny rock-and-roll band; they were kinda cartoonish. I liked them, they had great energy. The Ramones show inspired Billy. Got him all excited. Billy was a real good guitar player. Sometimes that's a detriment. He said, "Punk is really cool. You could be real good and nobody would notice." The next week he put an ad in the *Recycler* and Johnny Doe answered it.

BILLY ZOOM: I put an ad in the *Recycler* for a drummer and bass player, and John Doe was the first to answer. He was the second to show up and audition, but he seemed better than the first guy. John also had an ad in the same *Recycler*. He was looking for a guitar player and drummer. I can't remember what the ads said, but they were very similar.

TOP JIMMY: They'd rehearse out in the garage, and then John Doe started bringing his girlfriend by.

EXENE CERVENKA: I dropped out of high school when I was sixteen. My friend Fay helped me get into this program. I was eligible for some kinda women-who-don't-have-nothin'-going-on program, and I found out about Beyond Baroque, the literary center, and it sounded like a good thing, so I applied to work there, and the state paid for it. They'd teach you stuff like typesetting or something, and then the state paid you. I rented the apartment right above the poetry workshop. I worked there and got to read all these really rare poetry books, from the beatniks and all these chapbooks people had made, all this Bukowski stuff. Up till then, my sister was my only influence as far as writing and art. As far as the poetry scene, there were people reading, hanging out . . . people of all ages and all backgrounds. The very first night I went to the Venice Poetry Workshop was the first time I met John. It was his first night, too. We ended up accidentally sitting next to each other.

JOHN DOE: She was the youngest, most interesting other person there, besides myself, of course. She was immediately attractive in her eccentricities, wearing jeans. I thought, "Wow, who's this?"

EXENE CERVENKA: The first thing they asked us to do was write down a list of the ten poets we were most influenced by and I was just sitting there with the piece of paper going, "Let's see . . . um . . ." I had no fucking idea. And he was just like writing all these names down. And I was looking over at him. Looking at his list. And I saw that he had one of the same people down twice. I had nothing on my list, but I criticized him for his list. I said, "You know you wrote that name down twice." And he was like, "Oh." And then I said, "Can I have some of your names for my list?"

JOHN DOE: Exene and I began exchanging poems and writing and looking at each other's material. There were a few pieces that she'd written that were obviously songs. One of them was "I'm Coming Over." I said, "That'd be a great song. Can I sing it in my band?" And she said, "No, I'll sing it. It's my song."

KITTRA ALLEN: Billy liked John and thought he could work with him. They rehearsed together a few times and all was going well before John insisted on adding his girlfriend to the band as a singer. Billy was appalled. Fuck. The chick couldn't sing! But they were already committed to working together, so he figured he'd do the best he could and pray that John would come to his senses at some point.

EXENE CERVENKA: Physically I was taken with Billy 'cause he's so incredible-looking and he was such an amazing guitar player. He is such an eccentric genius.

BILLY ZOOM: I admit it. I was originally horrified that John was bringing his girlfriend into the band.

EXENE CERVENKA: I think everybody is a bit on the fence at the beginning. You know, it's like when you're auditioning a drummer, you're wondering, "Is this guy gonna be good?" It's the same thing. Sure, of course. I'd never even sung before except around the house, and Billy and John had been in so many bands and were so well versed in music. They knew big band, country, jazz, and rockabilly . . . they'd seen Jimi Hendrix play, and I was just a little bratty poet. I didn't know anything.

TOP JIMMY: I was renting this big old house on South Van Ness and it was just too much for one person. It was a mansion near the city's official mayoral residence with built-in cedarwood closets and two staircases going up and all this shit. I moved out so Kittra and Billy and half of X could move in.

EXENE CERVENKA: I had been living with Fay and this other girl behind Circus Books right by the Starwood, and then she decided to move to England.

KITTRA ALLEN: Fay Heart, who called herself Farrah Faucet-Minor, was Exene's best friend from Florida.

EXENE CERVENKA: Farrah Faucet-Minor, yes. I guess Farrah Faucet-Minors would have been more correct, but . . .

KITTRA ALLEN: Fay or Farrah and Exene were best friends. Farrah had a rep among guys as an aggressive tigress in bed, and she is the racist bigot John wrote about in the lyrics to "Los Angeles." You know, "She started to hate every nigger and Jew."

JENNY LENS: Farrah hated me because I'm Jewish. Farrah and Exene were walking in West Hollywood and Farrah just started spouting all these anti-Semitic remarks about how Hitler was right, and I just started crying. I was twenty-seven years old and nobody had ever done that to my face.

KITTRA ALLEN: I always felt Farrah was just doing some psycho Lucille Ball performance and that she didn't really believe a word she said. Farrah was very entertaining and fun to be with, but she could also be a neurotic, high-maintenance nightmare. Average looks to pretty, but she was charismatic with a very clever mind. She was also very obnoxious. A terrible instigator. Total drama junkie. Fiercely loyal to Exene. They loved each other very much. It was a sad parting.

EXENE CERVENKA: I moved in with John at the house on Van Ness after Billy moved out. There were four or five other people living there, too. We came up with a lot of the early X songs in the garage behind the house.

KITTRA ALLEN: What a beautiful house. Paneling and huge pocket doors in mahogany. Crystal pulls and beveled glass throughout the dining room and study and an oak staircase with mahogany trim. Outside was a detached garage and a gorgeous glass atrium. The maid's room had a cedar closet for furs when John and Exene moved in. They were already rehearsing in the garage with Billy and needed a place to live.

BILLY ZOOM: I remember doing "Blue Spark" and "It's Who You Know," and a bunch of rockabilly and R&B covers. I wanted to do something like the Ramones, but a little more . . . well, more something, I didn't really know what.

KITTRA ALLEN: Both John and Exene badmouthed Billy constantly. But it was Zoom who wrote the music for X and made their disjointed poetry come to life. There were control issues and I think they were intimidated by his talent and extensive musical training, so they just bludgeoned him emotionally.

JOHN DOE: The objective was to create something for our own personal satisfaction, because everything else in our youthful and limited opinion sucked, and we knew better.

DAVID ALLEN: Exene was a good gal and I hated that Billy badmouthed her behind her back. Once he called her a sack of potatoes. She heard about it and wore a potato sack next time they played.

KITTRA ALLEN: I let Billy continue rehearsing in the garage after we'd broken up and he'd moved out. I figured he'd dump the conniving [chick] he was screwing and come begging back sooner or later.

BILLY ZOOM: I moved out of the house on Van Ness after my girlfriend broke a guitar over my head, and then John and Exene moved into the maid's room so that we could keep the rehearsal studio.

TOP JIMMY: I don't know if Kittra broke a guitar over his head, but it could be true.

KITTRA ALLEN: John and Exene were mostly quiet with occasional bursts of loud conflict. I once remember Exene screaming at John: "Fuck you, fuck you . . . I never chose to be a woman!" No doubt he was projecting some stupid sexist stereotype upon her. He goaded her. I think he loved to see her rage and reel and bounce those exquisite tits of hers all over the place. There were also beautiful moments of calm serenity with John sitting at his desk in the atrium writing or laid out on the couch reading a novel. John and

Exene kissed and cooed and danced in the kitchen just like all lovers do, but they were a terribly poisonous pair. They loved each other, but there was a constant power struggle. Exene usually wrote while propped up in bed beneath the large black swastika she had painted on the wall over her head. She always looked like a rumpled rag doll, but she wore beautiful flesh-colored silk slips across those beautiful breasts, a massive pair of perfectly formed globes that defied gravity. Exene and I worked together at Jerry Piller's dress shop on Santa Monica Boulevard. It was like a military camp. Exene was depressed. I was depressed.

JOHN DOE: Everybody had day jobs, and then we'd rehearse two or three or four times a week. X's first gig was in our house, this old Craftsman house built in the '20s that we shared with David Allen, Kittra, and some others.

KITTRA ALLEN: John Doe was the most success-driven. Obscenely, ruthlessly ambitious. But nearly so was Exene.

JOHN DOE: We'd put flyers out and just play. We'd call around. Word of mouth. The audience was a mix of runaway teenagers and mid-to-late twenty-somethings. We knew most of them. They were either in a band or working on a fanzine or just hanging out, so they'd show up to these parties and we'd play. Nobody could afford drugs. It was mostly alcohol. We drank a lot of gin, which has a hallucinogenic high because it isn't a grain . . . it's a berry, like tequila or absinthe.

KITTRA ALLEN: I think K.K. played with X at their first-ever show, during Farrah's bon voyage party at our house in Hancock Park. I know he was there. I remember Exene performing. Moaning and lumbering back and forth stiffly like a theatrical exorcist in a hypnotic trance.

K.K. BARRETT: I played the first half of the set, three songs on drums, and Pat Garrett played the second half.

DAVID ALLEN: Bobby Pyn was there at the first X show in our living room at 601 South Van Ness. Back then, he was a very sweet young kid. I think it was probably him or Kickboy who started a big spaghetti fight. I remember scraping the mess off the walls afterward. Similar slapstick food fights seemed to become a tradition at L.A. punk parties after that.

KITTRA ALLEN: I remember Darby—when he was still called Bobby Pyn—smearing spaghetti on the wall of the living room as if it were an expressionist's canvas, and Farrah kept lifting my blouse and announcing to the entire room how large my nipples are.

DAVID ALLEN: Other guests I remember were John Denney and other members of the Weirdos, Margot Olaverra, Tomata du Plenty of the Screamers, Brendan Mullen, Claude Bessy, and Todd Rundgren. It was surreal. I overheard Todd on my phone saying, "I gotta get out of this place . . . and fast," probably because Claude had insulted him, or maybe he was just afraid of getting smacked by a stray meatball! I have no idea how he came to be present. Some pre-Go-Go's gals were also there. Music in the background was by the Stranglers, the Clash, and the Ramones.

HAL NEGRO: X was playing in the middle of the parlor of this big house. I remember thinking, "What a great name for a band—weird but effective." They played on one of those big oval American rugs, it was really an all-American parlor. Very Norman Rockwell. They had this whole American vibe going. John Denney said Billy Zoom was like a semifamous rockabilly country star. There was no CBGB new waviness about them, and even better, there was absolutely nothing English about X at all. And that setting, with the wooden furniture, only added to the atmosphere. They were awesome even then and they only played a real short set. I remember X played around with a bunch of drummers after that, Mick Basher, people like that. But they really came together as a great band when they got D.J. Bonebrake from the Eyes.

D.J. BONEBRAKE: I was playing with the Eyes and John Doe saw us play. They were looking for a replacement drummer. Mick Basher was in the band and had just quit. This must have been near the end of '77. John said, "You wanna try out for my band?" I played in five bands at the same time 'cause I get bored, so I said, "Oh, yeah, I'll do this." I did a rehearsal with them and I liked the music. So I was playing in the Eyes and playing in X, sometimes at the same show, until John said, "You need to be in our band exclusively. You need to commit." They pressured me to do that, and I agreed. The Eyes, I was getting tired of them. They were a really good band, but X had more variety.

Pass the Dust, I Think I'm Bowie: A Few Words About Black Randy (1977-78)

chapter 12

Black Randy, 1978. Photo Credit: Scott Lindgren

DAVID ALLEN: Black Randy also performed for the first time at Farrah's farewell do. Randy playing in the living room is still my most vivid memory of that night, playing his ode to African despot Idi Amin.

HAL NEGRO: He declared Idi Amin a hero and a saint . . . the crazed cannibal president of Uganda who drank blood and ate his enemies' entrails to show everybody who was boss.

EXENE CERVENKA: Black Randy was this amazing personality. A wild, dangerous, fucked-up guy who would do anything. Really fun to be around. I was very shy 'cause I'd never been in a big city and I wasn't used to these personalities from all over the country that were such outlaws.

JOHN DOE: John "Jackie" Morris, better known as Black Randy, was a figment of his own imagination. He was friends with people like Cherie the Penguin, who was a dominatrix. Randy was friends with her and with this guy Tony, who was this male hustler who worked Santa Monica Boulevard. Randy was just one of these incredibly colorful characters. He was a compulsive liar with a sort of Don Rickles type of insulting humor, who was constantly cutting people down, but he would always have everyone in stitches laughing.

HAL NEGRO: Black Randy was a bigger-than-life figure. The legend was that he was this white kid raised by black people in a black neighborhood in Long Beach.

GORILLA ROSE: He just wanted to be a Negro. It would've made him happier because he thought black people were doing all the cool things. So just be one!

BLACK RANDY: My stepfather was a horrible man. He was a gun collector and a violent geek . . . a racist, truck-drivin' pigfucker who kept a raccoon in the garage and about thirty guns around the house. He was at a Ku Klux Klan level of insanity, and he beat me and my mother up all the time. Every time I came home there was some new goddamn thing. I ran away a couple times and was caught with LSD, but Napa was such a conservative place that they sent me to the youth authority. Why would my mom marry a creep like that? She was a born insecure twit, that's why. My real father was a junkie. He's a well-known petty thief, creep, and dope dealer. His nickname is Morphine Jack. He lives in Long Beach. He looks like the skankiest dog. I didn't meet him until I was twenty-four. As soon as I met him he was borrowing money and shooting me up with dope. He borrowed money from me and shorted me on a heroin deal within an hour of meeting me, I swear to God. He was on welfare. He'd lived with Lenny Bruce in Laurel Canyon for a time in the '50s. They were good buddies. He got Lenny interested in heroin from speed. That was my old man's contribution to twentieth-century entertainment culture.

HAL NEGRO: Another part of the Black Randy legend was that he'd grown up hustling on the street for money. He'd sold his ass, done petty crime, and had been heavily involved with nasty drugs.

BLACK RANDY: El Duce from the Mentors always said that I got butt-fucked in the youth authority. Well, I have gotten butt-fucked, but never in jail. I did it on the street for the money.

JOHN DOE: Randy romanticized the whole street-hustler, drug-culture, criminal dark side of L.A. in his writing. But he didn't live on the street and he wasn't a hustler. He wasn't good-looking enough to be a hustler. Still, he totally embraced it, saw it as something that was pure and totally countercultural. It was antigovernment, anti-society, antieverything.

HAL NEGRO: Randy was very charismatic and intimidating with that street thug thing. His band the Metrosquad was like tight rhythm and blues punk rock, and Randy would do these sick-out raps like "Loner with a Boner," "Beershit," and "Trouble at the Cup" . . . he even had a tune called "I Tell Lies Everyday" set to some Sly Stone rip-off. Randy always had scams going. He'd steal neon signs from old buildings and sell them to antique dealers. He had an office supplies telemarketing company. He was always a little more flush with cash than the other punks.

K.K. BARRETT: Black Randy was a diabetic smart-ass who made his ends through phone sales. He was the most brilliant phone actor. He could sell anything to anybody. He could set up a phone room anywhere and make money, but because he was diabetic and alco-holic he'd always get too much sugar and pass out and end up in the drunk tank.

BLACK RANDY: I was a natural for lying over the phone because I was good at convincing people of things, and I like talking on the phone. I tell the truth even when I lie. Listen to the cut "Tellin'

Lies Every Day" on my album. Phone sales are just this side of dope peddling or something . . . just this side of acceptable white collar crime . . . we're a nuisance . . . it can't be stamped out. There's no law against what we do. We're just thieves, and that's what I do for a living.

JOHN DOE: Black Randy was a precursor to punk rap. He was all about an ironic take on Iceberg Slim, Donald Goines, Dolemite . . . blaxploitation movies, black pulp literature, and the whole pimp culture underworld . . . and his lyrics were creative in their rhymes and their rhythm. He was a great writer who wasn't afraid to be funny. Writing a song about Idi Amin, who was obviously a monster, was an example of the extremely dark humor that Randy loved. He loved the sheer preposterousness of someone eating part of their enemy to make a point.

K.K. BARRETT: Black Randy was the original prankster. If he thought something was boring, he'd call the cops and say, "There's somebody here with a gun." That was his idea of humor. His other big thing was he'd go to a party and if a girl had her purse down, he'd take a crap in it . . . they'd go into the bathroom to freshen up and they'd get their brush and drag it through their hair and Randy would be in the background dying laughing.

BLACK RANDY: My drummer Joe Nanini told me, "The first time I ever saw you, you were with your best friend John Doe, drinking beer, and you were supposed to be getting a ride in his car, but John was passed out drunk in the dressing room and you were pissing on him." I said, "Listen up, man . . . everybody knows it's not cool to crash out at a punk party."

KITTRA ALLEN: Black Randy was a total deviant. He was an abused and angry kid struggling with sexuality. He liked to shock people. He was very vulgar. And coming from me, that's quite a statement. I remember going to a party at his house and he'd made all these home movies of himself blowing up a plastic sex doll and shitting in its mouth. Randy was also a blustering bully. Brilliant but sick.

D.J. BONEBRAKE: One day I got a jury notice in the mail, so I asked Black Randy for advice! I must have been crazy. I said, "What do I do about this? I got jury duty. I don't want to go to jury duty." And he goes, "Well, here's what you do. You get a big, black felt pen and you write in big letters across the form VIVA LA ANGEL DUST and you send it back in. They'll never bug you again." So I did that and sent it in. I didn't get another jury notice for ten years.

BLACK RANDY: Everything I was doing at that time was a calculated type of behavior. I was a very rowdy, frustrated guy. I was big and fat, and I was very frustrated by this culture that I felt excluded from that had grown up in the '70s, the disco culture and the hippie culture that had grown up and given up. I was drunken and rowdy. I tried to steal the cash register at the door on my way out from a *Slash* benefit. I had to be restrained by a bunch of security guards, and I had to beg the editor of *Slash* to let me go. This was my way of social gesture. It was a calculated move in the sense of "I'm a punk and this is what punks do." The punks certainly responded to me in the right way, because it made everyone talk about me immediately.

GEZA X: Cuckoo money is SSI, Supplementary Security Income. Basically the government gives it to crazies or disabled people. It's really hard to get on it. I tried to show them I was crazy by acting so crazy that I didn't know I was crazy. It took me five years to get on it. I'd go down to the Social Security office and fill out all these forms. Black Randy smeared himself with excrement when he went down to get it. He was on it a long time, but Randy really was crazy. I was never really like schizoid crazy, it was basically putting on a show.

BLACK RANDY: I once shat right in the middle of the dance floor at an X show because I'd spent the whole day with X and they were really patronizing me because they didn't want me to do anything bad. They were buying me beers and driving me around, being best buddies. They even followed me into the bathroom at the hall to make sure I didn't do anything with the toilets. So I took a shit in a Dixie cup and went out on the floor when everybody was jumping around and dropped it. The hall was owned by some New Age Sufi subcult. After the show there were all these Sufi ladies in white robes and turbans standing around and there was this thin layer of shit all around their club and they're going, "This our church. This our church. What are we gonna do?" I have a tape of that show. You can hear Billy Zoom going, "What's that?" and you can hear

Exene go, "It's *shit!*" Then I had the balls to make John and Exene drive me home after I passed out in their car waiting for them.

GEZA X: Black Randy and I spent a good year raging on speed. It was one of the most colorful, interesting, creepy, brilliantly bizarre periods of my whole life. Randy was one of the most intelligent but borderline dangerous people I've ever known. I met his dad, who was this battered old hot-rod biker dog, and I eyeballed him shooting his son up with morphine. He had these spectacles with this little chain around his neck and Randy was blubbering like a baby, something he would do every single time he shot up, without fail. It was the most bizarre, ritualistic reenactment of some deep psychological thing. His girlfriend would tell him to go in the other room and shut up. He had tracks as thick as inner tubes. His dad had these square glasses and he'd say, "Now, son, just hold still."

GORILLA ROSE: He made a couple of records. Did his day jobs. Then years later he married this girl and they both died of AIDS from shooting drugs. I saw him two months before he died. I hadn't seen him for a year or two and he was real thin. He told me about this horrible toe surgery that he had had where he had his toes cut off because they were getting infected. He was still drinking like a fish. It was just real sad to see him like that. I don't want to say that all his sins had caught up with him. It was just unfortunate that he had this AIDS that came along and seemed to punish everybody for doing what they'd been doing for ten years and managing to survive. It was a tragedy.

chapter 13

The Germs perform at Kim Fowley's New Wave Night at the Whisky, 1977.
Photo Credit: Diane Grove

JOHN DOE: Despite the growing number of bands, there was no live music scene in L.A. The Whisky was closed and the Starwood was for cover bands. If you were lucky, Cheap Trick was playing there. And there was Quiet Riot, this weird Slade tribute band, three years after glam, or something. It was all so terrible that it demanded we create a new scene of our own.

STAN RIDGWAY: I used to go to the Whisky and talk to the owner, Elmer Valentine and say, "Please let our band play here!" And he'd say, "Oh, well, I don't know."

KIM FOWLEY: One day in the summer of '77, Elmer Valentine said to me, "We need a gimmick to get tickets sold. What do you have?" And I said, "Well, punk rock," and he said, "What's that?" "English stuff," I said. "Oh, yeah, well, put punk rock in here—whatever it is." I said, "Okay." So I called up Rodney and said, "Rodney, you gotta put me on the air, so we can invite all the garage bands to show up at the Whisky. We'll call it punk rock no matter what it is, okay?" So I went on Rodney's show and said, "Attention, unsigned new bands in garages! Guys and girls who are playing the weird underground music. Whoever shows up at the Whisky this coming Friday will automatically be guaranteed a spot. In other words, if you show up, you get to go onstage, even if you're horrible. I don't care. English punk is horrible and they get to go onstage—so if you're horrible, you get to go onstage, too. English punk and American punk can't be that much different." So KROQ pounded this thing for the whole week. We put a sign on the Whisky that read KIM FOWLEY PRESENTS NEW WAVE NIGHTS.

GREG SHAW: Fowley made a deal with Peer Music [song publishers] to pay to record the whole Fowley-promoted Whisky show on remote 8-track with the idea that if anything historic happened, it would be documented, and Fowley/Peer would own the publishing. I was to cover the record-releasing side of the deal, and all the bands signed recording/publishing contracts. There are still unreleased tapes by a lot of good bands, including the Weirdos; somehow it was only the Germs session that got released. I don't have the tapes.

GUS HUDSON: Rodney introduced the Germs and was mercilessly heckled by the crowd of kids from Uni High, Newbury High, and from God knows where else. They weren't diggin' on the new wave hype or the fact that many of the bands were these funny, beaten-up old bar bands that had about as much to do with punk as Donny Osmond or Led Zeppelin.

KIM FOWLEY: It was a crowd of displaced persons, refugees from the suburbs. It was urine-stained, safety-pin-wearing, shit-ass mother-fucker out-of-control fuckboys, fuckgirls . . . pissing, puking, shit-ting, farting . . . it was anger angst madness . . . white dopes on punk. It was like Kosovo meets Auschwitz.

PAT SMEAR: You should see some of the scums we attract.

GUS HUDSON: One of the songs the Germs were gonna do was "Sugar Sugar" by the Archies. The old bubblegum pop hit. I was to hand Bobby the bag of sugar on cue so he could dump it all over the room. Rodney was backstage and threatened Bobby, "If I get any peanut butter on me, or any of that whipped cream crap gets on my clothes, you guys are banned from the Strip forever. I mean that." During the rest of the Germs' set we were opening up condiment packs and throwing them at the audience. Afterward they made me clean up all the mess. I think Belinda was helping out, too.

RODNEY BINGENHEIMER: At the time, Belinda was fat and ugly with really short hair.

GUS HUDSON: Then on the second new wave night the Dils played. They were this group who flirted with Marxist imagery and played in front of a red-and-yellow hammer-and-sickle banner. But it just seemed like it was a subject they really might have not known very much about. It just sounded cool.

TONY KINMAN: I'd gone to UC San Diego and I think every one of my college professors were Maoists. I remember reading an awful lot of that stuff. When we moved to L.A., we met a guy named Peter Urban who became a buddy, and back then your buddy would end up becoming your manager, and it happened our manager was a hardcore communist. We'd sit around and talk about it and we started writing songs with more aggressive themes. It was never as important to us as some people thought, but at the time it seemed that trying to create some sort of change was a good thing. I considered myself a communist for about a year.

KIM FOWLEY: The Dils were these two shit-assed rich kid Marxist clown brothers, the Kinman brothers. Chip and Tony. This double-headed commie punk act from San Diego County who pouted and were obsessively anal about everything.

TONY KINMAN: The Dils hated Kim Fowley and his sidekick Harvey Kubernik. I thought people like them and Rodney Bingenheimer were repulsive and only on the punk scene to get laid. To them it was "Here's another little scene we can strut around in." I remember Fowley and Kubernik walking around with that leering look on their faces, and the rest of us were just so young. This was our punk rock revolution, and here you've got the same old stupid people stumbling around in their stupid old glam clothes. I don't know how they saw their roles in this, but I know other people saw them as liaisons from the old scene to help them get into the regular clubs. When Peter called us and said, "Do you wanna do Kim Fowley's night?" our first response was "Fuck, no. Fuck those assholes." But of course we did it, 'cause it was the only way we were ever going to get to play the Whisky.

GUS HUDSON: The Dils slagged Kim from the stage, calling him a trendy-assed exploiter. Afterwards they said that he demanded an apology or else he'd ensure bad press, no recordings, and no club bookings.

TONY KINMAN: We were into a punk rock revolution to destroy the way things were, to destroy the status quo, and to me people like Kim and Rodney were the status quo. However they saw themselves, I saw them as part of the problem, 'cause to me it wasn't about a career, or self-promotion, or chasing girls. It wasn't about getting a record deal. It wasn't about being on television.

KIM FOWLEY: Venom was everywhere that night!

CHRIS ASHFORD: Later Kim Fowley and the Dils almost had a fight. Kim was doing his usual bizarre posturing, and Peter Urban wasn't gonna take any of that bullshit and got up in his face. I don't remember how it cooled off, but they were like pecking red roosters in front of each other for a while. Kim and the Dils had openly despised each other ever since Kim's big new wave fest at the Whisky.

TONY KINMAN: A bit later on the Dils were at the Whisky. We're there watching the Zeros, and Rodney was sitting there with his clique of people, and he walked by us and he had his shag hairdo and it had some altitude on it with hair spray and of course back then you could smoke in nightclubs and I walked by with a little Bic lighter and set his hair on fire. And one of Rodney's friends, this goony guy, was beating on Rodney's head going, "Rodney, man, the Dils set your hair on fire, the Dils set your hair on fire." We would do stuff like that. "What's Rodney doing here? Set his hair on fire. Punk rock!"

KIM FOWLEY: So this went from the garage, through the radio, onto the stage, and into the *L.A. Times* and *Time* magazine. And of course, L.A. being a media center, everybody else soon picked up on it, and soon the rest of America was told about punk rock. Californian punk rockers, these throwing-up, open-sore, suburban callow youths, were suddenly the new cock-swaggering shit-asses after one gig apiece. Which is remarkable when you think of the Beatles and the Stones, who actually toured horrible night-after-night gigs over a period of years to get a record deal, you know? And here these fuckers were going right into *Time* magazine.

HAL NEGRO: *Time* magazine ran this totally lame punk article which carried a single unidentified photo of the Weirdos backstage at the Whisky and a bunch of shots of punks in all these different cities like London, New York, Boston, and Chicago. What was going on in L.A. wasn't even mentioned, Kim's show sure wasn't, and the caption never even identified the Weirdos as an L.A. band, but lumped them in under "bands with bizarre names like [sic] Clash, Stranglers, Damned, Weirdos." The writer focused entirely on the scenes at the Roxy in London, CB's in New York City, and the Rat in Boston . . . L.A. was shit out of luck.

BRENDAN MULLEN: Although the indigenous Los Angeles punk scene was fast expanding during the summer of '77, *Slash* still continued to look toward the Sex Pistols and their London-burning ilk for inspiration. Look at the third issue. Who's on the cover? Johnny Rotten.

LEONARD PHILLIPS: There used to be a magazine TV show in the '70s called *Weekend* hosted by this pock-faced guy. One weekend, probably around June of '77, he did a show about the punk rock phenomenon in England. The show concentrated primarily on the Sex Pistols 'cause it was the queen's Jubilee and "God Save the Queen" had just come out. The weekend after that show aired snippets of early pogoing with kids doing all that mock violence, dressed up with safety pins in their heads, strangling each other on the dance floor . . . boom, the very next weekend the L.A. kids were doing it at the Starwood club.

BIBBE HANSEN: New York punk was all about these lower-middle-class white kids suddenly becoming smart-asses. There were always more garage bands here in L.A. because we have more garages.

TRUDIE ARGUELLES: I had moved to New York for a while but had decided I didn't want to stay there after all. L.A. was much more exciting than New York. It seemed like the scene out here was just being born. When I traveled to New York during the summer of '77, Patti Smith and Television and the Ramones had already been the big thing for a while. It just didn't seem as much of an exciting, new, growing thing, it had already happened, all the bands were already signed and all their record companies and publicists were just gearing up to try and sell a ton of records to us new kids, record business as usual. The people going to CB's were much older people, but we were all really young. We were just teenagers. It was a new thing for us. We felt like everybody else was kind of jaded.

HAL NEGRO: If there was a media schism between New York and L.A., the Ramones became the only untouchable New York band on a level unbound by provincial limitations, and the entire L.A. new underground rock scene bowed down, enthralled by a series of shows they did at the Whisky in the spring and summer of '77, all of them unforgettable. The timing for this band was exquisite. L.A. gave the Ramones an audience at least as big and enthusiastic as they got in England.

EXENE CERVENKA: Joey Ramone was much more than a symbol of punk rock. There was something about him. He was the leader.

JOEY RAMONE: Los Angeles was great. We blew their minds. We were an instant hit. They totally related to us. A sick bunch. The L.A. kids were really wild and insane, much more like the English audiences than the hip New York crowd.

DON WALLER: Look how long it took X to get that deal with Elektra! Does anyone really think it would've taken them that long to get a major deal if they'd been in New York all those years?

GERALD CASALE: I think X suffered reverse prejudice from coming from here. Had X been from Indiana, all the top A&R people would have been salivating to sign them.

DON WALLER: The whole CBGB scene hogged all the media attention and those acts got bigger-budget major-label deals and access to proper recording studios and engineers—mostly because of Sire Records chief Seymour Stein—but most of 'em didn't have careers. Here in L.A., the punk bands got no national media, and certainly fewer major record deals. It made the L.A. bands more willing to do things themselves, to start their own labels.

EXENE CERVENKA: It definitely helped the scene that there was no major label involvement early on. I think an artist working in a vacuum has got to be the healthiest thing.

HAL NEGRO: The near total lack of major label attention produced an indie label boom. It's a natural extension of the punk ethic. Anybody can make a record. Fuck it. Anybody can sell that record. Some people waited for the majors to come around. But most bands didn't wanna wait. And some of their enterprising friends didn't want to wait either. There was too much excitement about what was being created.

CHRIS ASHFORD: The first single on my label, What? Records, was "Forming" by the Germs. It came out at the end of July in '77. When they recorded "Forming," they just got a roll of tape and they set up in Pat Smear's garage and recorded three versions and some other song. We used the version with the most echo on the voice. The echo was an accident. Somebody hit a button by mistake. It was just a two-track recorder. The voice was on one side and the music was on the other. We were gonna put mono on it, but we realized it's just real crude stereo. The first batch was a thousand. And they all had the labels on the wrong side. Reversed. The A-side, "Forming," was listed on the B-side, and the plain black "Sex Boy" live label on the A-side. There's only a few of those around 'cause they threw about six hundred of them at this one house. It's the ultimate Germs record geek collectible.

PAT SMEAR: We recorded "Forming" for a single. The only reason there weren't many indie records then was because it was down to how were we gonna sell them. Out of our homes? But Chris Ashford worked at a record store and made a deal with the Peaches record store chain. We'd been listening to Rodney whose show started up the year before punk happened. He was the first to play punk out of England. So when our single came out we called him and asked him to play it. We were like brats. We called him all night, every night, and he finally just got mad and said "Look, I'll play your record if you'll stop calling me." So we made this deal and stuck to it and he played our single, and it started selling.

NICKEY BEAT: This terrible little Germs record made it onto Rodney's show. It was a novelty. It was played because it was so horrible! It was real slow and boring and wimpy-sounding compared to what they became.

CLAUDE BESSY: Beyond music . . . mind-boggling . . . inexplicably brilliant in bringing monotony to new heights.

PAT SMEAR: At the time *Billboard* had this new wave chart, and the single made it onto the new wave top ten. Which was hilarious, of course, since there were only 1,000 pressed. This chart must be pretty fuckin' weak if we're charting on it, you know it had the top five—Blondie, the Ramones, whatever—and it had this bottom five which was these dumb little nobody bands like us . . . but we got shows from it.

TONY KINMAN: Chris Ashford was putting out the Germs record and he wanted to put out our record, too. The Zeros were our buddies. They lived near us in Chula Vista. They'd already put out the "Don't Push Me Around" single on Bomp, which they'd recorded in this cheap little studio down there. So we went there and recorded "I Hate the Rich."

K.K. BARRETT: Dangerhouse Records became one of the most important indie labels of the day, but it started up under somewhat strange circumstances. There were emotional boyfriend/lover things going on in the Screamers between David Brown and Tomata, and Tommy Gear disapproved. Something happened, and all of a sudden David was out of the band. They just told me. I didn't have a say in it. I was like, "Fuck, there's not enough musicality going on to carry it without him." The entire rhythm section was me playing floor toms and rack toms and sixteenth notes on the bass drum pedal with David playing the bass and the melody on the distorted Rhodes. The whiny synth on top of that was a single note at a time, a lead guitar part played by Tommy. With David gone, I thought, "Fuck, now what are we gonna do?" But David soon hooked up with my friends from Oklahoma and started up the Dangerhouse record label to do stuff with Black Randy and the other new bands.

EXENE CERVENKA: I was busy drinking and fucking around and goofing off, when John came up to me and said, "I met this guy David Brown. He says he'll put this record out." And I said, "Oh, good." I didn't really negotiate much back then.

JOHN DOE: David and Pat Garrett would set up recording stuff in hotel rooms. There was one Black Randy Dangerhouse session that we did that was in two empty hotel rooms. Sort of like Robert Johnson—put the recording unit in one room and the band in another, then fight with the hotel manager because we were making too much noise.

HAL NEGRO: These indie records were starting to get played on KROQ, and Cheech and Chong's producer, Lou Adler, saw these new punk bands as an opportunity to drum up extras for a Battle of the Bands scene for their movie *Up in Smoke,* which was shooting in Hollywood in August of '77. Adler put out a Fowley-style open cattle call for punk bands.

EXENE CERVENKA: Bobby Pyn and I were both extras on the Cheech and Chong movie . . . that's where I met him. It was fifty dollars, an open call . . . fifty bucks for a couple of hours, so it was a big score for me. It was boring as hell, and they didn't even feed us.

ANDY SEVEN: It was so boring, sitting and waiting around, so Bobby started throwing stuff around, screaming, and tearing shit up. Maybe he knew that the joke was on them, but that was the way the Germs played shows anyway. They always trashed stuff. As soon as Bobby started singing he was kicking stuff over. The stage-hands freaked out 'cause they realized it wasn't a joke, it was the real thing. I'm not sure they even finished one song before they turned off the PA and threw the Germs out of the club while the audience was booing the stagehands big-time 'cause they came to see these bands at the Roxy for free.

GERBER: The whole *Up in Smoke* thing turned into one of those take-the-walls-down moments. I just remember being very fucked up and roarin' out, "O-o-o-kay, it's time to fight!"

RICK WILDER: Oh, God, that thing with Lou Adler. The Cheech and Chong movie. I was drinking Jack Daniel's early in the morning, and by the middle of the day I was sick of these people throwing water and trying to be punk, so I started throwing the water at the cameras and breaking shit, so Uncle Lou got mad and threw me off the set.

TONY KINMAN: I never liked Cheech and Chong.

HAL NEGRO: The Dickies, the only L.A. punk band to get signed to a major label, A&M Records, about a year later, was formed by Iggy Pop's drug dealer. They were great, but they were a novelty act.

TONY KINMAN: The major labels decided that the one band on the West Coast that was really gonna be huge, the best punk rock band in America, was the Dickies. That was the only band that got signed to a major record deal. That was the corporate music business's idea of what was good and vital and totally cool. A band that sings songs like "Gigantor."

STEVEN HUFSTETER: Stan Lee of the Dickies was a wheeler-dealer. Not just in drugs, but in all kinds of contraband. He was a legendary person on the local rock scene and he'd been working it for a while. Iggy used to show up at Stan's window at his parents' house in the Valley, stumbling about on the front lawn in his bikini underwear moaning, "Stan Lee! Stan Lee!" Iggy was trying to get off heroin and was always trying to get Quaaludes from Stan.

STEVEN HUFSTETER: One day Stan Lee suddenly decided that he wanted to play guitar. I was giving him lessons. He wanted to have a band like Bad Company. He wanted to be like Ritchie Blackmore from Deep Purple. I told him, "Stan, you can't play that stuff. You gotta be punk rock. You're not good enough . . . it'll take too long for you to be that good. Why don't you just play punk rock?" He was real skeptical. At first he thought I was insulting him, but then he listened to the Ramones and that's when he decided to form a punk band. I kept reassuring him, "Stan, it's okay, it's very cool to be a punk rocker." I said the same thing to Leonard Phillips, who later became their lead singer. He is an incredibly gifted keyboard player who wanted to be Keith Emerson to Stan's Ritchie Blackmore. Leonard even had a Keith Emerson haircut and stuff, and he'd been in the Quick . . . he used to crack us up during rehearsals with his weird comedy sketches and parodies of singers in other bands. So I'd already seen the whole Leonard show, but he didn't think of himself as a real singer. So when Stan decided to

form this punk band, I told Leonard, "You should be a punk rock singer." I put the two of them together. And that was the core of the Dickies.

LEONARD PHILLIPS: I idolized Steve Hufsteter as a serious musician because in the '70s if you were a young wanna-be rock musician, you practiced your ax. You didn't spend as much time writing songs as you did running up and down silly scales trying to get faster and hotter on the old frets at the expense of honing any compositional or writing skills. You just wanted to be hot with the licks so you could jam and get girls, but Hufsteter was one of these rare guys who was a superb player who paid more attention to just getting three or four musicians together, irrespective of their ability, so he could show them actual songs—not just showing off scales—things he'd write and arrange himself, and he was real good at it and I was totally impressed.

STEVEN HUFSTETER: I was pretty domineering with the writing in the Quick and the rest of the guys were dying to get their songs done by the band, so it was only a matter of time before there was a big outburst of frustrated creativity . . . and the formation of the Dickies was real timely. Here was finally an outlet for their songwriting talents, and the early Dickies became like a side writing project for the Quick. The earliest Dickies' rehearsals were with Danny Wilde singing. The Dickies were a spin-off of this little Valley scene where the Quick coalesced first and the Dickies second. Danny and Ian and Billy Bizeau and our roadie Scott Goddard all wrote for the early Dickies.

LEONARD PHILLIPS: I knew Hufsteter in junior high as this weird, goofy, different-looking kid. He had these very, very large lips and very weak eyes that he had horn-rimmed glasses for and he kind of had bad acne, too, but I saw him turn his weaknesses into strengths at school. He grew a shag haircut and started wearing these effeminate low-cut skinny knit shirts. Steve very much had this rock-and-roll affectation, and had this rep for being quite the rock-and-roll wizard on guitar. So I eventually approached him and we got together. He'd give guitar lessons to Stan Lee. He didn't have a car, so he'd come over to my house and we'd work on songs, then he'd have Stan pick him up from my place, go over to Stan's, where he'd give him a quick guitar lesson and get a steak dinner out of him and then a ride home to his part of the Valley.

STEVEN HUFSTETER: The Dickies never really thought of themselves as punks even though they were completely embraced by that scene. The Dickies were a spoof of punk rock. Not so much making fun of it, but using it as an opportunity. Embracing the silliness of the form ever since the Ramones had made it deliberately silly. Karlos Kaballero, the drummer, came up with the name the Dickies, and he also came up with the song "Doggie Doo." The Dickies did the same routine as the Quick, with every song having a different prop: "This song has the monkey mask. This song has the dog puppet." We wrote "If Stewart Could Talk," which had the dick puppet. That came from the Tubes and the Sensational Alice Harvey Band . . . but also *Wallace and Labmo*. There was a kiddie show broadcast out of Arizona called the *Wallace and Labmo Show*. And every kid watched the *Wallace and Labmo Show*. These guys were very hip kind of bohemian types. And all the members of Alice Cooper and the Tubes grew up watching them. I grew up watching it, too, and the humor of bands like the Dickies and the Quick is all directly attributed to *Wallace and Labmo*. They would do parodies of everything that was out. They had various kids' shows broadcast out of L.A., too. I remember one called *Shrimpenstein*.

STAN LEE: Our only goal was to make a single. John Hewlett came to one of our early shows and told me he thought we were the best band he'd ever seen. I laughed, but then he told me he managed Sparks. I really liked the *Kimono My House* LP. I thought, "Well, what did you have in mind?" He asked if we had a manager. It didn't hurt that he was short, British, and charming. He had an instant plan to take us in the studio to cut some tracks for a single on a label he was starting. Soon we were recording at Brothers Studio (the Beach Boys haunt in Santa Monica with Earl Mankey). When we were done he looked at me and said, "This is far bigger than I had imagined . . . I'm gonna take this tape to England and get you a major deal." I thought, "Okay, what can it hurt?" Island Records was interested, and he had an appointment with Derek Green, president of A&M Records U.K., who'd just kicked the Sex Pistols off the label and was looking for another punk band,

preferably one that wouldn't throw up on them. After hearing the tape, he flew to L.A. with John to see if we were for real and to meet us.

GERBER: I loved the Dickies' goofy punk rock and I liked to party with Karlos and Billy Club. I shot a lot of Desoxin with Karlos and had a big affair with him. I never really was too connected with Leonard and Stan Lee. They lived with their fucking parents, you know? They lived with their fucking parents in the Valley. I think they still do.

STAN LEE: Meanwhile a local TV writer who saw us at the Whisky wrote us into an episode of *CPO Sharkey,* a nationally syndicated sitcom starring Don Rickles. The timing was perfect. The plane landed at 7 P.M. Hewlett ushered Mr. Green over to NBC by eight o'clock and into the live audience just in time for the taping of the show. Afterward we met, but the checkbook didn't come out yet. He wanted to see the band live doing a full-length show with a real club audience. We set up a showcase at the Whisky. He showed up with Jerry Moss (the *M* in A&M). I put them in a booth and told them in my most puffed-up posture, "You have no business in the record business if you don't sign this band."

HAL NEGRO: Punk was ridiculed nationwide in the Don Rickles sitcom *CPO Sharkey* when the Dickies appeared surrounded by some punks from the Masque mingling with movie punk extras. It was just like in those '50s-style teen exploitation quickies where actors are obviously way too old to be real kids . . . the "punk" extras were in Alice Cooper makeup, leather motorcycle jackets, ballet leotards, and tennis shoes! It was totally hokey, but the show gave the nation's kids ideas on how to dress punk.

STAN LEE: The *Incredible Shrinking Dickies* album came after they put out the demo tape as a ten-inch white vinyl EP with three tunes, "Hideous," "You Drive Me Ape," and "Paranoid." The Dickies also covered a lot of '60s songs punk rock style, as an affectionate piss-take of hippies and the old culture. Critics dissed us as an air-headed novelty act, but we were the first L.A. punk band to sign with a major.

LEONARD PHILLIPS: The adventure of the Dickies, as well as the detriment of the Dickies, was that it all happened too fast. We went from rehearsing in someone's garage to selling out the Whisky and the Starwood in about two months. Two months after that we had a hundred-thousand-dollar major label deal. Within a year we had a Top 10 hit in England. A few months after that heroin raised its ugly head. Stan and Billy had already dabbled with it, but we all started using it as a band on that first trip to London. It just seemed like the hip rock-and-roll thing to do. I was just a drug addict waiting to happen, and as soon as it hit me, it proceeded to fuck up the next twenty years of my life.

chapter 14

Inside the Plunger Pit. On bed (*left to right*): Trixie, Hellin, Trudie, and Mary; front (*left to right*): Billy Club and Rock Bottom, 1977. Photo Credit: Jules Bates

BRENDAN MULLEN: I moved officially-unofficially into a ten-thousand-square-foot basement in mid-June '77, the Hollywood Center Building at 1655 North Cherokee Avenue, off Hollywood Boulevard, and agreed to take it as is—thrashed to hell—and got a free month's rent to clear out fifteen years of debris from this multi-roomed labyrinth whose last known occupant had been the Don Martin School of Radio and Broadcasting in the '40s. This architecturally wonderful big-little building had gone up circa 1923 bankrolled by Hollywood's first important mega mogul, Cecil B. de Mille, now flush enough to build his own five-story headquarters right on Hollywood Boulevard. The real Hollywood is one square mile, and everything else is the aftermath of movie gold rush madness. If you took a pin and stuck it dead center of Hollywood, it would be Cecil's Hollywood Center Building. We were literally dead center in the bowels of Hollywood. I had been trying quite hard to find a place to beat on drums and percussion anytime, any kind of drums, any kind of percussives, night or day. Punk rock, British, American, or otherwise, was not the main agenda. I recruited various runaways, musicians, welfare people, artists, and other street people from the boulevard like Mark Hazlewood (son of Lee), Don Bonner, Pat Flaherty, and others to help me open a rehearsal room rental business, which quickly morphed into probably the first illegal club space (excluding those "ethnic" all-male hoo-bangin' storefront card joints) since Prohibition. The Boulevard of the '70s was a whole other underdog downscale nonentity to the Strip, which worked its own sick street magic.

BIBBE HANSEN: My father, Al Hansen, came out to L.A. at the end of '75, beginning of '76. Al had that extraordinary knack for being right on the edge of everything, and a little beyond, a little ahead of everybody, without even trying. My husband at the time, David Campbell, Beck's dad, was working with all these people like Linda Ronstadt, Carly Simon, J.D. Souther, Rita Coolidge, Andrew Gold, Jackson Browne, James Taylor, you name it . . . the quintessential California singer-songwriter stuff, but I just didn't relate to that music at all. The only thing from the early-to-mid '70s that touched me musically was Iggy and Bowie. I had completely tuned out from commercial radio. My father and I started going to clubs after he moved to L.A. to check out bands, but the scene wasn't really punk yet. It was that weird indeterminate '75–'76 area after glam had totally fallen out. We'd see the Runaways, the Quick, Cheap Trick. Soon Al told us about meeting this guy carrying lumber down an alley and he followed him. And it was Brendan Mullen, this Scottish guy who was setting up this huge practice facility in some basement with all these different rooms where six or seven bands could rehearse at the same time, and wasn't that fantastic? This Brendan guy also knew who John Cage was. It was just several blocks from where we lived on Lanewood Avenue.

SEAN CARRILLO: The fact that Al Hansen arrived on the scene at that precise moment when Brendan was trying to come up with a name for the place was the genius of Al.

BIBBE HANSEN: While Al was there with Brendan, the Controllers came and rented their room, and I think they were one of the first people in, and that's how Al met the Controllers and they all became fast friends. Al became the center of their little clique and ended up managing them.

STAN RIDGWAY: I don't want to speak for him, but Brendan had something else entirely different in mind for the Masque. He was a drummer, and it was also a place for him to play if I'm not mistaken.

JOHNNY STINGRAY: The Controllers needed a place to play loud, so we found a rehearsal studio in the heart of Hollywood (under the Pussycat Theater on Hollywood Boulevard) for $2.00 an hour, provided we didn't mind practicing in the middle of the night. We didn't. The place was run by a disheveled Scotsman named Brendan Mullen who was impressed enough by our tenacity and cash flow to rent us a tiny room on a monthly basis. By the Fall of '77, Brendan was hosting regular shows and we were trying our best to be the house band by weaseling our way on to as many shows as we could.

GEZA X: I'd slept on the floor of a recording studio and had learned a little from second-engineering jobs at Artists Recording Studio on Cherokee. I offered to do sound at the Masque and I also had some PA gear, so I traded my equipment and services for a room at the Masque and Brendan quickly agreed.

BRENDAN MULLEN: The Masque space began literally as somewhere for me and my cronies to experiment with beating on drums and anything else that showed up, undisturbed by neighbors or cops, 24/7.

BIBBE HANSEN: We all started going to the Masque almost immediately. I took Beck one afternoon. The Masque probably wasn't a suitable place for a seven-year-old kid on a wild Friday or Saturday night, but it was a pleasant way to spend a Sunday afternoon, and we'd go there to watch the Controllers rehearse. I don't know if Beck liked their music or not; I think he just liked watching them practice.

GEZA X: The rates were so dirt cheap, a bunch of poverty-stricken unsigned local underground bands were able to move in as well as all these bikers, freaks, runaways, early gutter punks, record collectors, and a slew of other barflies and bizarre street characters from the Boulevard that Brendan liked to hang out with. The Masque was the catalyst for L.A. punk rock to make a break from the past and to explode with its own music and its own social identity.

BRENDAN MULLEN: I advertised cheap band rehearsal facilities in the *Recycler*, and the Berlin Brats, Backstage Pass, and the Motels were my first customers. I filed the dba paperwork and the bank account under New Era Productions but rechristened the space the Masque after a few open-door parties following a drunken argument with the ever-contentious Al Hansen, the New York Fluxus "happening" artist who was currently on the outs with Andy Warhol in New York.

BIBBE HANSEN: Al always thought the name the Masque was fruity. He hated it because it didn't sound punk. He said it sounded like a Victorian private sex club for homosexuals, the haunt of a bunch of old British queens with poodles and too much time. But then again, Al was the first to admit he didn't always call these things correctly. Back in New York in the '60s Lou Reed had a copy of this book about Victorian bondage called *The Velvet Underground*. At the time he was looking for a name for his band. He asked Al what he thought of calling it the Velvet Underground, and Al told him, "The Velvet Underground? That sucks! That's a terrible name!"

BRENDAN MULLEN: We were in my office with guys from the Skulls and the Controllers getting plastered and trying to come up with a name. I was compiling a list of insane names that people were coming up with . . . like the Pit and the Pendulum, the Toilet, Wankers Disco, the Hellhole, Slime-O-Rama, the Puke Bowl, and God knows what else . . . the Masque was on the list, too, and I wasn't even that gung-ho on it until Al kept on about how bad it was, and since I have a major contrarian reaction to authority, any authority, like some psychological allergy (to do with my father), Al saying this was like waving a red flag. The more he bad-rapped the name, the more contrarian I'd react. I said the dictionary definition of *masque* was a form of "cheap, amateur, histrionic medieval entertainment." Finally Al stormed out in disgust, saying, "Where the fuck is the punk meaning in that?" And so Masque it was, literally because an older man (in his early fifties) seemed to be telling me what to do, and as fate would have it, I never saw Al the Jewish art leprechaun again.

RICK WILDER: The Berlin Brats was one of the first bands to move into the Masque rehearsal playground, then we broke up in early '78. I thought I was gonna form another Brats until I met Rod Donahue, who convinced me that the Brats' legacy was too glam-damaged for the new punk scene, and so we formed a band called the Mau Maus instead.

BRENDAN MULLEN: All the early gigs were no-cover, open-door BYO parties until the Weirdos demanded, "Why do we have to play for free?" And I said, "I really don't know . . . hadn't really thought about it." Cliff Roman told me, "Well, the Weirdos need to be paid if we're going to play here," and I said, "Well, shit . . . I guess we better start charging money, then. How much do I charge?" We charged $2.50 for four bands, but hardly anybody paid to get in, because everybody was a musician or in a band or running a fanzine, so they all wound up being free gigs anyway. Even though Paul Collins from the Nerves was a pretty tough doorman, it was like getting blood out of stone. We were lucky if there was a hundred bucks in the kitty at the end of a busy night, a hundred fifty max. Everybody was on somebody's list somehow. At the end of the Weirdos' night I triumphantly handed Cliff about a hundred thirty-five dollars, or something, thinking he'd be stoked, yet all he did was to whine about how little it was . . . and he never even said thanks.

JOHN DOE: The real turning point was Brendan Mullen opening the Masque during summer of '77. At first there were only fifty people there. Then there were seventy-five. Then a hundred. By the end of '77, when the Whisky had ten people at their club and there were two hundred people at the Masque, our bands started getting booked at the Whisky. Then the *L.A. Times* got behind it.

BLACK RANDY: The Masque became the focal point for everything. Everybody I knew started going there on weekends, and all these people were getting drunk and getting high and fucking in the bathrooms and the practice rooms . . . they were pogoing and literally bouncing off the walls and it was just insane. The cops didn't know about it for a long time, it was so underground. And they did keep it pretty quiet.

EXENE CERVENKA: You got a sense of something really big going on and you'd go, "How come I'm one of these people?" There was an overwhelming sense of awe that it was even happening . . . mingling with those people from many different backgrounds was great. Claude Bessy was so completely different from Belinda Carlisle, and there they were.

PLEASANT GEHMAN: All the people who were well read in art or pop culture didn't have Internet resources. We'd find weird art movies at the Nuart, or hear a Lou Reed or Bowie song and there'd be some literary reference, so we'd think, "Oh, Bowie was reading this book." By the time we all met each other, and not just me, Darby, and Pat, but all of us in punk, we all had this similar frame of reference that we'd stumbled upon completely independently of each other, something that definitely helped unify all the diverse elements of the early scene into the one L.A. punk unit when it started to really come together as this weird little community at the Masque.

HELLIN KILLER: The Masque was like heaven and hell all rolled into one . . . it was the greatest thing since sliced bread. You could always go there . . . it was like the clubhouse. It was like a bomb shelter, a basement, all these weird rooms, stairways going up to a cement ceiling . . . it was so amazing, such a dive, but it was our dive.

X-8: I remember falling asleep on the Masque toilet quite a bit and getting my picture taken. Partying too much for a little boy. I wasn't into high school garage parties, so just going to Hollywood was a whole new world. But the early Hollywood punk scene definitely had its own identity. We were well aware of New York and London, but most people made a concerted effort to make it our own. A lot of the people who hung out side by side with the new punk kids were middle-aged and from suburbia . . . all of us brought together by true boredom with the shit on FM radio.

BLANK FRANK: The Masque was like no other place ever was or is ever likely to be. Some of the early punks were the smartest people I ever met in my life. Inside was the best graffiti in the world. It had to be seen to be believed—every square inch, including the floor and ceilings, top to bottom, was covered. Once I saw a band that the crowd didn't like, so they started tearing their clothes, breaking their instruments, then Bobby Pyn, or maybe it was Kickboy, got a fire extinguisher and hosed them down. Amazingly, no one was electrocuted, especially Bobby himself, 'cause there were bare live wires everywhere. It was insanity like that all the time.

HAL NEGRO: Sometimes the Masque went on all night on weekends, with bands showing up on the doorstep unannounced wanting to play at four in the morning. There might be three or four shows a week. On the nights where there wasn't a show, that was an excuse to have a party anyway, and there wasn't a single soul from the music industry or any of the major record companies within miles, unless you count Kim Fowley, I guess.

EXENE CERVENKA: Soon there was enough people who would pay to get in and that's all the club owners cared about, so they started booking bands into other venues.

GERBER: It was just about gigs, every night . . . wherever, whoever, however, whatever—the Weirdos, Germs, the Bags, didn't matter. Just gigs.

PLEASANT GEHMAN: The hallmark of every punk rock show or party would be Philomena Winstanley from *Slash* standing there at the end of the night with Claude passed out cold on the floor or dumping a pot of spaghetti all over the house or pissing in the punch, and she'd just be wringing her hands and going, "Oh, Claude." One time cops were raiding the Masque and Claude was out front jumping from the roof of a car to the hood of a car, seven or eight cars in a row, screaming "Feck all you peegs! Feck all you peegs!" Whenever he said *fuck* it was like f-e-c-k. "Oh, Claude!" She was like his nanny.

PHILOMENA WINSTANLEY: The punks had no money to buy drinks at clubs and would drink anything from paper bags outside in the parking lot. We'd just lie on top of cars and whoever got drunk would slide down the roof of the car and lie under the car. Everybody was very drunk. That's how I remember the beginning of the whole punk thing . . . drinking on the pavement outside the Whisky and stumbling around the Masque.

STAN RIDGWAY: More importantly, from my point of view, many great musicians came to the Masque eagerly looking for the opportunity to play original music for a crowd that seemed to want it no matter how loose or inexperienced the band was.

TRUDIE ARGUELLES: Around the time the Masque was starting to happen, I got this place with Hellin Killer and our friend Mary Rat. Kid Congo was supposed to move in, but that didn't happen. Then we met Trixie at the Tropicana with some other girls she was hanging out with and we wound up inviting her to move in.

TRIXIE: I think I was complaining about my father, or the distance from my home in Norwalk to all the fun, and one of them said, "You should stay here." The three of them were already living there at the apartment on La Jolla. So the next time I got into a tiff with dear old Dad, that was it. I took my records, my clothes, and makeup, complete with three-way mirror, and moved into the infamous Plunger Pit.

TRUDIE ARGUELLES: One day when we were bored Hellin and Mary and I tried to dress up as weird as we could. Collars up, '60s sunglasses, and I was holding a plunger in the picture just to be really stupid, and we were like, "We look like a band. How about we call ourselves the Plungers?" I was learning how to play the guitar, but it never went too far. We were never disciplined enough to really become a band.

HELLIN KILLER: We were a band that never played 'cause we couldn't be bothered to learn to play anything, but we lived together and had the biggest party house . . . the Plunger Pit.

TRIXIE: The Plunger Pit was paradise for a short while. We slept in one bed like four peas in a pod. It was Hellin, Trudie, Mary Rat, and me who paid the rent. There was a constant stream of people and hardly anyone was ever turned away.

MARY RAT: People were always crashing. You never had many moments to yourself. The police raided us one night. I guess they thought we were selling drugs because people were always coming and going.

HELLIN KILLER: There was constantly people there, sleeping every-where. Food was like spaghetti or instant mashed potatoes or whatever you could get. We'd wake up at three in the afternoon when somebody would show up at the door, and we'd say, "Go buy a bottle of alcohol and bring it back here and let's start the party now." And people would do it. Bands would come to town and they'd be playing at the Starwood and we'd go, "Party at the Plunger Pit!"

MARY RAT: We had no money. We couldn't afford drugs. I don't know how we lived. I remember Leonard from the Dickies baked us a turkey for Thanksgiving, which was really nice.

X-8: I lost my virginity on the roof of the Plunger Pit. All I remember is that the girl helped show me where it went. The Plunger sisters were Mary, Trudie, Hellin, and Trixie, they all slept in the same bed. They were the center of the world, they were fabulous, they were the cutest girls on the scene, and everybody wanted to be seen with them and to hang out with them because they knew every-body and they knew everything about new music and they dressed sexy and partied every night.

TRIXIE: The Plungers were just a group of fun-loving girls with an aura of chic that people gravitated toward, and we were carefree enough to do as we liked.

BRENDAN MULLEN: The Masque was temporarily closed down by cops for no entertainment/cabaret license early on. I was trapped in doublespeak because of recent creepy close encounters with the landlord, City Hall officials, and cops where I'd consciously avoided usage of the word *club* fearing a rejection of permit applications because legally converting a space from one usage to another is a majorly expensive bureaucratically controlled project. I'd told sev-eral police inspectors and referred to it in bureaucratic paperwork as a "cabaret" and as a "theater" to try to lower the profile as much as possible. So I called it the Masque Theater right at the very beginning . . . but it never caught on, and I never used it on any of the early Masque flyers, which I designed by hand myself. The best thing ever written on the wall of the Masque? TO ESCAPE HELL YOU MUST FIRST BURY YOURSELF IN IT. Taken from Genet. The descent below was well on its way.

chapter 15

Hellin Killer, Pleasant Gehman, and Bobby Pyn at the Starwood club, 1977.
Photo Credit: Jenny Lens

CLAUDE BESSY (*SLASH*, SEPTEMBER 1977): Thank God there ain't no spokesman or leaders yet.

DARBY CRASH: Well, basically I'm bored with all these people, so in order to make them how I want them. Right? Look. When you have people for friends and they're not the kind of people you want, what do you do? You make some better ones. So I'm going to take all these idiots out here and make them into better ones.

BRENDAN MULLEN: A big landmark event was the Labor Day weekend party in '77 when the Germs headlined their own gig at the Masque with the Alley Cats, the Skulls, and Needles and Pins playing also. It was the biggest turnout so far. I was shocked . . . I had totally underestimated how much pull the Germs actually had, since they'd been written off as a bad joke who couldn't play for toffee. Their notoriety from the Orpheum show preceded them.

GEZA X: It was the Masque that put the Germs smack in the middle of what was happening at precisely the right moment, but it was the buzz on the Germs as a social force more than a musical one that caused a line to form outside the Masque for the first time, so it was a two-way symbiosis. Many people, myself included, began to take the Germs more seriously rather than viewing them as a talentless mess of punk rock wanna-bes. The Germs that night were Bobby Pyn, Pat Smear, Lorna Doom, and Cliff Hanger on drums . . . I remember Bobby or Pat christening Kim Fowley "Penis Face" and they sent him and his entourage packing.

BRENDAN MULLEN: I was flabbergasted by the Germs at the Labor Day gig . . . with a few Guinnesses in my belt I thought they were absolutely hilarious . . . rock and roll could never be serious again for the rest of my life . . . Cliff Hanger's drums collapsed and were rolling all over the stage and there was feathers and confetti everywhere. I defy anyone who could've been present that night not to have fallen in love with them.

NICKEY BEAT: After Donna Rhia left, Cliff Hanger was working out as a pretty good drummer for the Germs, and then he either quit or got kicked out after the first Masque show. I had become a friend and a bit of a Germs fan, so I filled in for three or four months. I never committed full time because I thought the Weirdos were the band for me. I thought the Germs were a bad career choice. I thought, "They're never going to do anything. Their stuff just isn't marketable."

PLEASANT GEHMAN: [On September 23, 1977,] the Hollywood Palladium hosted the Punk Rock Fashion Show. They billed it as "A new wave of sound and style." Blondie played. Devo played, the Weirdos played, and the Avengers from San Francisco. It was an ill-conceived, underattended fiasco where Bobby Pyn came out onstage wearing only a leopard fur jockstrap and announced to the crowd that his new name was Darby Crash, but nobody paid heed at first.

RIK L. RIK: He started off as Bobby Pyn before I knew him. Everyone needed a punk rock name, and that was his. After a while, he recognized the limitations of Bobby Pyn, that it was too cute, not heavy enough. And so he came up with Darby Crash. He never told me about the derivation of it or anything. Darby was one of the most outrageous-looking people I'd ever seen. He had six safety pins in his ear. He was really into the whole look. His hair was bleached blond and cut really severely. That look is pretty much universal at every high school nowadays, but at the time it was way out on the edge, even compared to some of the other kids who had the punk look back then. I remember thinking he sounded like the biggest on-fire fairy I'd ever heard in my life. I would go to a club and afterward we'd go to his mom's house in West L.A., where he lived. We'd stay up till like five in the morning, then we'd get up around one in the afternoon. Darby had foil covering his windows, so it was pitch black all day. We'd get up late and talk on the phone all afternoon, listen to records, then somebody would come by in the evening to pick us up and we'd go out all over again. He never had a straight job.

DARBY CRASH: I completely control a number of people's lives. Look around for the little girls wearing CRASH-TRASH T-shirts and people like that.

RIK L. RIK: Darby Crash completely resocialized me. He taught me to question everything and how to make up my own mind by evaluating reality and drawing my own conclusions, rather than just accepting the way society wants you to see it. He did this for everybody he came in contact with. It was a whole retraining program. And it wasn't some malevolent Charles Manson thing, either, although Darby's clique, the Germs' Circle One people, were seen as being like a Manson family type of situation. Darby was so intelligent. I was overwhelmed by the way his mind worked, and the way he would design the conversations you were having with him, or with whatever group of people you happened to be with.

DARBY CRASH: What we're going to do is get lots of . . . what do you call them . . . allies in key positions and, um, if you get somebody that works for the post office, I mean somebody that's just even a mail clerk, you can really screw the post office up bad . . . or the newspapers. If you go to the newspapers and they have those big machines that print them and you shoot a rubber band into it, it rips the paper; it ruins the whole day's edition. So if you can get enough people to do that, one day you can go to the government and say, "Look how much control I have. You've got the armies, but we can just stop this country from working." I don't know which country we'll start with. It's just as easy when you go to Japan and they can't understand what you're saying. I mean, it makes it a lot easier. You bring them in ten at a time and teach them English, you know? We're trying to get Reverend Moon to back us to go to China . . . because we want to play on the Great Wall and you have to have special permits and stuff to even go up there, unless you're a tourist. Yeah, well, as far as I know, as far as the government's concerned, and as far as Moonies are and whatever, he'll just say, "I'll show them how decadent America is, we'll put these people up here to play on this wall and they'll make fools out of themselves." And after that we're going to play the Berlin Wall, right? Is that the next one? Any more walls we can play? Marianas Trench? We used to go there in high school.

MATT GROENING: The punks that came into Licorice Pizza, the record store where I worked, were a combination. There were very idealistic kids who were totally into the scene. And then there were these kids who would create a ruckus in order to distract us so they could shoplift. Most of those kids were associated with the Germs.

RODNEY BINGENHEIMER: One day Darby came on my show and he was giving out satellite numbers over the air so people could make free long distance calls.

PAT SMEAR: Darby was intrigued by the concept of fascism. He was such a leader that people would follow him around and do what he asked. Whatever it is people like that have in them that enables them to attract a following, he had it in him. I'm not talking about the hate part, I'm talking about some guy coming from a log cabin and ending up being president of the USA.

K.K. BARRETT: I had a lot of one-on-one conversations with Darby about religion as a business, the whole idea that you could start your own religion and make money off of it, which was an obvious L. Ron Hubbard reference Darby had picked up on . . . he brought me books on Scientology and he also talked about how religion was just basically a funnel for lost souls. But his songs kept getting better and better. The Screamers even did a cover of the Germs' "Sex Boy" at our shows, which was the equivalent of the Stones doing "I Wanna Be Your Man," written by the Beatles.

JOHN DOE: The Germs became scary after Bobby became Darby. They began to fuck stuff up. Their audience fucked stuff up. Their music and, in particular, Darby's stage persona was very different than his private personality. The stage was where he could do whatever he wanted. Onstage, he was much more violent. The music made people feel that way. It was incredibly dark. The Germs were much darker than most of the other bands. Darby's writing is nothing like the kind of person he was. He was much more of a kind of Valley kid, a goofy, California kid, but obviously there was something behind him that was very secret and weird. You didn't know the words because it was all like "Warrrrrrrwarrrwarr" when Darby sang them live. So everyone was just astounded later on when they got that first Slash record and actually read the lyrics. They were great! I know that he cheated a lot. He used a thesaurus! He'd take Nietzsche books and pick stuff out that sounded cool, and reflected his feelings, and he was able to put those words together really well. He'd never use words like he'd write in regular conversation.

HAL NEGRO: Germs burns were inflicted with a lit cigarette. You were supposed to get one from somebody else who had one. It was like pledging allegiance to Darby Crash.

PHRANC: Darby gave me my Germs' burn himself.

TRIXIE: No Germs burns on me. We Plungers preferred razor slashes.

PAT SMEAR: I didn't know what the circle meant. He had some little speech at the time, but I can't recall. I always thought the blue circle was like his blue eyes, but I might be wrong. The burn was the circle. It was his idea of something permanent, so that in ten years you'd be at the supermarket, and some lady would give you change, and you'd see the burn and make a connection. It was a circular thing. I gave the first one to a fifteen-year-old girl. The rule was once you got yours, you could give it to other people.

DARBY CRASH: Everything works in circles. You know, like something you've done maybe eight years ago, but all of a sudden it feels like you're at exactly the same place doing the same thing. You may not be doing the same thing, but, you know, it's just that feeling. Well, that's circles. So everything works in circles. I think we should make a new shape for flags. Round flags.

KIM FOWLEY: California was wide-open sex—no condoms, no birth control, no morality, no guilt . . . "flaming schoolgirls" describes the look and age group of the most desirable female. Most of them were over eighteen, but they all seemed to want to remain eternally junior high. Even twenty-somethings were trying for that perennial high school teen popularity crap, and that's why the Germs were able to flourish as local celebrities in that community.

PAT SMEAR: I never knew whether Darby was gay or not. All I remember is that all the girls wanted to sleep with him and didn't get to.

GERBER: I fell in love with Hellin Killer, how about that? She was horned in trying to be Darby's girlfriend, and I was really close to her, so I didn't really want to tell her, "Don't even, you're wasting your time."

KIM FOWLEY: And I must talk about that filthy goddess Gerber, who was the Germs' sexual poodle girl that they drug around. Gerber was Sandra Dee meets Leslie Caron on a French poodle porno level. To attract girls of her bacterial beauty I thought was really important. I said, "These guys are gonna be big—they have dirty pussy around them, dirty pussy is worshiping their cock stink and their slime." I always like bands that have dirty women, like with the Germs. They pulled pudgy white girls from the Valley, from the suburbs, from the beaches, from the South Bay, from Orange County, affluent porker chicks who didn't want to marry the doctors and the lawyers—the future farmers of America, or the future schoolteachers. They wanted to go get pissed on and shit on and beat up and shot up and desecrated in Hollywood. And there were the Germs to do it for them. That was their appeal. You'd hear Germs records at a party or on Rodney's show, or you'd go into punk shops or weird jewelry stores and there'd be their music all around. It was the sound track to getting dirty pussy, and if that's what you wanted, you had to put up with the Germs' music. Sex with the Germs playing in the background was like, "Hey, are you finished puking? Okay? Now I'm going to fuck you in the ass and then your girlfriend can puke on me and then we can have a three-way and then I'll flog you and bleed you a little and then I'll jizz all over your dirty little hole a second time." Then it goes like this: "Oh, no, that's okay, my mom's waiting for me." Then it would be like, "Oh, okay, how about your dog? Can I fuck your dog?" "Would you like to?" You know, for that kind of ambience the Germs' music was essential. Toilet sex. Toilet culture. Toilet rock culture has its own Elvis—Darby Crash.

RODNEY BINGENHEIMER: Darby was always really nice. He was a gentleman. He was really sincere.

BRENDAN MULLEN: Right when Darby Crash's star was rising, his original inspirational heroines, the Runaways, were falling apart. That fall they played the Whisky, debuting their new image, the ill-timed heavy-metal style: black leather, studded chrome, Judas Priest look. The Weirdos were on the bill in order to bring in the new punks. Acrimony between the band and Kim Fowley sparked rumors that Kim was looking to sell off their contract.

JACKIE FOX: Kim only wanted us to do songs that he'd written 'cause he'd own all the publishing. The second choice was for us to do songs by people whose publishing he controlled. If you look at all our albums, Kim has written most of the songs and the others are either written by us or by other songwriters whose publishing Kim controls, like Marc Anthony and Billy Bizeau. Kim owned their publishing. We started fighting with Kim so much that he turned everything over to Scott Anderson. Bill Aucoin, who managed Kiss, was interested, but he said, "You have to get out of your contract with Kim because I'm not gonna front fifty grand to get you out and then another fifty to work on you. You guys get rid of Kim Fowley and I'll manage you." I was probably the only one who paid any attention to what was going on on the business side, but I was still just a sixteen-year-old girl. I knew we needed to get someone high-powered and I couldn't get the band to do anything about it.

CHERIE CURRIE: After *Queens of Noise*, we went to Japan. There was a lot of problems in the band. Jackie couldn't take it anymore.

JACKIE FOX: We got to Japan and found out that nothing had been taken care of. My bass was really valuable, even back then. It was a Gibson T-Bird from the '60s, one of the rare white ones, a magnificent instrument. I was about to go onstage and the roadie told me that my bass was broken. And it was kind of like, that was the last straw. Nobody was looking out for us.

CHERIE CURRIE: Jackie took pieces of glass and hacked her arms up 'cause she wanted out. We ended up doing the Tokyo Music Festival without her.

JACKIE FOX: The rumor got out when I came back that I'd tried to commit suicide. Every time I went out I'd see people staring at me or coming over and grabbing my hands to look at my wrists. I got so fed up with it, I stopped going out for a while. Darby Crash dedicated a song to me for trying to commit suicide in Japan. It's on the Germs' live album. Which is a great irony because I didn't and he did.

CHERIE CURRIE: We replaced Jackie with Vicki Blue. By this time I was miserable. The band members didn't like each other, and Kim was playing one member against the other. We were doing a photo session and I told the photographer up front that I needed to leave on time immediately after the session 'cause my sister and I shared a car and she needed it to go to acting class. Lita blew in a couple of hours late and the photographer threw a fit 'cause I had to leave and he hadn't gotten the pictures he wanted. He threw his camera down in frustration and broke it and Lita went berserk. I went into the dressing room to get ready to leave, and Lita kicked the door down right off its hinges and pointed at me, saying, "You have to choose between the Runaways and your family. We've chosen the band." And I said, "Forget it, man. I choose my family. Bye." Kim called and asked "Are you really quitting?" And I said, "Yeah."

LITA FORD: Joan took over lead singing and she did a great job. I didn't miss Cherie at all when she left. But it just got more and more druggy, we were just getting so stoned . . . and more and more people in our lives were pulling us in different directions.

TOBY MAMIS: Joan's passion for the new punk scene was dominating the band's direction, while Sandy and Lita were more passionate about hard rock and heavy metal and suspicious of punk. This sowed the seeds for the final destruction of the Runaways.

KIM FOWLEY: I didn't go on the Japanese tour and the group broke up because mean old daddy bear wasn't there controlling everything. I was only told, "The group broke up tonight." I was like, "Oh, okay."

chapter 16

Tiny Rosen, the security guard who was hired at the Masque after the Hillside Strangler murdered club regular Jane King, 1977. Photo Credit: Al Flipside

BRENDAN MULLEN: The Hillside Strangler embarked on this lunatic murder binge of kidnapping, torturing, raping, and strangling ten girls around Halloween '77 and continued until February '78. During Thanksgiving weekend five more bodies turned up. The cops didn't know till later there were two of these dumb shits whose mommies didn't like 'em, but the carnage hit close to home when they got Jane King, a friend of Berlin Brat Rick Wilder and a regular at the Masque.

RICK WILDER: I first met Jane King when she was still Matt Campbell's girlfriend. There's stupid things you do, that you regret, and going off with your best friend's girl is one of them. The last time I saw her was at the Masque on Halloween night 1977. She died the next day. Her mother called me and said she was missing and she thought she was dead 'cause the police had called. At that time, that wasn't a common thing to have happen, a serial killer out there on the loose. Jane King was my first love . . . I can't talk about it . . . I can't even read the book on the killers . . . what they did to her, oh my God. Why? I'll wonder for the rest of my days.

BILLY BONES (STEVE FORTUNA): My band the Skulls played the Whisky with Sorcery, some sick acid metal band from '72 who promised special appearances by the Black Wizard and Satan on their flyers! After the show two cops from LAPD Homicide investigating the Hillside Strangler murders followed us back to the Masque posing as art dealers who said they were interested in investing in a punk band. I'd been screaming at the audience Jim Morrison style during the intro to the song "Victims," a song we'd written about the Hillside Strangler . . . I was yelling silly, crazy-assed shit like "You're a victim, baby, and you're gonna die." That was their big clue that we were some weird punk cult in league with the killer. But Brendan had them sussed right away. He took them into his office and told them that going undercover was pointless. He told them you better believe it that if a single person from the Masque knew anything, one tiny shard that could help them, they'd be calling the cops in a hot second. The killing was too sickening for words. They seemed satisfied that he wasn't harboring a killer, although they said they knew the Hillside Strangler went carousing punk gigs looking for girls. They left LAPD business cards for him to call them direct if any of the punks heard anything.

BRENDAN MULLEN: The killers pretended to be cops and picked Jane King up at a bus stop outside that creepy Scientology Celebrity Center Building on Franklin Avenue at Bronson.

RICK WILDER: She wasn't a prostitute. She may have been, but she wasn't when she was with me, and who cares? You shouldn't take somebody's life like that. Jane thought she was the greatest actress in the world. She was taking singing lessons.

HAL NEGRO: After that Brendan hired a security guard for the Masque. The crowds had been getting bigger anyway, and I think he realized that he had no idea who some of these people coming and going were, and there was no way to tell, either.

BRENDAN MULLEN: I hired a 350-pound, six-foot-four uniformed security guard named Tiny Rosen after it occurred to me, in a moment of panic, how would anybody be able to hear anything, a girl's screams, if somebody was strangling her in one of the many dark corners of the Masque? Nobody would hear a thing if the Skulls were thrashing away at 130 decibels . . . the horror of Jane King weighed heavily on me . . . even though they'd picked her up elsewhere, it occurred to me, what if I found a girl dead on the floor after a night of revelry? It was a major turning point for me . . . the idea of the utopian punk playpen of endless mad fun was over, violated forever by the arrival of pure evil in our midst. The bogeyman had come early. Cops knew he cruised Hollywood Boulevard . . . it was a wake-up call. I decided maybe I should party a little less, that I should take on some responsibility for the goings-on in the basement, after all, rather than just hanging out like everyone else. I had badly wanted the space to be inclusionist of everyone, but how do you account for malevolence on that scale? Tiny patrolled around and sort of became a mascot for the club, he became a bit of a celebrity on the scene himself because of his girth. He kept an eye open when everybody was all fucked up, and I'd have him walk girls to their cars . . . plus he was good at talking to cops.

TITO LARRIVA: I'd pick Blank Frank up for rehearsals with the early Plugz while he was turning tricks on the corner of Highland and Santa Monica Boulevard. That was how he got his junk. He'd just suck a few cocks and then go out and get high. I'd pick him up there 'cause I knew that's where he was. I'd pull up to the corner and say, "Hey, Frank, you wanna rehearse?"

HAL NEGRO: The Gold Cup was this sleazy coffee shop a block away from the Masque and the Canterbury on Hollywood Boulevard, and Arthur J.'s was another big chicken hawk hangout on the corner of Santa Monica Boulevard and Highland. Male hustler hot spots. A few Masque scenesters like Blank Frank, Bruce Barf, and Tony the Hustler turned tricks there. So Arthur J. and the Gold Cups became the name of the Masque house band, made up of people that worked there, it was a Hollywood in-joke if you knew what was really going on with the street.

TITO LARRIVA: Danielle's coffee shop was another one. It was primarily a transvestite hang out. For a while, I worked there . . . fed the Plugz there. They'd come in at night and I'd get them free dinners or steal steaks from the fridge. I worked the night shift and I saw someone die at my station one night. This pimp staged a fake fight in the back, and while they were throwing shit, he shot this transvestite under the table with a .22. And she was so high on Tuinols that she didn't even know she was shot. We thought she was asleep.

BLACK RANDY: My record "Trouble at the Cup" is about this fantasy I had that all the male prostitutes in Hollywood would become punks and overthrow the LAPD. It went, "They say the Boulevard is no place for me / Pinball and coffee is all right with me / I can't live at home / I gotta be free / I hate my parents more than they hate me / Schools and factories make me sick / I'd rather just stand here and sell my dick / Trouble at the Cup, trouble at the Cup." The Gold Cup was a restaurant on Hollywood Boulevard at Las Palmas where all these male prostitutes hung out, who I admired and fraternized with. I was closer to them than most of the punk rockers walking around in their punk army suits.

ANDY SEVEN: When I saw the bulletin at the Masque for Arthur J. and the Gold Cups, everything that was listed in that ad was right up my alley, and I said, "This is the band of my dreams," 'cause it mentioned Ornette, Sun Ra, James Brown, the Soft Machine, T. Rex, the Dolls, the Pistols, all in the same band! I couldn't believe it!. This in some bombed-out punk rock basement? A pretty sick concept. Then I found out it was Brendan and Spazz and Geza and a bunch of other people that worked at the Masque who jammed there all the time for fun, so I rushed home to get my horn.

HAL NEGRO: Brendan got Spazz Attack, this skinny guy with spiky hair who crashed at the Plunger Pit and who was famous for being able to land flat on his back without hurting himself after throwing 360-degree back flips, to be the lead singer of Arthur J. and the Gold Cups.

MARK MOTHERSBAUGH: That's Spazz Attack doing 360s in our video for "Satisfaction." How he didn't kill himself or break his spine doing that, I'll never know.

BRENDAN MULLEN: Spazz Attack was coached by legendary street dance coach Toni Basil, and he later moved to New York to design clothes. He also danced with David Bowie on the *Glass Spider* tour in 1987.

HAL NEGRO: Geza X played guitar and Brendan played drums in Arthur J. and the Gold Cups. I played trumpet, and the rest of the lineup shifted. It was a punk rock big band, with a three-piece horn section, a keyboard, and backup singers. We'd play covers by Little Richard, James Brown, and George Clinton; we'd do surf instrumentals, TV jingles like *Green Acres* and the "Cal Worthington and His Dog Spot" theme, but we'd also play Ornette Coleman's "Theme from a Symphony." There were very many different musical ideas in the band. It was really out there for the time, but nobody wanted to commit the time to writing original material. Arthur J. and the Gold Cups was never taken seriously, unfortunately, but it had a few moments where we hauled ass live at the Masque and the Whisky. An Arthur J. and the Gold Cups show had been booked with X and the Deadbeats at Larchmont Hall and nobody wanted to do it, so Brendan and I and Kelly Quinn, the piano player, decided, "Fuck 'em, we wanna play . . . we'll do the gig without 'em." And we renamed ourselves Hal Negro and the Satin Tones and showed up at the hall ready to play instead of Arthur J. to show we could pull off the gig without them. Satin Tone was the name of a can of paint. We were gonna do this suave Sinatra/Dino/Darin saloon thing one time only, but it was such a blast, we had such a good time doing it, we stuck around just for the hell of it. Our gigs were always messy but fun, and girls seemed to like it. We had matching tuxes, and some girlfriend of Brendan's stitched fake zebra fur onto the lapels and all of a sudden we had this identity. And we had the hot girls, the Punk

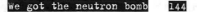

Bunnies, Allison Buckles and Shannon Wilhelm, who were the first really cute punk girls.

HELLIN KILLER: I was brutally shy, so I didn't talk much. I'd stand around with a bottle in one hand and just stare at people, just leaning against a wall, so I developed this reputation for being scary, like, "Don't go up to her!" It became part of my whole thing. I was really fearless, never got scared of nothin'. I used to go around kicking in windows and stuff. That's where my reputation comes from. I'd just kick in windows on the street . . . put my fist through them . . . and carry switchblades. I was the silent deadly type, I was always the one: "Hellin will do it—if nobody else will, she will."

HAL NEGRO: One thing about punk rock, it wasn't the greatest look for some girls. The girls that we started out with were pretty homely types. Trudie, of course, was the goddess of punk rock, but Hellin was very tough-looking. Hellin and Trixie. The look was very hard and antipretty in the beginning. Some of the punk rock girls weren't sexy with the short spiky hair and fucked-up makeup, but Shannon and Allison were curvy, sexy girls. Allison had long red hair. We started calling them the Punk Bunnies after they came onstage with the Satin Tones as part of our Vegas lounge act, dressed up like deranged parodies of Playboy bunnies. At first there weren't as many girls, then they started coming around 'cause it became cool to hang out with punks. This girl named Paula—we called her Stripes—was this feather-haired rock chick, but she came out and started fucking all the punk guys and she'd say, "I can't stand the music, but the guys are hot."

chapter 17

Former cheerleader Belinda Carlisle of the Go-Go's, 1979.
Photo Credit: Frank Gargani

DAVID ALLEN: Margot Olaverra, who took over John and Exene's room at our house on South Van Ness, had designs on learning bass and had already started an all-girl punk band, and so Kittra's days as the Go-Go's discoverer/manager began. The early publicity material, logo, et cetera, was all Kittra. She was involved with Herb Cohen's brother Martin, who got the Go's all connected.

MARGOT OLAVERRA: I'd just gotten back from a trip to London where I saw the Sex Pistols. I was a new punk rocker, still a little self-conscious about being around these wild catwomen of London, but I always wanted to play in a band. I thought starting a girl band would be less intimidating because being a nonmusician was okay in punk and that was what was so beautifully democratic about it, but that's what made me think in those terms. It wasn't the commercial value of having an all-girl band. I met Elissa Bello through a friend from high school. She played the drums, so I said, "Oh, great."

ELISSA BELLO: I came out to Los Angeles from Buffalo on my own. I wanted to put an all-girl rock band together. I initially wanted something more rebellious. More political . . . not English political. I couldn't understand the obsession with everything that was English. I had a cousin out here who was about my age and we went to a party one night and she introduced me to Margot. Margot and I talked about it and we got together and started writing songs in her house.

MARGOT OLAVERRA: I was also attending Valley College, where Gerard Taylor, a classmate and friend, told me, "My friend Jane wants to start a band. Why don't you meet her?" So I talked on the phone with Jane Wiedlin, who was calling herself Jane Drano at the time, and we decided to meet.

HAL NEGRO: I had a little crush on Jane. She lived right near me in the Valley, so I'd see her waiting for the bus back from Hollywood. She called herself Jane Drano. I asked for her number and she wrote it down on the back of the first Generation X single, which I'd just shoplifted.

EXENE CERVENKA: Billy Zoom would always give Jane guitar lessons and she was just the cutest, most sweetest person.

KITTRA ALLEN: I found out that Jane was fucking Billy Zoom and it really pissed me off. Billy had used her. Jane came to the Go-Go's rehearsal one day and said, "I went over to Billy and Pandora's and took groceries. It's so sad. They didn't have any food in the house." To which I responded, "You are kidding! What makes them any better than you that you go to work every day to pay for your groceries but Billy Zoom is too good to get a job. The only reason they don't have any groceries is because they spent their money on drugs. That is their problem, not yours." I'm sure Jane thought I was a cold-hearted bitch and saw herself as a wet-pussied compassionate.

ELISSA BELLO: Then Margot suggested Belinda. She introduced me to Belinda, and I was opposed to it 'cause she couldn't sing and I didn't like the way she looked at the time. She had green hair and the dye was all dripping down her neck and I just thought, "No, I don't wanna work with her." Margot was determined. Margot liked her look and wanted her in the band. Belinda wasn't into music. It was just obvious. And she couldn't sing. But I'm an ass-hole and a pushover and Margot got her way.

MARGOT OLAVERRA: Belinda Carlisle was someone I just met on the scene. The first time I met her was backstage at the Whisky for a Black Randy show. She was wearing this black priest's tunic with a pink bow tie and had really really short hair and a big head, and we proceeded to call her "Big Head."

KITTRA ALLEN: To me Belinda seemed like this out-of-control compulsive overeater who knew her parents would be very disappointed because she wouldn't be making the cheering squad that year. So she just drank and partied instead.

MARGOT OLAVERRA: The Go-Go's first gig was at a birthday party for Hal Negro. I remember seeing Darby in the Whisky parking lot and he said, "Hey, so you're playing at the Masque tonight." I said, "What?" So we just got there and played, I think one or two songs . . . one of them we played twice, "Living at the Canterbury" was one . . . "Living at the Canterbury . . . da da da . . . fighting off the roaches . . . da da da . . . ." We didn't have Charlotte yet.

PLEASANT GEHMAN: Charlotte was the only one who really knew how to play.

CHARLOTTE CAFFEY: I was born and raised in Los Angeles. My first concert was the Beatles at Dodgers Stadium. Right before punk exploded, I was in college, studying classical piano, but I was also in bands. I remember seeing the Runaways at the Whisky and thinking, "I can do that better." That made me very competitive. It kicked me into gear. I met Belinda and Margot one night at the Starwood and they asked me to join the Go-Go's.

GINGER CANZONERI: I remember going with Kari Krome to the Masque. And there was this horrible screech coming from one of the rehearsal studios. We followed the sound and pushed open this door, and I'll never forget the sight of Belinda awkwardly holding this microphone with this sheepish look on her face and she said, "Oh, we've started a band." They were working as the Misfits briefly and I think the name the Go-Go's was Jane's idea. My friend Robbie Fields said to me, "You should manage the Go-Go's, you'd be perfect." I was interested in getting involved with the music scene and was working at CBS Records, and wasn't interested in being in a band myself. When I was all set to approach them, Robbie stopped me and said, "Oh, you're too late. They've already got a manager. They've got Kittra Allen."

PLEASANT GEHMAN: Ginger Canzoneri was with Kari Krome. She started doing some artwork for the Go-Go's, and it seemed like a normal step that she would be doing other businessy stuff. She was a bit older.

ELISSA BELLO: Ginger became one of these people that would hang out with us at shows. I never really paid much attention to her until we were playing at Club 88 and Kari Krome approached me and started to come on to me really heavy. I'd never had a lesbian experience. So I said to Kari, "Where's that girl you hang out with?" And she said, "Oh . . . she kicked me out of the house." Kari passed out in my car so I took her back to my apartment and we became friends. Ginger found out about it and got really upset.

GINGER CANZONERI: I became friends with the band. I don't know at what point Kittra left, but there was a reshuffling of band members. Gina had arrived from Baltimore and within a few months of putting her in place as the drummer, they didn't have Kittra Allen, their first manager, anymore, so they asked me to collect money at the shows. I became very protective of them, and it just became a gradual trust situation. I thought the Go-Go's was the most perfect concept.

ELISSA BELLO: Ginger started to hang out with Belinda and cry on her shoulder that her girlfriend was at my house . . . and the next thing I know we had this meeting and they said, "Well, Ginger's going to be the manager," and the next thing I know, they said, "We're having a meeting to figure out if you're going to stay in the band." I was working in Brentwood and didn't get out till seven-thirty and they were like, "Well, we want to rehearse at seven," which was impossible for me.

GINGER CANZONERI: Elissa wasn't fired because she started going out with a girlfriend of mine. There was no way a Go-Go's decision like that would be made over something like that. I wasn't even managing the band yet. I'd just begun to become friends with them and to actively help them with things, like counting money at shows. I think they were mad because there was some interview that she didn't show up for, but really they just weren't that happy with Elissa's abilities as a drummer. The Gina segue was pretty seamless. I wasn't even consulted.

ELISSA BELLO: Ginger found Gina, who had been playing with Edie the Egg Lady in Baltimore. Gina had her own truck and her father had made her drum cases and she was all set up, so it was "Let's get rid of Elissa and put Gina in. She's been playing a lot longer." And I was ousted from the band.

MARGOT OLAVERRA: It may have been Ginger's ethic, this really serious thing that took hold in the Go-Go's . . . the seriousness to make it at whatever cost . . . and because of things like Elissa's notorious lateness we reached the decision to replace her and I felt really bad about it . . . she didn't put up much of a fight but that was part of her personality. Of course, I eventually became the next victim of the same cutthroat drive for commercial success.

GINGER CANZONERI: Margot wanted the band to have this cooler, darker, edgier side, but the Go-Go's were already evolving into more of a fun, pop thing. It was never about me saying, "I think you girls would make more money if you did more bubbly pop songs." They all got along well at the beginning when they all hung out together . . . but Margot gradually was hanging out with different people and had different interests and maybe took different drugs. Margot did not approve of the band's musical style, and she would sigh and go, "Oh, can't we do songs that are more like X? Can't we do songs that are more like the Germs?" The Go-Go's were evolving as a musical entity, and there was a sense that Margot wanted the band to be more rough, and I think that Belinda always had her eye on the prize and wanted desperately to succeed.

PLEASANT GEHMAN: The only way a band could have gotten signed and marketed was to say they were new wave and to abandon the punk stuff. The Go-Go's had to cut off their past to do that. That was the only way you could get signed. They weren't going to sign a girl band like Castration Squad when Pat Benatar was the big thing.

CHARLOTTE CAFFEY: We didn't want to be just an L.A. band. That was not our goal. I never wanted to fucking stay in L.A. and play clubs.

BELINDA CARLISLE: We wanted to be rich and famous.

"Ever Get the Feeling You've Been Cheated?": The Sex Pistols in California (1978)

chapter 18

The Sex Pistols' final show at San Francisco's Winterland Ballroom (L.A. punks Rik L. Rik, Dim Wanker, Gerber, Darby Crash, and Basho Macko are in the crowd), 1978. Photo Credit: Kerry Colonna

HELLIN KILLER: The Plungers talked somebody into driving us to Dallas to see the Sex Pistols. We drove in a Volkswagen with five people and a spare tire in the back, from L.A. down to Dallas, just switching drivers. We headed straight for the place, Randy's Corral or whatever, and that's where we met 'em . . . we were buying tickets and they were arriving for sound check. Sid came up and he was like Joe Friendly, like, "Hey, what's up?" I just had my sights set on Sid, I guess, and we somehow hooked up.

HAL NEGRO: You know that famous photo of Sid Vicious playing bass with blood all over his face and chest? Hellin did that.

HELLIN KILLER: It was a total accident. It must have been a head butt to the nose that did it . . . they had a corral around the stage and I had my knees onstage and I was hanging on to that and I slipped off. I was smoking and we were sharing a cigarette and I think he bent down just as I slipped off and jumped up and the top of my head smashed into his nose really hard and blood just started pouring all over him. I think that picture circulated around the world.

MARY RAT: Johnny Rotten was actually kind of nice in Dallas. We were all going to this restaurant to get some food and the car was full, so Malcolm McLaren told me to sit on Johnny's lap, which made him kind of mad. So I sat on his lap. I was embarrassed the whole time, but he was really nice about it.

HELLIN KILLER: After the show Sid was like, "Stay, stay," and I'm like, "My ride is leaving and I don't know anyone in Dallas," and he was like, "Just stay," so I said okay, and he was swell enough to have them buy me a ticket back and he gave me cab fare to the airport. We planned to get together in San Francisco . . . we really hit it off . . . it was really weird, like a dream come true, suddenly you're best friends with the person you like the best out of anybody.

HAL NEGRO: Everyone was excited that the Pistols were coming to town. I guess we were excited that they were playing in the state of California, 'cause they decided not to play any L.A. dates.

SEAN CARRILLO: We were devastated when the Pistols didn't play here. I was seventeen. I wasn't thinking about Malcolm McLaren's clever little strategy. All I was thinking was, "Why aren't they playing here?"

BIBBE HANSEN: I was totally bummed. I've never forgiven them for that. It was like a slap in the face.

BRENDAN MULLEN: When the Sex Pistols arrived in Los Angeles during their U.S. tour in January 1978, Johnny Rotten skulked secretly at the Hyatt/Riot House, apparently in the company of his mother, without once emerging to meet and greet the entire time the band was in town, a whole week prior to their swan song at the Winterland Ballroom in San Francisco. Sid, Cook, and Jones at least hung out at night, if only for the abundance of willing punkettes. The three prowled L.A. by night on boozy doped-out bird-shagging expeditions to the Masque. Sid's favorite cocktail: peppermint schnapps and Southern Comfort with tall-can chasers of Olde English 800 Malt Liquor and Rainier Green Ale! Such a gross-out combination would even cause a hard-boiled serious drinker like Top Jimmy to blow chunks. And that was just the booze part of his consumption! Try mixing that lot with heroin, coke, and speed and, well . . .

RENE DAALDER: During the week the Pistols wastefully hung around L.A. doing nothing before the big Winterland show in San Francisco, we were driving Sid around while he was kicking. He kept saying, "Bring me to the hospital or the nearest bridge." We took turns baby-sitting him at the Sunset Hyatt Hotel, where Lydon was hanging out with his mom, glad to be away from the hated McLaren . . . who in turn called John a "Catholic twit."

MILES COPELAND: When I was a booker for the Sex Pistols, I would go up to Malcolm McLaren and say, "Gee, Malcolm, I just read another article about how you can't get the band gigs. But I just got you three gigs." And finally one day he looked at me like I was out of my fucking mind. He said, "Look, you cunt, I don't want this fucking group to play because then people can see that they *can't* fucking play. Don't you fucking get it, you fucking asshole?! I'll get more press saying that they can't play than if they fucking play! Don't you fucking get it, you asshole?! This isn't about playing. It's about press." And then a lightbulb went off in my head: "This was not a band about music." Of course, the group thought they were because they'd call me up and ask, "Oh, Miles, oh thanks. Can you get us some gigs?" I'd say, "Well, I've got a couple." They'd say, "Oh wow, great. That's really fantastic." And then of course it wouldn't happen because Malcolm just didn't want them to play. Every time I'd get them a gig, he'd say, "You're fucking up my whole rap, you bastard!" That's why they didn't play in New York or Los Angeles, the real media centers. Malcolm thought it would have ruined everything.

RENE DAALDER: Russ Meyer, the filmmaker who was the best man at my wedding, was asked to make a Sex Pistols movie. He called me because of my teenage movie *Massacre at Central High*, which anticipated punk, *Heathers,* and Columbine back in '76 . . . and so McLaren, Russ, Roger Ebert, and myself were supposed to collaborate on developing a movie concept for the Pistols. Roger and myself were to write the script with input from Russ and Malcolm. It was an improbable mix. Russ wanted the movie to be the follow-up to his outrageously campy masterpiece *Beyond the Valley of the Dolls*, written by Ebert. Roger was, of course, totally into Meyer's thing. Malcolm had no idea what he had gotten himself into, since the Sex Pistols came from an entirely different world than Russ. I worked for months writing and rewriting different versions of what came to be called *Who Killed Bambi?* but I couldn't bridge the chasm that existed between the band and their management at one end and Russ at the other. I shuttled back and forth between the two camps, but there was no way to avert the clash between Malcolm's anarchistic art-school earnestness and the camp sensibilities of the King of the Nudies. One day Russ yelled at Johnny Lydon to have some respect. He shouted out: "We saved your limey asses in World War II!" It all ended in bitter tears of rage and lawsuits, and Russ would never make a film again. It also cost me my dear friendship with Russ because ultimately I had to root for the Sex Pistols. Our house became the U.S. headquarters for the Pistols and I was hanging out with them a lot, especially Malcolm, Sid Vicious, Paul Cook, and Steve Jones, who crashed with us and at other houses. Warner Brothers' Mo Austin was seriously wondering if punk could be the biggest thing since the Beatles.

HAL NEGRO: The L.A. punks weren't so upset with the Pistols that they didn't organize a mass exodus upstate to see them play the Winterland Ballroom in San Francisco. Nobody knew it would be their last show ever . . . well, until those reunion shows twenty years later, anyway.

NICKEY BEAT: The Germs booked a gig at Mabuhay Gardens in San Francisco coinciding with the weekend when the Pistols played Winterland. Knowing that Sid was in the audience, Darby pulled out all the show-stopping moves. We opened up with "Circle One." The song starts with sixteen beats before the band comes in. As I hit the first note, Darby ran onstage, put his hands on my shoulder, jumped right over me, grabbed a glass full of booze, downed the whole thing, carved a circle in his chest, grabbed the mic, and started singing the first word of the first verse in perfect time. It was amazing. From there on it was pandemonium.

PENELOPE HOUSTON: The Avengers opened the Pistols' Winterland show. We ended up playing after the Nuns and right before the Pistols. That show was insane. There were about six thousand people there. Sold out. The biggest show the Pistols had ever played . . . and the biggest show we'd ever play. People came from the whole West Coast, but counting all the people from L.A. and even all the punks in San Francisco and Seattle, there was probably only six hundred of us, so who were the rest of those people? Suburban kids or just people who'd come to see the freak show, basically. The Pistols didn't show themselves backstage. Sid came out, but Johnny Rotten didn't come out of the dressing room at all. It was so packed, you couldn't lift your feet off the ground, and you were covered in sweat within one minute of going into the pit. We were pretty scared, and also pretty disgusted with the whole thing. It was the first time that Bill Graham, the famous promoter, had gotten his hands on punk.

RENE DAALDER: Bill Graham thought it was some weird violent rehash of his '60s shows, and Russ thought the Pistols were the British version of the Strawberry Alarm Clock or the Carrie Nations. Personally, I thought they were the greatest thing I'd ever seen.

PENELOPE HOUSTON: We saw somebody get beat up. Richard Meltzer, the MC, this really obnoxious guy, he was out there swearing and trying to get the audience riled up after introducing the Nuns, and after he came off, Bill Graham had some of his goons start pounding on him. Wow, getting thrashed at a Sex Pistols concert, how weird was that? That was kind of disturbing. It was a weird show. It was kind of like supposed to be this real high point for punk, but . . . I mean punk went on after that, but we felt dirtied . . . we felt somehow the purity was gone.

RENE DAALDER: I remember one conversation at my house with Malcolm and some of the others, just before San Francisco, about how everybody in the Pistols camp was completely at odds, how the band had managed to outlive its usefulness in such a short amount of time. Even before Winterland there was talk about breaking up. The relationships were totally fucked up, especially between John and Malcolm, and Sid was completely strung out. There was a lot of creative competition and jealousy between Lydon and McLaren. I think John Lydon was much smarter and much more developed as an artist than Malcolm recognized or bargained for . . . I think he may have thought of John as a malleable puppet like the others who'd passively go along with anything.

PENELOPE HOUSTON: I think they were burned out. They were partying hard and getting into all kinds of trouble. But I didn't see any indication that this was going to be their last show.

HELLIN KILLER: In San Francisco, Sid was a wreck. All he wanted to do was get drugs, and all we wanted to do was keep him from getting drugs at all costs, and at this girl's house after the show, someone brought him heroin and he OD'd. We were at the party after the show and Sid just went flat out in the bathtub.

LAMAR SAINT JOHN: After the Winterland show, the Warner Brothers' muscle men who were taking care of Sid just let him go and said, "Fuck it. Let him party." Sid wanted to get high and they let me take care of him. I knew where to get drugs. I took him there. He got high, I wasn't into it then. We got to my house. Hellin Killer was there holding his hand. He was just drinkin' and drinkin'. He was gone. The next day, Johnny calls Sid, and they get into a big argument. After this, Sid wants to get high. Hellin says, "Yeah, I got money." I am like going, "Don't do that to him" because he hadn't eaten and he was drinking like a fish. So I called Malcolm and Rory and I tell them to get over here, because the guy is going to get loaded and he is going to go out you know, you got to stop this. The connection comes over. Him, Sid and Hellin go into the bathroom. The connection leaves, Sid turns blue. He just went out. I lived a block from the Haight Ashbury Free Clinic, so I run over there and said, "Sid Vicious is in my house and he OD'd." They came over and hit him up with Narco, or whatever it's called. After this Malcolm and Rory finally came and got him, and that was the last time I saw him.

RENE DAALDER: After Winterland Sid stopped by the house to say goodbye to everybody. He was in great spirits, saying things like, "It was nice working with you," and only the next morning did we learn what had caused his cheery demeanor—he OD'd again on the plane to New York and upon arrival he was rushed to the hospital. Malcolm had nothing left but the loyalty of Cook and Jones. They took off for Rio, and by the time Malcolm made it back to London, receivers had taken over his Glitterbest company.

MARK MOTHERSBAUGH: Richard Branson called me up in Akron in the winter of 1978 and said, "Hey, you wanna come down to Jamaica?" And I looked out the window and said to myself, "Well it's snowing about thirty inches here. Sure, I'll come down to Jamaica." So he flew Bob Casale and I down there to meet him and Ken Berry. We were all just sitting around in the Kingston Holiday Inn and he brought out this big stash of pot and Branson is rolling these gigantic joints on a newspaper and we're used to being in Akron where you get enough to make a pencil-thin joint. We were talking to him about playing Mabuhay Gardens the night after the Sex Pistols' last show at Winterland and how we were staying over at *Search and Destroy* magazine, we were using *Search and Destroys* for mattresses. And we talked about how the Sex Pistols came over to the office, Sid and Nancy, and we were hanging out. And Branson said, "What do you think of them?" And we said, "They were all nice guys. You know. It was fun meeting them. It's too bad that they broke up." And Branson said, "I'll tell you why you're here. Johnny Rotten is down here at the hotel. He's in the next room, and there are reporters downstairs from the *New Musical Express, Sounds,* and *Melody Maker.* I'd like to go down to the beach right now, if you're into this, because Johnny Rotten wants to join your band . . . and I want to announce to them that Johnny Rotten is the new lead singer for Devo." And I'm going, "Oh my God, I'm really high right now." Regrettably, I didn't just go, "Yeah, sounds great. Send him to Akron. He can do it for a week or two, just for the hell of it." It was a weird time for us.

chapter 19

The trashing of the Troubadour, 1978. Photo Credit: Unknown

BRENDAN MULLEN: Things got off to a bad start when the Bags played at the Troubadour. It was the first punk show ever at this once jolly country rock cowboy club in West Hollywood, which was the birth spot for post-Burritos/CSN&Y country vocal groups and the new Hoot Night Asylum artists hawked by a cute, fresh-faced future renowned multinational corporate power broker named David Geffen. This seedy roach-infested joint had recently been knocked out of the water after a long run as the premier industry haunt when Lou Adler opened the Roxy. Now the club was desperate for business, so desperate they were reduced to booking punk! The Troubadour was owned and hands-on operated by Doug Weston, this fabulously outlandish cocaine-addled old hippie queen, a lumbering giant who was six foot six and stormed around in caftans, beads, and bells over open-toed leather sandals in 1978. Knowing or caring naught for this club's revered folk and country rock history, punks arriving for the first time balked at the two-drink minimum and responded by upending all the tables and chairs to create a pogo dance floor in front of the stage! When [Tom] Waits allegedly tried to pick up on Alice [Bag] by asking what a beauty like her was doing with an asshole like Nickey Beat when she could enjoy the thrill of being with him instead, things only got worse.

ALICE BAG: A group of us were standing in the entrance of Canter's Deli, ogling the pastries we couldn't afford. Tom Waits came in and started talking to my friend Lauren, who introduced us. We made small talk. Then I said goodbye and left Lauren talking to him. I didn't know that he was supposedly a celebrity, so the whole meeting seemed perfectly ordinary. The next time I saw Lauren, she told me that Waits asked what I did. When she said I was a singer, he asked when and where my band was playing and he told her he would go see us. He also asked Lauren who the "dipshit" was that I was with. That "dipshit" would be my then boyfriend, Nickey Beat. Nickey was furious when he heard about it, but it seemed that we had forgotten it. It had blown over by the night of the Troubadour show. That night, we were in the dressing room getting ready when one of our friends told us that Waits was sitting at a table right in front of the stage. Then Nickey went up to the mic and verbally abused Mr. Waits. I believe he called him "a fucking asshole." Tom sat coolly at his table during the entire set. Punks were throwing chairs into a pile at the back of the club so that they could pogo in front of the stage. The whole area at the front had been cleared, except for one table. Tom was on one side, sitting with a very serious look on his face, and on the other side was this unruly rabble who every now and then shoved his chair or threw a table over his head. But what was really weird was that he didn't even move the entire time. He sat there until the show was over, and he was still there when everyone left. Meanwhile, we were up in the dressing room thinking, "What a great show." But when we start trying to load up our equipment these brawny guys told us that we couldn't. Tom and Nickey started arguing. Members of our band tried to break it up, but the brawny guys were shoving us out of the way, saying they wanted to let them fight, and so Tom and Nickey started sluggin' it out like Neanderthals. And no, I didn't cover my eyes. Eventually the brawny dudes decided they'd had enough entertainment and broke it up. Tom was taken to another part of the club and we were allowed to leave, vowing never to play the Troubadour again.

CHUCK E. WEISS: I was in Canter's Deli the night before the trashing of the Troubadour episode, sitting with Waits when this chick Alice from the Bags came up to our table and was flirting with us and then she invited us to come and see her band the next night. I didn't know what she was doing exactly, but I knew something was wrong. So we get there the next night anyway and she calls out Waits from the stage and said, "Tom Waits is down here trying to pick me up." She tried to embarrass Waits in front of the crowd. She stopped her show specially to say this. Afterward that Nickey Beat guy called Waits out to further embarrass him—he called him an asshole from the stage, as I recall—but you know, the guys at the Troubadour were all pretty tight, so we just said, "Okay, if that's what you want." So we shut the door and locked it after all the punks had gone outside so's Waits and Nickey Beat could have it out one on one. They had their little scuffle . . . it was pretty soft-handed . . . it was like watching two girls fight, pulling hair and open-hand slapping. I'd say it was pretty much a draw. Outside the club the punks kept trying to get back in, and John Sanborn, one of the doormen, was poking them in the face to keep them away from pushing the door open. It was like the movie *Night of the Living Dead* except with angry punks trying to kick the door down. Nickey disrespected Waits, but Alice did it first. She invited us to come down; we would have never come to see her otherwise. The place got trashed, all right, but the place used to get trashed nearly every other night anyway.

BRENDAN MULLEN: The next day the entire Troubadour staff signed a petition threatening to quit if punk wasn't banned. The petition referred to punks as "vermin" and the bands as "anti-artists." Weston deferred to his employees' demands, and so a show featuring the Zeros, X, and the Flesh Eaters set for the following week was canned.

CHUCK E. WEISS: Man, I seen things happen when country and western bands would play there and brawls would break out—a huge slugfest broke out when Willie Nelson played there, with glasses flyin', tables and chairs upended, the whole nine yards. I saw Doug Weston do more damage to that club than any punk rocker did that night. Once Doug came out onstage brandishing a shotgun directly at the audience; another time he was kicking things over. I saw Phil Ochs kick shit all over that joint, and I saw a duke-out between Bennett Glotzer, Albert Grossman's partner, and Dr. John at the front bar. Things like that happened all the time, so the punks kicking over tables and chairs wasn't more radical than Doug Weston getting onstage and pointing a gun at the audience. Later that same night there was the legendary food fight at Canter's between the punks and the Troubadour guys . . . I got into a verbal exchange with Brendan Mullen at the cash register with matzoh balls flying in the background.

✳ ✳ ✳

LEE VING: By the time I'd put my band Fear together, I'd already gone down to the Masque to see what was up with this new punk scene, and what I saw didn't look like shit at first. I thought: "Aw, man, this punk rock shit sucks, man."

BRENDAN MULLEN: During early 1978 another hilarious band came out of the Van Nuys area of the Valley. This was one was named Fear, who played their first show in Hollywood with the Skulls, the Deadbeats, and F-Word at a show I promoted at Larchmont Hall. But Fear was a different kind of punk band. Not influenced by Bowie or the Pistols, Fear fused an aggressive, revved-up take on punk with unapologetic out-and-out heavy metal riffs pulled from the Unholy Book of Sabbath and Motorhead, and there's no doubt they helped to prime SoCal audiences for speed-metal, speedcore, or speed thrash nearly a decade before Metallica, Slayer, and their post-Venom ilk generated hundreds of millions of dollars in record and concert ticket sales.

LEE VING: The second time I went to the Masque, it was even worse, but then on my third try I saw Black Randy and the Controllers and I immediately thought, "This is way closer to what I'm thinking." Good, strong rhythms is what I wanted to bring to it. A total all-out metal assault. You can thrash and still be in tune, musically speaking. Why not? Part of the Fear concept was to put the fear of God into the punks. We made a lot of enemies in San Francisco. They were surprisingly ready to fight up there, I had to put more than one uppity Clown Alley joker in his place . . . at the edge of the curb. Mostly it would be juiced-up jar heads trying to stir up beefs because of my hair color, but rankling people wasn't strange to us, it was definitely a part of what Fear wanted to do as a band. And we weren't just looking to wig out bank workers and straight people only; we were looking directly at the punk audience as a prime target as well.

BRENDAN MULLEN: I once witnessed Lee Ving in a pink hair rinse staring down three drunk marines in San Francisco, saying, "Yeah, it's my real color, d'ya like it?" Watching these fuckers back off was the finale to one night on the town! Although most Hollywood punks were amused by Fear, many curled their lips and rolled their mascaraed eyes in horror, and I was slagged for booking an "uncool" band of macho metalhead dicks that weren't "one of us."

DARRELL WAYNE: Lee came off as a tough, street-fighting New Yorker type, but was actually a very kind and respectful man. He became a good friend and we hung out a lot at Barney's Beanery, trying to drink every kind of beer they had.

LEE VING: We had enemies everywhere we went. A lot of promoters got shit for booking us. We didn't physically ruin the place we worked in; it was because the music was just too weird and aggressive for some. So we went looking for bands we could talk into opening shows for . . . not necessarily because we admired their musical direction, just that we thought it was close enough that we could pick up new fans of our own if we could just get out and play for them. And X supplied that many, many times, as did the Dils, the Plugz, and the Bags, and we were real happy to be involved.

CHRIS D.: I remember there was kind of a backlash in Hollywood, not in terms of the music, because a lot of people appreciated how aggressive they were, but it just got so much more violent. Some people embraced it and some people really hated it.

BRENDAN MULLEN: Fear's blatant heavy metal leaning with angry punk lyrics (early Metallica member Cliff Burton had a Fear sticker on his bass) was equally as controversial as their gay-baiting, between-song banter. Fear alienated some among the mostly closeted but considerably large don't-ask-don't-tell homo constituency within the old Hollywood/Masque scene, which was probably as much as 30–35 percent gay, maybe even more.

LEE VING: We did the fag shtick 'cause we thought we'd found a source of humor. I thought everybody would get the joke pretty easy, 'cause there was Philo Cramer, our guitar player, wearing a dress onstage. It was strictly a joke, a confrontational tack to get these big boneheaded jocks all riled up. We decided it was our job to throw these bozos into states of mass homosexual panic. The more "mature" punk sophisticates found us "vulgar," "too heavy metal," "too macho" . . . oh, and "puerile" was another one, I think. Okay, whatever, but what we were doing was never mean-spirited, it was not meant to be taken personally by anyone, we were never putting out any hate messages against gay people at all. How could anyone be offended by a band whose guitar player is in a dress offering people in the audience a dollar to be his friend? He'd say in this little pleading voice: "We just want you guys to like us . . ." We were goofs, cutups, and we were willing to delve into any area for a laugh. Philo is a great musician who had a real twisted sense of humor and we happened to think he was very funny. I don't know what image people had of us. I was going to the gym and my arms were big, but we weren't into beating anybody or having people be physically intimidated by us. The idea of Fear was that it was something we all knew about and everybody would be able to relate to it in some way. We just wanted to be entertaining and to play this music and maybe sell some fuckin' records. It wasn't about fag bashing or hurting anybody, for fuck's sake.

RIK L. RIK: It just wasn't acceptable to be gay in the early L.A. punk rock scene. Even though it was obvious in his manner that he was such a raving queen, with the way he talked and everything, Darby's party line was that he was asexual, and we pretty much believed that. But then I'd be alone with him at night and he'd try to get me loaded so he could have an easier time taking advantage of me.

JOHN DOE: There was an undercurrent of not accepting the gay lifestyle with bands like Fear.

PHRANC: I was always out as a lesbian. I can't remember any other out queers at that time. There were the Screamers, but nobody ever really talked or sang about being queer. The punk scene was the only time I felt I had a peer group. All the dykes I'd hung out with before were about ten years older than me. I was young and angry and political. It was the first time, maybe the only time I ever felt I fit in.

GORILLA ROSE: All these young California kids were coming out of their folks' houses to view this wild music scene that was happening in alleys and ripped-up clubs and funky old places. You'd leave home and find out there's more than what your parents had told you. You can either be an asshole and stay Beach Boys, "California Rules" and "babes, babes, babes" and "I'm a guy, I just drink beer and play guitar," or you can start exploring alternative ideas. Start taking drugs. Start experimenting sexually.

RIK L. RIK: The relationship I had with Darby ended because he had this big crush on me and I wasn't feeling it back. I knew I was kidding myself that he liked me for me and only wanted to be like my best friend. He finally tried to put a move on me at his house, but he did it in a really elaborate, mind-controlling way. The whole time he was talking about Rimbaud and Verlaine, and how the greatest men in the history of our culture were homosexual. He talked up the Greeks, how they were like the apex of civility and that it was a totally homosexual culture where women were only used for procreation. He'd also read up on a lot of mind control techniques. He would keep the lights off, then turn them on at certain key moments. He had this whole system he was experimenting with, but it didn't really work on me, although it freaked me out enough that I told my girlfriend about it. She was only fourteen and when she saw Darby at the Masque the next night she said, "Hey, I heard you tried to pick up my boyfriend." Our relationship died after that; Darby completely cut me out of his life. I was devastated because he was my best friend, and to this day, he is the most important person I've ever met.

K.K. BARRETT: It was a time of gay fear and there were a lot gays in the scene like Tomata, Tommy, Darby, Maicol Sinatra, Kid Congo, Craig Lee, but it was all hidden, 'cause there was a lot of homophobia going on.

GERBER: Darby was very freaked out about his own sexuality, and I know this from our early acid trips when we tried to figure out if we were even capable of having sex at all. For many years he just claimed to be abstinent; he just was unable to admit that he was gay—other than to me when we were on acid.

TRUDIE ARGUELLES: The only openly gay punks I knew were Maicol Sinatra and Craig Lee. Darby never said, "I'm gay." We kind of figured it out later, but he was very closeted.

K.K. BARRETT: So was Tomata. You've got a scene that's so close-knit, you're fearful of judgment. It was descendent from the glam era when Bowie publicly said, "Oh, hi . . . I'm bi." Girls could do it both ways, sure, and that was very cool, but guys couldn't, no way.

TRUDIE ARGUELLES: Punks were getting away from that whole wimpy glam thing. Now it was supposed to be mean and tough.

K.K. BARRETT: Even though Dee Dee Ramone wrote "53rd and 3rd," it was tough. He wasn't announcing that he was a gay hustler. Dee Dee was doing it for money.

BRENDAN MULLEN: Most of my gay drinking pals actually became some of Fear's biggest fans and shared my perception that Fear's alleged homophobia was less about hate-driven g-boy bashing; it was more akin to someone yelling "Faggots!" into a roomful of drunken rednecks in a southern cowboy bar at 1 A.M. on a Saturday night and then watching all hell break loose.

chapter 20

The courtyard of the Canterbury Apartments, just north of Hollywood Boulevard on N. Cherokee Avenue, a block away from the Masque, 1978. Photo Credit: Jules Bates (*pictured himself in forefront*)

TRUDIE ARGUELLES: The Canterbury was this amazing old apartment building in Hollywood with the cheapest rents you could find. We were still living at the Plunger Pit when Rod Donahue came over one day and said, "I found this apartment. This place is only a hundred fifty bucks a month and it's only a block away from the Masque."

TERRY GRAHAM: The proximity to the Masque was the whole reason the Canterbury flourished as this tiny punk colony.

MARGOT OLAVERRA: The Canterbury was this classic old Hollywood apartment building, but it was so run-down. It was a haven for underclass marginals, especially punk rockers like myself with no regular income. It had a really big hallway with staircases going on both sides, and these rickety elevators that smelled of mildew and petrified soggy mattresses and this red carpet that wasn't shag and wasn't flat, in between—perfect to capture dust and dirt. There were Vietnamese refugees living there and you could smell the rice cooking all the time. This crazy girl from Detroit named Sheila was there. We used to get into all kinds of trouble. The Plungers moved in there, too. Hellin had an apartment there. Alice and Nickey Beat had an apartment there. Belinda lived with Lorna Doom from the Germs. Darby used to hang out there all the time.

JANE WIEDLIN: We'd run around from apartment to apartment. It was like a dormitory for punks.

TERRY GRAHAM: I was dating Jane Wiedlin when she was living there. I always had to make sure that she actually stayed in her bed at night. She would get up and sleepwalk nude around the apartment. People would find her walking around the halls either completely nude or with a sheet around her. I'd notice the door open in the middle of the night and go catch her.

TRUDIE ARGUELLES: It was 50 percent blacks, then all these criminals, pimps, junkies, and a lot of insane people who talked to themselves and didn't wear shoes.

K.K. BARRETT: The burned-out glam rockers Zolar X lived there, too. At one time they'd worn silver space suits with antennae, but now they were just burned-out drunks.

TRUDIE ARGUELLES: As soon as we moved in, the building manager was arrested for shooting someone, and we got a new manager called the Reverend. He had this weird religion that was called Animalism, which didn't believe in killing any living things, including bugs, so there were cockroaches all over the place!

K.K. BARRETT: Animalism was some strange, self-invented Islamic sect. We'd signed up to move in, and the week before we were to move, the landlord shot somebody in the lobby and killed him, but we still moved into this place anyway.

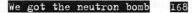

TRUDIE ARGUELLES: The Reverend was this big black guy, and he brought all his Muslim friends with names like Omar and Mohammed.

K.K. BARRETT: Loaded on PCP.

TRUDIE ARGUELLES: They'd call us the "punk rocks."

K.K. BARRETT: You'd run into them at night in the hallway and they'd be like, "You punk rocks stay away from me. You crazy! You insane! You stay away from me!"

TRUDIE ARGUELLES: And in the daytime, they'd blast Marvin Gaye.

K.K. BARRETT: One time the Rev came up to us while we were playing Coltrane's *Ascension* very loud plugged into an amp and it was filling the whole courtyard.

TRUDIE ARGUELLES: Across the hall from us lived these Okies named Buzzard and Li'l Bit, who'd come out with her gun all the time— "I'm gonna git you." There were these collisions of culture all the time.

K.K. BARRETT: Buzzard claimed to be the drummer on "Wipe Out" by the Surfaris. Total burnout paranoids. "What are you doin'? What are you doin'? Don't be loud."

TRUDIE ARGUELLES: There were Hell's Angels there, too, and full-on transvestites. Jane had a big war going on with Buzzard and Li'l Bit. Belinda and Lorna had an apartment together. Margot lived there, too.

MARGOT OLAVERRA: I remember Black Randy howling right on the roof of the Canterbury. A girl got raped one night and she was screaming these bloodcurdling screams, and because everybody used to scream all the time, nobody thought there was anything unusual going on. It was that kind of environment. Very crazy.

K.K. BARRETT: The Reverend let us set up a rehearsal room in the basement, so me and Paul Roessler set it up, and all the Reverend's friends came down and ripped off our instruments. We had to go from apartment to apartment to get them back. That same room was where the Go-Go's rehearsed. Jane Drano lived down the hall.

SHAWN STERN: Darby Crash was a little wuss. He stole some of my band's [the Extremes] equipment from the rehearsal room in the basement of the Canterbury, and we confronted him, and he took us to where he hid it real fast 'cause we were gonna kick his ass. It wasn't the Black Muslims who lived in the building who took our stuff . . . it was Darby. People thought Darby was tough. He wasn't tough at all. He was a pussy. The Muslims were pretty cool. I didn't have any problem with them at all. We'd say to them, "What's up?" when we saw them.

BELINDA CARLISLE: At least fifty punks were living at the Canterbury. There were a few homeless street people hanging out there, too, but there was music coming from every room. You'd walk into the courtyard and there'd be a dozen different punk songs all playing at the same time. It was an incredible environment.

JENNY LENS: It was an age before Reagan where one week's work paid for your apartment. Now it's three weeks' work. Many people squatted or paid cheap rent at the Canterbury, where there were several people to an apartment. The people who were really involved with the scene got little part-time jobs here and there, but God knows what some people were doing to make money.

MARGOT OLAVERRA: We were so deeply embroiled in the scene that everybody was really supportive of other bands. The whole thing was such a close-knit community—that's what I value about those days so much. We were really supportive of each other; it wasn't competitive at all.

TERRY GRAHAM: You slept all day 'cause you were up all night. Parties were anywhere and everywhere and there was an ever-present search for sex with a different person every night. Jane and John Doe were together on some intimate level, and when I found out I didn't like it, and I was like, "It's John's fault," but then I thought about it a bit and decided that it's really not John's fault because if some gorgeous young girl came up to me, basically offering me her body . . . those things happen, you know? I recall very little fighting in the early days. Everybody was too busy laughing, drinking, shooting speed and dope, and having some kind of sex.

BRENDAN MULLEN: One night Darby Crash got into a heated argument with Alice Bag outside the Canterbury over the role of the performer, with Darby maintaining on the one hand that a performer is supposed to cultivate a deitylike untouchability, a larger-than-life persona, while Alice took the fundamentalist punk rock line that separation between performer and audience should be eliminated. It came to blows literally. Alice punched Darby's lights out.

ALICE BAG: Darby and I had been getting into arguments ever since we first met outside the Orpheum Theater on the night of the Germs' debut. We were both living at home, but we'd talk on the phone. We could talk about anything and disagree about it. Usually the disagreements led to a rousing argument, and sometimes to a good laugh. Both Darby and I were interested in philosophy, so our arguments were frequently inspired by whatever we happened to be reading that day. By the time I was living at the Canterbury, Darby and I had established a love/hate relationship. We could have a lot of fun together as long as we stayed away from discussing anything that meant anything to us. We also drank a lot. We could always agree on having a drink, and if we had that drink we could always count on getting into a fight. That night at the Canterbury we had been sitting inside on the stairs, drinking. It used to really bother me that Darby enjoyed trying to control people. I felt it was demeaning not only to his followers but to himself. It used to bother Darby that I treated my fans as equals. He would lecture me on what people expect in a leader. We had very, very different views on this subject. I think we had both really thought long and hard about the responsibilities that went along with having a bunch of kids look up to you. We were both committed to our beliefs. Anyway, we took ourselves very seriously, and we were very drunk, so we started arguing, then shouting at each other, and finally throwing punches. Although I can't say for sure, I'm willing to say I probably started the fight. I was quite a hothead in those days. Did he hit back? Of course he did. It was a good scrap! When I was younger I knew a lot of people who thought that most other people were basically stupid and required a benevolent dictatorship to keep them in line. At some point in my life I'm sure I agreed until I realized that in the long-term nothing much good can come from absolving people from thinking and making their own choices. I don't know if Darby aspired to be a benign dictator—I do know that he felt that people who could be controlled should be controlled. I am sure he would have been flattered if someone had compared him to Manson or Hubbard or Hitler. We got drunk. We got in an argument. We duked it out. And, of course I won!

HAL NEGRO: A bunch of junkies calling themselves the Youth Party began spray-painting swastikas in the lobby and in the basement rehearsal facility in the Canterbury, where the Go-Go's sometimes rehearsed. The swastikas were countered by a series of Star of

David emblems sprayed adjacent to them, since there were several Jewish punkers also in residence, but nobody made anything further of it until "America's favorite Jewish lesbian folksinger" protested in her song "Punks Take Off Your Swastikas."

TOMMY GEAR: At that time the use of the swastika had a different significance as far as its application by youth was concerned. It was an interesting transformation. Then it was about the rejection of icons and their meaning. We wanted to subvert or transform accepted meanings or appropriate them for other purposes. In appropriating the swastika we were not trying to be neo-Nazis, but trying to be proactive, challenging the discourse which gave that icon a particular place and meaning in cultural sensibility.

PHRANC: I wrote the song "Take Off Your Swastika" as a response to a lot of people wearing swastikas just to piss people off. That's when I started introducing myself as "The All-American Jewish Lesbian Folksinger." I started performing acoustically so people could hear the words. *Some* people took off their swastikas.

KIM FOWLEY: The scene at the Masque and the Canterbury got into a lot of decadence and debauchery, and all of the fucking and sucking, and the heroin and the dog fucking and obese shit-assing with the Go-Go's and their early circle. Somewhere in the vomit, the blood, and the vaginal pus, somewhere among the filthy hypo syringes and the blubber, there probably was poetry. Scene cheerleaders got to have their scabied cunts eaten on dirty roach-infested floors while this loopy music raged and the worms crawled, you know? It was excremental existential sexual shit at death's door.

GEZA X: Kim Fowley is a great poet. His poem "Hollywood Trash" absolutely brings tears to my eyes.

TERRY GRAHAM: The Canterbury period makes me think of three things: mildew, stale vomit, and soiled panties.

MARGOT OLAVERRA: I had to move out of the Canterbury after a fire when the ceiling collapsed and drenched all my belongings. The whole apartment above burned out and caved into mine. They wanted to renovate the building, and so they started driving out all the punks by starting fires in the hallways near the apartments . . . I had to move that very night.

BELINDA CARLISLE: There was a vibe there, an energy before the whole drug thing divided the scene.

chapter 21

Proto hardcore: Orange County's the Middle Class, 1977. Photo Credit: Mike Atta

JOHN DOE: From '77 to '79 it was an inclusive scene, and from '79 onward it became splintered. People went to the kind of shows that they identified with. There became a more defined rockabilly crowd and a more defined hardcore crowd. It used to be inclusive just because it wasn't Linda Ronstadt, Ted Nugent, and the Eagles.

BRENDAN MULLEN: The first casualty from the original '77 punks were the Skulls, the sloppiest and most fun of the original Masque bands. Marc "Conehead" Moreland spent the next six months writing songs with Stan Ridgway from the Model Citizens. The collaboration emerged in December '78 as the electropop Wall of Voodoo.

STAN RIDGWAY: Marc Moreland was the guitar player in the Skulls, one of the thrashier Masque bands who played loud, fast downstroke punk rock. Although Marc was an amazingly accomplished musician behind all the feedback and chaos onstage, I'm not sure most of the punks knew just how much more advanced as a musician Marc actually was. We bonded over similar interests in Kraftwerk and Eno. As musicians, we both knew the three punk rock chords oh too well, but by mid-'78 hale and hearty hi-ho punk rock, fun as it most surely was, just wasn't enough to keep our interest musically much longer. I began coaxing Marc into playing more experimental styles of music with me. I had a Farfisa organ and a bunch of rhythm machines, Marc had his guitar and a wonderful musical imagination. I didn't even want to be the singer. I tried out various vocalists, but nobody would sing what I'd written because it wasn't like Iggy or Johnny Rotten. When Voodoo eventually started playing out in late '78 we were not well liked by the punk rock crowd. They dismissed us as new wave. I thought, "Gosh, like the French New Wave? Like Jean-Luc Godard? That's cool, man." It was their way to discount a music that wasn't proletarian enough for them, but it was the energy and the take-charge DIY aspect of punk, not the sound or the fashion aspect of it, that informed what we were doing. We were cast as "art punk."

MILES COPELAND: I never heard the term art punk. To me, bands like Voodoo were certainly new wave, because new wave basically meant a new way of looking at things. What Wall of Voodoo did, for example, still strikes me as the most brilliant and creative exciting musical thing that I ever signed. They were very eccentric in their own way, which prevented them from being as big as they could've been, but musically, and what they did, the marriage of spaghetti Western and techno, and Stan's lyrics and singing style—I mean the whole thing is still brilliant. It's still some of my favorite music ever.

MIKE ATTA: The Middle Class might have been the beginning of the second wave, but it was the same typical story: high school losers find guitars. As far as being an early hardcore band, we'd heard about the Hollywood bands like the Bags and the Skulls. We didn't consciously try to play faster. I think it was because we had more energy than you can imagine. I had just turned seventeen. Our drummer had just turned fifteen. And we were the straightest people in the world. We were drinking lots of Dr Pepper.

MIKE PATTON: The Middle Class was sort of like the Zeros and F-Word, not musically alike, but because we were really young and from the 'burbs . . . and because we weren't art students, either. The Middle Class was just kids from Santa Ana in Orange County, but it didn't take us long to get shows. When we first showed up at the Masque around mid-'78, we felt like we were from Montana or something, but once we got our first show everybody thought we were cute. We weren't fashion punks, we didn't dress the part, and we were openly from Orange County . . . we were not putting on any sort of image. We were just who we were, and to us that was what punk rock was all about—something honest and pure. We didn't drink. We drank Dr Pepper and we played really fast and people thought we were unusual, so bands put us on opening up their shows. We didn't have a hard time getting in. When we first showed up in Hollywood, it was a fairly small group of people who lived at the Canterbury apartments and everybody was very nice. Everybody was cool, there were very few attitudes. The Bags, especially, and the other Hollywood bands were real friendly to us.

MIKE ATTA: We came up before there was any bad feelings about bands from Orange County. That would happen a bit later. But they liked us when we first came out, the Hollywood crowd. I think they respected that it was more about music than fashion to us. I thought the whole bondage pants thing looked cool, but I also thought that it would look really stupid on me.

POISON IVY RORSCHACH: The Cramps weren't thinking of this weird subgenre when we coined the term "psychobilly" in 1976 to describe what we were doing. To us all the '50s rockabillies were psycho to begin with; it just came with the turf as a given, like a crazed, sped-up hillbilly boogie version of country. We hadn't meant playing everything superloud at superheavy hardcore punk tempos with a whole style and look, which is what "psychobilly" came to mean later in the '80s. We also used the term "rockabilly voodoo" on our early flyers.

JEFFREY LEE PIERCE: The arrival of the Cramps in L.A. convinced us that there was plenty of American culture out there that needed to be destroyed. I highlighted this period by smashing a hundred-dollar Ersel Hickey single on Sunset Boulevard and shouting "Fuck rockabilly!" According to Phast Phreddie, I then promptly hid in the brush beside the Cinerama Dome at the sound of police helicopters, convinced that I was a Viet Cong cadre escaping the Americans.

KID CONGO POWERS: I nearly dropped dead when I saw the Cramps . . . it seemed like they were from outer space or something . . . there was no comparison. I'd never seen anything like it. Jeffrey and I thought they were the shit . . . they were the only band that was really reconfiguring what was going on with the old and the new, all the way from the '50s to present-day punk rock.

POISON IVY RORSCHACH: Roky Erickson, Suicide, the Ramones, and a bunch of old '50s rockabillies were our biggest musical influences, but we never really fit in with the New York punk scene as such. We were always able to get good gigs at all the best punk clubs, we'd sell out multiple nights, and kids loved us, so we're not complaining, but the rock writers hated us, and we were written off as some sort of clown act. Once we even did a benefit for *Punk* magazine, and they never even bothered to list us as playing, nor did anyone even say, "Hey, thanks, you guys" after the gig, in print or on the phone, or whatever. Mediawise, it was like we didn't even exist in New York, yet we'd sell out everywhere we went just by word of mouth.

MILES COPELAND: People definitely took to them here. Walking down the street in the hot Los Angeles sunshine with Lux and Ivy and Bryan Gregory in their vinyl suits and white was something else. People looked at them like they were from another planet.

POISON IVY RORSCHACH: The New York punk scene was in its death throes. It was all over, it had been for a while, whereas in L.A. it seemed like it was just getting going. We decided to move here for a number of reasons: the climate, and we had friends here like Pleasant Gehman and Kid Congo Powers. What clinched it was when we discovered we could live twice as well out here 'cause everything, especially rents, was becoming so expensive in New York. We weren't particularly trying to align ourselves with the scene out here or to become an "L.A. band" or anything because we travel so much, nationally and internationally . . . we just saw L.A. as the most practical place to be based. Our friends were here, so was our label, and we've been based here ever since. Moving here just made everything easier.

BUNKY KIRCHENHEIMER: The punk scene started to slowly move beyond Hollywood toward downtown L.A. because of the Atomic Café, this grimy old noodle café with a cool still-functioning neon sign on East First Street in Little Tokyo. This joint originally opened in the '40s . . . now it was becoming the after-hours focal point of the scene after Tomata du Plenty from the Screamers told everybody that it was his favorite place to go to wind down after shows.

PAUL GREENSTEIN: Nancy, the daughter of the owner of the place, targeted the punks with a full page in *Slash* after she told me that her family's business was facing closure because the landlord had just jacked the rent 300 percent. I told her if she'd put up for expenses, I'd design ads for placement in *Slash* and reprogram the jukebox. Nancy and her family were eagerly amenable. Soon after you'd see punkers and new wavers rubbing elbows with cops, insomniac hyper Japanese restaurant workers, cab drivers, and other graveyard workers. Nancy encouraged bands to put up flyers and posters for their gigs, and we programmed the jukebox with local 45's.

BRENDAN MULLEN: The place served chow till 4 A.M. Nancy reinvented herself as Atomic Nancy and courted more members of the punk scene at the urging of Paul Greenstein, who had previously worked at Pasadena Arts Center as a nude model for budding artists.

PAUL GREENSTEIN: I liked the bar at Madame Wong's in Chinatown, an area which was adjacent to the Atomic Café in downtown L.A. I used to go there at three or four in the afternoon during my rounds downtown and have a beer. I'd just hang around and talk to George Wong about China. I told George I had a great idea and he said he'd have to talk to his wife, Esther. She of course said no.

NICKEY BEAT: When the Bags played with X at Madame Wong's, this kooky little Chinese restaurant downtown, the place got trashed—not as bad as when the Troubadour got trashed, but tables and chairs got knocked about to create a pogo space, and the Bags were like kinda hardcore before there was hardcore. Paul Greenstein gets on the mic and says: "The Whisky and Starwood are fucked, and if you don't behave, we'll close you up, too." The Bags got the plug pulled on them, and Greenstein blamed me and my girlfriend Barbara James for starting shit and had us thrown out, but it was Craig Lee who kept trying to incite a riot. Chairs were thrown, a few glasses got broken . . . I got into it with Paul in defense of Barb . . . he was trying to physically restrain her from throwing things.

PAUL GREENSTEIN: The next week the Alley Cats played and somebody banged into the cigarette machine and Esther went off on me again. Then this wimpy power pop group from Oklahoma called 20/20 was bugging me to play a residency, but I wouldn't let 'em do it, so they snuck around my back to Esther. After about three months I'd had it with Esther's tantrums, and since she'd never really hired me in the first place, I was ready to quit. One of her classics was "No girl singers. All time girl singer make people too crazy . . . no good." This came a week after a show with the Bags and X where we had a minor insurrection during the Bags' set. That and the night two birds duked it out while Dianne from the Alley Cats was singing convinced her of the infinite wisdom of this edict. Of course, the dear, sweet Motels were a whole different story.

MARTHA DAVIS: The new wave thing came along and the Motels fit in somehow. We were too raucous to be like the regular California sound, we were way too weird for that, but we weren't playing three-chord punk rock, either. We gigged at Madame Wong's constantly.

BRENDAN MULLEN: In June of 1979 the Hong Kong Café, another Chinese restaurant in a tight business jam, approximately the same size as Wong's, opened up to punk right across the same courtyard, and the bookers began ruthlessly pirating Wong's bands. Esther quickly declared that any band who dared play the Hong Kong would never play her room again. The two clubs were in the same mall, within sight of each other. Wong's ad slogan was: "Home of the Motels, the Knack, 20/20, the Naughty Sweeties, Sumner, Bates Motel, Great Buildings, Bugs Tomorrow, Shandi, Sensible Shoes" . . . and at least two dozen third-rate bar bands trying to catch the new wave with bland pop rock songs, Blondie and the Cars being their protos. Thus the punk rock which-side-are-you-on dichotomy was even more intensified: Are you punk (self-taught, self-contained DIY) or new wave (musically comprised of shitty theoretical pop songs drenched with three-part harmony la-la's supported by major-label hype)? Somebody ran a piece in the *L.A. Times* called "The Chinatown Punk Wars."

GREG SHAW: At some point back in '77, Warner Brothers acquired distribution of Sire, with all of Seymour's new bands, and was signing the Pistols as well, so they'd already made a corporate decision to get into punk. I was invited to give an orientation talk to Warner's creative people. I went over the ways this "new wave" music differed from the "album rock" they were more familiar with and discussed the politics. They went on to market "punk" under the name "new wave" and quietly forced Sire to drop the rest of its punk roster.

BRENDAN MULLEN: Seymour Stein followed his punk ethnic-cleansing operation with an open letter he circulated to the nation's FM program directors. . . . Sy, or maybe it was Shaw who hacked it for him, wrote, "One of the most significant trends in recent years has been 'new wave' rock, all-too-often wrongly referred to as 'punk' rock." The term "punk" is as offensive as "race" and "hillbilly" were when they were used to describe "rhythm and blues" and "country and western" music thirty years ago.

DARRELL WAYNE: Both Tom Petty and the Heartbreakers and Elvis Costello were considered punk rockers before they sold a bunch of records. After they signed to major labels, all of a sudden they were new wave. Same with local bands like Devo and Oingo Boingo.

D.J. BONEBRAKE: Some hardline punks even said X was too poppish for the old Hollywood scene. Somebody once said, "You guys are like Elvis Costello." That was a big put-down. It meant you were candy-ass new wave opportunists rather than true punk. I didn't care, I just wanted to play music that I liked.

BRENDAN MULLEN: Then Greg Shaw's *Bomp* magazine put out their famous issue, touting power pop as the next big thing. There may have been no Beatles or Stones in '77, but in '78 it was back to suits and three-part harmonies according to Uncle Greg.

DON WALLER: I liked some classic power pop records—the early Who, Raspberries, Small Faces, the Jam, the Buzzcocks, all the usual suspects—but that music's been basically just a cult jam for almost thirty years. A good song in any style is a good song, but that's a real limited style and you're competing with Pete Townsend and Ray Davies and even Big Star and Paul Weller, and you have to do something more original than just imitating the records you love. The pop groups of L.A. in the '70s were a little bit older and so were their fans. I think Greg was doin' more than his share of wishful thinking 'cos you know rock 'n' roll theory is one thing and actual events may vary. . . .

PETER CASE: I hated that power pop versus punk shit. I didn't want to have anything to do with power pop. When Shaw came up with that power pop cover of *Bomp*, I hated it. I liked punk 'cause it was a much better word with a much wider scope for interpretation and he was talking up its "built-in obsolescence" . . . its limitations, for fuck's sake. As if "power pop" or new wave weren't even more incredibly stunted and limiting terms bound for surefire overnight disappearance. I'd been around these things that took off as fads that didn't include me before, and once again I didn't fit in. I felt a lot closer in spirit to bands like Black Randy, the Weirdos, X, the Germs . . . and the records Geza X was producing for Dangerhouse. All those things were much more important to me than any power pop. I just liked rock and roll. The punk versus power pop was hype, but it was fun to have a battle and everybody had a club or a side to be on. Greg wanted to push that angle so he could be the boss of it, I guess, but I think he's really basically a good guy.

DOUG FIEGER: The Knack had the idea to do band uniforms, which nobody was doing at that time, so everybody had a white shirt and black pants. Bruce's girlfriend worked in the clothing trade and she got us these skinny black ties. When we got successful, it became something that people copied, but it wasn't a conscious thought to say, "We're gonna create some kind of look." It was to differentiate us from the bands who dressed punk, and the L.A. casual bands who wore Hawaiian shirts.

PAUL GREENSTEIN: Esther Wong declared that any band who dared to play the Hong Kong Café would never play her room again. The two clubs were in the same mall, within sight of each other. Wong's ad slogan was: "Home of the Motels, the Knack, 20/20, the Naughty Sweeties, Sumner, Bates Motel, Great Buildings, Bugs Tomorrow . . . and a host of other loser bar bands trying to catch the new wave" . . .

TITO LARRIVA: I don't know why, but we were the only band who could play both the Hong Kong and Wong's. I guess it was because we had a slow song. We had "Electrify Me." It was a ballad. Maybe that was it. I don't know. Beats me.

SLASH MAGAZINE, "LOCAL SHIT" COLUMN, "WONG VS. KONG" (SEPTEMBER 1979): Ever since the Hong Kong Café opened its upstairs room and bar to punk we've heard rumors that the neighboring club across the plaza, Madame Wong's, has been pressuring bands with ultimatums: "Either you never even try to be booked at the Hong Kong, or my doors will forever be closed to you and your music." Of course most of the bands playing the Hong Kong regularly these days were already banned ages ago from the Wong place, but apparently the old lady never tires of adding new names to her prestigious black book.

PAUL GREENSTEIN: Yeah, Esther's edict made no sense at all since most of the acts who played the Hong Kong were harder-edged anyway and she had already banned all punk shows long before the Hong Kong even opened.

GREG SHAW: There were pop bands alongside the most extreme punks in every music scene in the '70s. The two mixed as easily as Blondie and the Dead Boys sharing the stage at CBGB.

MARTHA DAVIS: The Knack single-handedly started a feeding frenzy in Los Angeles during the summer of '79. When "My Sharona" happened, the industry went, "Oh my God, they're here!" Once the record companies decided that they didn't have to go to New York to sign new wave bands, they came in and signed every band in L.A. . . . every little bar band that played Madame Wong's. Anybody who had a skinny tie got a record deal. You could be walking down the street in a skinny tie and you're getting signed. Six months later, most of them were dropped.

BRENDAN MULLEN: The Knack hit number 1 on the Billboard Hot 100 chart in the summer of '79 with "My Sharona." With an amazing Bruce Gary drum hook, a knockoff of a Zeppelin riff, the insufferably smarmy thing was the triumph of the "skinny tie" power pop simp faction over the messy true grit of the Masque type of bands.

DOUG FIEGER: *Get the Knack* went gold in thirteen days. It was the fastest debut platinum album in history. "My Sharona" went to number one within a month. It was a true happening all over the world.

BRENDAN MULLEN: The Knack's success was a crushing blow to bands like X, the Weirdos, the Screamers, the Go-Go's, and the Germs, all of whom had designs or dreams of going big time.

HARVEY KUBERNIK: Remember the Nuke the Knack campaigns? When you start selling two, three, four million records and everybody else collectively sold forty thousand, there's no camaraderie, nothing but hatred and anger and division . . . but the Knack were too busy touring Japan.

DOUG FIEGER: The Chipmunks did three of our songs on *Chipmunk Punk*.

BRENDAN MULLEN: Just as the scene was being split into harder-driving, superadrenalized extreme power metal-punk on one side and simpy new wave power pop on the other, the first L.A. punk compilation album, the one-sided *Yes L.A.*, was released by Danger-house, featuring X, the Alley Cats, the Bags, the Germs, the Eyes, and Black Randy.

NICKEY BEAT: There was this record called *No New York*, so we did *Yes L.A.*

RIK L. RIK: The *Beach Boulevard* compilation came out on Posh Boy Records like in the fall of '79 just as the suburban hardcore attitude was beginning to kick in. It had an accessible poppiness to it and a great sound, but the packaging didn't fit the sound; it was weird, like all the Posh Boy releases. Only one band on it was actually from the beach—the Crowd from Huntington. The Simpletones were from Rosemead, I was from Covina, and Negative Trend that I recorded with was even from the Bay Area! But sonically it's a great record, and it sort of documented the rise of suburban punk.

ROBBIE FIELDS: I got serious with the Posh Boy label after I began working with David Hines, a top-class engineer whose expertise enabled me to produce the Rodney on the ROQ series. The label also allowed me the luxury of cherry-picking the best songs from a slew of spanking new second-generation suburban California punk groups. Originally I had badly wanted to do a compilation of all the top in-crowd Hollywood bands, like the Screamers, the Weirdos, X, the Germs, the Bags, and so on, but couldn't get anybody to agree—they all thought they were holding out for major deals—

so I went out deep into the suburbs scouring for younger, fresher talent. Rik L. Rik, Negative Trend, the Simpletones from Rosemead, and Huntington Beach's the Crowd had already recorded tracks for me, so I threw together the *Beach Boulevard* compilation instead. In a time of New York black leather and London safety pins, I thought the beach remained a cultural icon that suburban teens could relate to.

chapter 22

Rockabilly kings Levi and the Rockats inspire temporary mania, 1979.
Photo Credit: Jenny Lens

BRENDAN MULLEN: In January 1979, following their sensational L.A. debut at the Other Masque, aka the New Masque, aka the Second Masque, the club I opened after the fire marshalls shut down the original Masque for live shows, Levi and the Rockats, managed by Leee "Black" Childers, former MainMan publicist and ex-manager of Johnny Thunders, became the toast of the town.

LEVI DEXTER: We came out to L.A. in early '79 and were an instant sensation at the Other Masque on Vine Street.

HAL NEGRO: For a while there, rockabilly was the it thing. Levi and the Rockats hit Hollywood like a mini British invasion. Rockabilly was going to be the next big thing, and a lot of the trendy-type punks completely jumped on it.

LEVI DEXTER: We were on the cover of the Sunday *Times* Calendar and the *L.A. Weekly*, too. We were on the *Midnight Special*. All first-time-evers for an unsigned band. It was all flukey. After the *Merv Griffin Show* the buzz on rockabilly was really strong.

LEEE "BLACK" CHILDERS: The press was waiting for the next big thing . . . it was rockabilly's moment. We did *Midnight Special* without a record deal. We kept the rock and roll philosophy that we'd play anywhere. So one night we were playing out in West L.A., at some crummy little joint called Club 88, and the Rockats were headlining and the Go-Go's were the support group, so the place was packed. David Byrne was there, all these people were there . . . it had become like "the thing" to go to, and so this guy came up afterward and said, "I'm from Merv Griffin" And we went, "Oh right, sure you are," and he said, "Will you come on the show?" And we said, "Well, what do we have to do?" He said, "Nothing. All you have to do is say yes." So the next thing we knew we were in the green room with Betty White and Barbara Cartland!

KID CONGO POWERS: I liked the rockabilly thing for a while . . . I liked wearing the flashy suits. It was all new to me, but it was important knowing about it. There was the constant search for the new fresh thing, so when anything new would come along there was a group of people who'd just grab onto it. So when Levi and the Rockats showed up, we were into them. Plus they were cute and sexy and fun . . . and they had great parties at the Tropicana, where the whole band was sacked out in one room.

LEEE "BLACK" CHILDERS: First Brendan Mullen, then Michelle Myers and Doug Weston really helped it explode in L.A. . . . they really got behind the band. L.A. was just ready for it . . . we used to go to this place called Oscar's on the Strip for breakfast . . . we'd just played the Troubadour the night before and the mobs had just been so big trying to get in, and this CBS film crew were there and it stopped traffic on Santa Monica Boulevard! At Oscar's the next morning I ran straight into Peter Brown, who used to manage the Beatles, and without even thinking of what I was saying, I said, "Peter, if only you could have been there . . . it was so wonderful! It was just like Rockat mania!" And he said, "Hmm, where have I heard that expression before?"

LEVI DEXTER: There were groupies and female fans everywhere we turned, but for me, that wasn't the cause . . . rockabilly was the cause. For our bassist Smutty, sex was the cause, and that little pup did everybody. They don't call him Smut for nothing. He was up for it, mad for it, all the time, but I was the serious one. I was more into hanging out with rockin' people and playing music, and discussing it, whereas Smut wanted to get his rocks off day and night, and many of the local chicks threw themselves at him and so he was kept busy. And Smut is hung like a horse.

HAL NEGRO: If the Plunger Pit and Joan's apartment was party central for the old Masque punks, the rockabilly house was definitely Disgraceland, where Pleasant, Marcy Blaustein, Iris Berry, and Kid Congo lived, among many, many others.

PLEASANT GEHMAN: For over a decade, I lived in one of Hollywood's most famous punk flophouses, Disgraceland. It was a buff-colored, stucco, '20s-era fourplex standing in the shadow of Frederick's of Hollywood, right around the corner from the Masque. By the time I moved in with my pals Kid Congo and Marcy Blaustein, the building—hell, the entire neighborhood—had seen better days.

KID CONGO POWERS: One time while I was living at Disgraceland we almost killed Kim Fowley when we were tripping on acid. We almost knifed him. Kari Krome was over and she said, "I just called Kim Fowley and told him to come over." And we were, "Oh, no, now you've done it! Now you've done it! Now what are we gonna do? Kim Fowley's coming over, what can be absolutely worse than that?" I don't know why we thought that was so terrible. Maybe just the thought of looking at him while we were tripping. Me and Pleasant used to collect knives and switchblades. He came over and we opened the door with the chain on the door and we stuck some knives out and he's like, "Okay, I'll leave."

PLEASANT GEHMAN: Billy Persons dubbed it "Disgraceland" because we had a Tijuana plaster bust of Elvis (with Alice Cooper makeup that I added) on the mantelpiece, surrounded by empty fifths of booze. DG Land was within stumbling distance of lots of major Hollywood nightspots, the Masque, Cathay de Grande, after-hours club the Zero Zero, Club Lingerie, and about five dive bars that all opened at 6 A.M., including some that are no longer there—the Firefly, the Frolic Room, and the Sideshow. My brother Chuckles called this Bermuda Triangle–like setup the "Circle of Death."

HAL NEGRO: Pleasant met Levi and they quickly became the "it" rockabilly couple of the 1979 scene. Well, one of many "it" couples. Soon after that, they got married and Levi moved into Disgraceland.

PLEASANT GEHMAN: I basically married Levi so he would not get kicked out of the country, but I was in love with him, too.

LEVI DEXTER: Everybody always asks me if I married her for a green card, but it's not true—I loved her. I was convinced that she was the one, the rockin'est chick of all time. I expected once we got married for things to change, but they got worse.

PLEASANT GEHMAN: The minute we got married he turned into an English working-class asshole.

LEVI DEXTER: The place had even more people in it all the time. The mess doubled, and I wanted basically to have my life in order, to have less of a constantly trashed-out, beaten-up crash pad. I wanted to fix the place up and have a cool crib, but it was impossible, there was a whole bunch of slobby drunks and junkies living like white trash, and eventually it just got overwhelming. Right about the time we got married, Pleasant joined the Screamin' Sirens, an all-girl rockabilly band which had some real raunchy out-of-control members who outdid the guys with outrageous behavior. Some of their sexual exploits would put Led Zeppelin's roadies to shame, but it just seemed a bad influence on her and it was bugging me.

PLEASANT GEHMAN: There was always crushed empty beer cans and broken bottles and smashed glasses with cigarette butts all over the floor and on the coffee table, and Levi was a neatness freak.

LEVI DEXTER: It was outrageous. I'd catch Pleasant and Buster from the Blasters in the shower when I'd go to take a piss and I'd ask, "Is this really happening?" I was like, "Hey, wait a minute . . . I'm supposed to be the husband here!" It got to the point where it was, "Look, you either get it together or I'm out of here."

DARRELL WAYNE: The rockabilly thing was kind of fun. Lots of guys running around with big country hair, but it didn't last long. Two-tone ska—bands like Madness, the Specials, and the Beat—were right around the corner. By late '79 that had become the next big thing.

BRENDAN MULLEN: One day you'd see someone walking around in their Elvis quiff and the next, they were hanging around outside the O.N. Klub on Vespa scooters with the star spangled banner on the back panier instead of the Union Jack. Steppin' out in their mod clothes, trying to look like the rude boy caricature on the cover of the Specials' "Gangsters" single.

LEVI DEXTER: *Merv Griffin* and the *Midnight Special* were broadcast nationwide. Everybody in the industry had seen us, and it really looked like we were gonna get signed, then the *L.A. Times* fucked everything up. They printed that we were holding out for a million-dollar record deal. I asked Leee about it and he said he didn't tell them that, they just put it in there, and it kind of killed us. All the labels just backed off overnight. There was very little interest after that. We were dead in the water, murdered by overhype.

LEEE "BLACK" CHILDERS: The rumor that we didn't get a deal because I was asking for a million dollars was not true. That's not why we didn't get a deal. Levi says a lot of peculiar things like that lately. Here's a good example . . . one night after a really good gig at the Troub, some guy came up from like the Flamingo Hotel and said, "Listen, I'll offer you a deal now to play one of the lounges, a six-week deal, we'll pay all expenses, ten thousand dollars a week. Will you come and do it?" And I thought, Oh my God, that means after six weeks, we would have sixty thousand dollars! It would change everything! We'd be able to eat! We could pay our bill at the Tropicana, but instead Levi said, "I'm not going to Vegas until I can walk in like Elvis!" And I said, "Are you crazy?!"

The Rockats broke up and three years later the Stray Cats turned into one of the biggest bands in the world. What's to say about that? You just can't harbor grudges. I stayed with Levi after the breakup and before he was in the Stray Cats, we actually got Brian Setzer out to Hollywood to be one of the new Rockats! He lived with us at the Tropicana Motel and they learned rockabilly from Levi, who really did know his rockabilly history. Levi would play him records and say, "What did you think of that." And Brian would say, "Oh, that was really cool" And Levi would say "No, that wasn't cool. That was really stupid. That was Pat Boone!" Not taking away from Brian's great guitar ability. The guy is a great guitarist, but he didn't really know his rockabilly history. Years later Smutty called me and said, "I'm looking at a copy of the *NME* with Brian Setzer on the cover wearing my clothes!" And he was, 'cause I'd given him a bunch of Smutty's old rockabilly clothes to make him look cool! But that's just show business. That's just the way it goes.

chapter 23

Claude Bessy restrained by the LAPD at the Elks Lodge "riot," 1979.
Photo Credit: Ann Summa

BRENDAN MULLEN: The Saint Paddy's Day Massacre, March 17, 1979, the Elks Lodge police riot. Another ominous shadow cast itself in March 1979 when law student Paul Sanoian and some friends promoted a punk concert at the Elks Lodge at MacArthur Park. It was St. Patrick's Day. The lineup was the Go-Go's, the Plugz, the Alley Cats, the Zeros. X never even got to play at all.

JANE WIEDLIN: There was no riot. The cops just came in slamming. They just started beating everybody up.

CHARLOTTE CAFFEY: The Go-Go's played the big Elks Lodge show on St. Patrick's Day at MacArthur Park. After us the Plugz played, and that was when the cops came in and tore the place up all right . . . and I was holding, too. I had drugs on me and now the riot squad comes stormin' in, I was flipping out. I was so scared. That was a frightening night.

KEITH MORRIS: I looked outside and saw all these battlin' SWAT pigs—otherwise known as the special SS branch of the LAPD—they're all lining up on the sidewalk, and I said, "This is not good."

EXENE CERVENKA: The Elks Lodge was so insane. There's the front doors and there's a big lobby area and this big stairway with this old rose carpet on it, wide enough that twelve people could walk across it in a row. I was sitting on the stairs with a bunch of other people and those doors flew open and all of a sudden there were these cops in riot gear, I mean helmets, shields, sticks, and everything, and they just came marching in. It was so odd 'cause I was just sitting there going, "I don't believe I'm seeing this." And then, of course, they just kept coming and coming and hitting people with the sticks. Everyone started running and yelling and screaming.

BARBARA JAMES: I was arrested at the Elks Lodge riot because I was so freaked out that cops had clubbed my sister Dorothy and Jeff, the two people I loved the most, and I just lost it. I picked up a NO PARKING ANYTIME sign and threw it at them and they cuffed me and hog-tied me but I broke the cuffs, and they hog-tied me and riot-cuffed me again. John Doe bailed me out from Sybil Brand because my dad wouldn't. He hung up on me, so I was locked up there for three days. Dad said, whatever mess I had gotten myself into, I'd have to get myself out. The cops beat me up and I was in the infirmary for three days. We never sued the LAPD like Rodney King or anything because we didn't know how. We didn't think that we could. Our parents were not really supportive that way, they never helped us figure out how to do something like that. It was so overwhelming, they thought it was just easier to put it behind them. I still don't understand what happened. It was X and the Go-Go's headlining. It wasn't like a bunch of those hardcore superaggressive guy bands that came later that made everyone wanna fight.

KEITH MORRIS: Suddenly cops flew through the front doors in full riot gear with shields and batons swingin'. They were cracking heads. Cracking skulls. Swinging at anybody who was in their way. Three or four dozen people got hurt, half a dozen seriously. I ended up hiding in the men's room. All of a sudden this guy Donnie Rose comes flying through the door, bleeding from the head, and he said, "Just stay where you are." It was really ugly. Really out of hand.

MARGOT OLAVERRA: We all went outside and watched these police choppers flying overhead. We were so used to this lifestyle and knowing it as so nonthreatening, 'cause it was such an isolated small community, but to all these city bureaucrats and to the repressive police force, it was very strange, all these freaks congregating near MacArthur Park. Who ordered this absolutely unprovoked assault and why is still a mystery.

MARK STERN: It was at the press conference held at the Masque after the St. Patrick's Day riot in '79 that I had the idea that we needed to start something to promote the positive things about this music, because all the media seemed to focus on was negativity and crazy kids with safety pins in their cheeks, starting riots, blah blah blah. That's when I started BYO, meaning Better Youth Organization.

SHAWN STERN: My brother Mark and I were teens among guys like the Screamers people and the people at *Slash* who were already in their late twenties and early thirties. Most of them were art school people and the music had a lot of different styles, but for us punk rock was everything, it wasn't just an excuse for a bunch of art groovers to party and get naked. It was like a religion to us.

MARK STERN: We began meeting other kids our age and we put out this two-page newsletter-comic thing saying "Join the BYO." We also had this big house in Hollywood, nicknamed Skinhead Manor, and that became the focal point for meeting people for a short time. We moved in during the fall of '79 . . . we were just sort of hanging out listening to music, and we had a rehearsal studio, a Coke machine filled with beer, we were gonna do a lot of things . . . we were gonna have a pirate radio station and a recording studio. By 1980, kids would drive in from Oxnard . . . from Ventura, San Diego, Orange, Riverside Counties for the Tuesday hardcore night at the Starwood and they'd hang out with us before heading over to the gig.

SHAWN STERN: Skinhead Manor was on Leland Way, west of Highland, south of Sunset, but we weren't white power, anti-Semitic, or anything racist at all, we were nearly all Jews at the beginning of Skinhead Manor. Adam Small, who made the documentary movie *Another State of Mind,* lived there. Robert Lopez, too. To us the word "skinhead" had more of a cool "oi!" soccer chant reference.

2-Tone was starting to get popular in England during '79. I had a skinhead but in those days skins and punks hung out together, there were no political or racist connotations, we didn't know about the National Front and all that British neo-Nazi shit at first, because we'd never have supported any crap like that.

MIKE WATT: The cops in Torrance figured we weren't really about gigging and making records, that it was all about moving drugs. Robo [Flag's drummer] would just drop off records at a store, and they'd think it was a heroin shipment or something! I was at the door when the entire Torrance PD waltzed into the SST HQ. They were so sure there was something else going on. We got thrown out of several towns—Hermosa Beach, Long Beach. The Black Flag thing with the cops was unreal—they were pigs who were totally into harassment. They had mug shots of kids just for having funny haircuts. As the scene expanded with more and more younger kids, people started to worry about this "lifestyle." Parents worried, but being working-class, the Minutemen never took on our parents—what the fuck was there to fight with them over, that they had too much?

Slam dancing and general crowd mayhem at a Circle Jerks show, 1979.
Photo Credit: Ann Summa

chapter 24

EUGENE: In 1979, I was living in the Holly-West building [on the corner of Hollywood Boulevard and Western] where the Chiefs and a bunch of other bands rehearsed. I got my first apartment there with my friend Dana, who was in a lot of heat with the cops and whatnot in Huntington Beach. Around that time there were a lot of kids from the beaches who were getting seriously fucked up by these long-haired redneck hicks in their 4x4 vehicles, real Lynyrd Skynyrd kind of guys. They were going to punk shows and hiding out in the parking lot and ambushing us, and I think a couple of people died, a couple got put in wheelchairs fucking forever, and nobody was doing anything about it. No disrespect against the Hollywood party punks who'd been around longer, but they just weren't prepared to defend us out in the 'burbs where kids were gettin' beaten on all the time. So Dana came up with this idea: "How about making a fight-back skinhead army?" And so we made this insular group of like maybe twenty to twenty-five guys. We were called the Wayward Caines—that was the inside inner circle, the fucking SS of the Skinhead Army, and Dana controlled the whole thing. One night he called up a war party. He called up all these guys from Huntington and Long Beach and just hammered out the big "Skinhead Army" plan. Originally, it comprised of skins, crewcuts, flattops, and we decided we were just gonna eradicate this fucking hippie threat by any means necessary. And within a couple of weeks, Dana had control of, fuck, maybe a hundred guys. Most of them went to Edison High, and then there was an extra amount of people that just wanted to associate with it . . . and that's where the hardcore shit really started. It was just a self-defense thing at the beginning and then we totally fucking took over.

JEFF MCDONALD: I know exactly how and where hardcore started. I remember the day! I was a teen with a couple of friends around my age who were all into punk rock. Somebody told me about this school in Huntington Beach where there was supposed to be over a hundred punk rockers. That was unbelievable to us, completely unheard of. One afternoon we went by that school, Edison High, looking forward to meeting all these cool new hip people. We were shocked and bummed instead when it turned out it was the same kids who'd previously been hassling us for liking punk and now they're all red-hot punkers emulating how the media portrayed punk rock, as really violent and fucked up. The Edison High punks all seemed to worship Sid Vicious and Johnny Rotten. All their bands sang with English accents, whatever was coming over from England, stuff that had nothing to do with their lifestyle in southern California. The entire New York punk scene just wasn't a factor.

MUGGER: Edison High is just this one school. There were a lot of schools in the Huntington Beach and Costa Mesa area that attracted the sort of kids whose families didn't care about them or whatever, and they just got crazy. Huntington Beach was the term the people used, but it was all over Orange County . . . it was basically a full-on white suburbanite rebellion. People were saying "fuck you" not only to these people that were trying to tell us what to do but to the establishment in general . . . the hippies did their thing and now the punkers were doing their things.

MIKE PATTON: Most of the new kids from the beach areas thought the Germs were cool 'cause they were so extreme . . . they had this mysterioso of being so dissolute, they had to be cool. Live they were a complete mess, but they had this mystique, so when the new kids showed up, the Germs were always cooler than the crowd. I don't know if they even liked the music, if they even cared . . . but it didn't matter, they were the Germs, you know? He was Darby Crash!

RAYMOND PETTIBON: Most punks from the original Masque scene in Hollywood were turned off by hardcore, and that's understandable, 'cause a lot of these new kids from various high schools in Orange County had their own bands that they followed.

KEITH MORRIS: I'm from Hermosa Beach, which is about twenty-five miles south of Hollywood. My dad owned a fishing tackle business. I was being groomed to be the future heir, but I just wasn't into it. My musical thing, if you can call Black Flag musical, was basically my protest against being geared toward this nine-to-five existence. I had no musical ability whatsoever. I could play a little drums. I just loved music. When Black Flag started, we looked like we were roadies for Peter Frampton. We were wearing flannel shirts and deck shoes. We looked more like Deadheads than punk rockers, and Greg Ginn was actually a big fan of the Dead.

JEFF MCDONALD: Black Flag's first advertised show was at the Moose Lodge in Redondo with the Alley Cats and Rhino 39 in January '79. There was probably only fifty people there, and that's how we met the other bands.

MIKE WATT: The Reactionaries were the first version of the Minutemen. D. Boon and I were inspired by the old Hollywood bands, but it took a while to get the nerve up to start our own. By early '79 we finally tried with the Reactionaries, a four-piece with a lead singer. We mostly played sped-up Blue Oyster Cult stuff. We were pretty tepid and unoriginal, but Ginn took us to play with Flag anyway at some show in Pedro which turned into a nightmare. It was in a heavy part of town at the Teen Post Center and people were writing on the walls and tagging the outside with spray paint . . . the cops locked everybody inside to save them because all the big dudes from the neighborhood were all riled up wanting to kill 'em all! It was us with the Plugz and the Alley Cats from Hollywood and Black Flag . . . it was Flag's second or third gig, and the Descendants' first . . . they were like fifteen-year-old kids. Our singer, Martin, had tagged a wall with "Reactionaries" . . . now the whole town wanted to kill the Reactionaries, which prompted us very quickly to change the name to the Minutemen! Very soon we dumped the BOC shtick and became a three-piece. D. Boon took over as lead singer and began pushing hard for us to be more bold in coming up with our own sound, doing our own thing.

KEITH MORRIS: When we formed Black Flag, we'd rehearse in Greg's living room, or in this office space. We had no goals. We had no idea what we wanted to do. We just wanted to play. We'd play for whoever would let us play. We played backyard parties. We played in basements. People's living rooms. Teen parties. Anything. Anytime. Anywhere. Anyplace.

JEFF MCDONALD: Redd Kross got Black Flag their second show, a sixth-grade graduation party in Hawthorne playing in somebody's living room. That was Redd Kross's first show before Janet Housden played with us. We were all pre-to-mid teen—one was twelve and one was eleven. It was definitely real teen music by and for other teens. We were inspired by the Runaways and the Ramones. The Runaways looked kind of tough, like you didn't screw with them 'cause they could probably beat you up. They were only sixteen when they started and they were playing their asses off, and that really inspired us to think we could get up and play, too. Black Flag was an inspiration, too, of course, but every band I can think of, even if they said they hated the Runaways, it was because of the Runaways they actually got up the nerve to start playing in a rock band with no musical training. In that respect the Runaways were much more influential on punk than most people care to admit.

KEITH MORRIS: Greg Ginn moved into this place in Hermosa Beach called the Church in February '79. It was an abandoned church in Hermosa that they'd turned into an arts and crafts center with hippie, sandal-wearing pottery makers wandering around.

JOE NOLTE: The Church got started round about the time the second Masque closed. Greg and Chuck had rooms there. The basement of the Church was the perfect place for parties . . . it was huge, it was soundproof. Anybody who was into things in the South Bay was hanging out at the Church because it was the only place to go.

KEITH MORRIS: Our bass player, Chuck Dukowski, sold pool tables out of the front offices while Ginn ran an electronics supply business from the back. I worked for Greg when I wasn't working for my dad.

JEFF MCDONALD: Greg Ginn was really into getting a scene going outside of Hollywood, and he was there for anyone who needed help—he was an adult with a job, and he had money, which he made from his own electronics company. Us and the Descendants were like little kids literally. If we needed to borrow equipment, Greg would loan it to us. Once Black Flag established themselves outside of the South Bay, playing gigs at the Hong Kong and stuff, they brought us along.

MUGGER: Ginn had an electronics company that made tuners, and I was a cheap laborer who would work for food. I didn't have any money and my parents were poor, but the band started growing—they put up flyers everywhere—and then the electronics thing kind of fizzled, and so that's when we really focused on the band.

MIKE WATT: The SST logo came from one of those guys . . . SST stands for Solid State Transmitter . . . Greg had a ham radio thing, one of the biggest ham radio magazines in the country. Him and Chuck were good at networking—they really got me and D. Boon thinking that maybe the world was two categories, just gigs and flyers. They had a huge influence on us, especially with the nonstop work ethic applied to music.

MUGGER: Greg was the leader of the tribe, he was the captain of the ship. Musically, artistically, and the business side . . . it was all Greg. Greg Ginn is a leader and everyone else sort of followed. He was really intense and he had a lot of faithful people. It was like a religion for us, and we were really into it. Straightedge, we didn't do a lot of drugs or anything. Drugs are what destroyed everything, when people started smoking pot and drinking. He had people who were like his lieutenants, his sergeants, who drilled out and got people going. Chuck was an intelligence officer. I was the motivator. I was the pusher, I would do basically whatever Greg said.

MIKE WATT: Greg Ginn is kind of internal—he doesn't say a lot. When I first played with Flag, I thought Keith wrote those songs, but when I got to know them a bit, I knew it was all Greg's band.

JOE NOLTE: The Church scene wasn't really as big a reaction against Hollywood as Greg Ginn has said. Once the Church was happening, it was like we could go to Hollywood or we could stay and do our own thing right there in Hermosa. But there were always so many great shows up in Hollywood, or at the Hong Kong in downtown, so the tendency was to go up there and then come back and party at the Church all night.

DON BOLLES: Greg Ginn said he never heard the term "hardcore" until '82, which is total bullshit. The Germs started Southern Californian "hardcore" and Black Flag codified it, and Greg knows it, but old BF had this brutal paleolithic quasi-Calvinist work ethic thing happenin' . . . they worked their asses off, night and day, twenty-four/seven, as opposed to the Germs, who barely even liked getting up in the morning. Fair enough, but working your buns off is still not a license for blatant revisionism, although nobody will deny that Black Flag took it to wider circles nationally.

BRENDAN MULLEN: I think many key people from the Hollywood scene embraced Black Flag and were totally supportive, even went out on a limb for them.

JOE NOLTE: Punk started to get going in Hermosa Beach in early '79, and kids from there started coming up to the Church pretty soon after that. We invited them to come up around the summer of '79, and it was weird because then there were only like fifteen punk rockers in the entire South Bay and I knew every one of them . . . then this new crowd from Huntington Beach started hanging around the Church. Yeah, it was the party place, all right, all the time, it was great, but nothing seriously violent ever happened. I think the worst thing was a window got broken one time. There was a kindred spirit because we were geographically distant from Hollywood. Hollywood to us seemed like Mecca. There were skinheads back then, but it wasn't like what it would become.

KEITH MORRIS: Black Flag wanted to make a record for Bomp, but we got so fed up with being put off by Greg Shaw. When he eventually submitted an offer it was hilarious and pathetic at the same time. We were gonna pay for everything, and he was gonna put it out and own the masters and the publishing. So Ginn, acting out of sheer disgust, finally financed the EP with his own money. That's where SST Records came from. We recorded the seven-inch *Nervous Breakdown* EP above a bar in Hermosa. Everything changed for Black Flag once the *Nervous Breakdown* EP finally came out and people started to know what we were about. Our first real gig was at the Moose Lodge in Redondo in January '79. We rented the hall and had the Alley Cats and Rhino 39 . . . the review for that show thought Rhino 39 was okay, and thought the Alley Cats were excellent, but my all-time favorite quote describing Black Flag came from that article: "Black Flag doesn't play their songs, they annihilate them." Rodney Bingenheimer was there and we handed him the EP and he started playing it. Kickboy from *Slash* loved it. Other things that helped us out a lot was Chris D. and "Ranking Jeffrey Lee" Pierce writing about us in *Slash* and it got us rolling.

JOE NOLTE: Mugger, who was around the South Bay from the beginning, ended up hooking up with Black Flag as a roadie, and later he became a key person at SST who worked as hard as Greg and Chuck to make the company grow into the most important grassroots U.S. indie punk label of the pre-alterna-nation of the early '80s.

MUGGER: Greg Ginn's brother Raymond Pettibon was behind the Black Flag logo—you know, the famous four black bars . . . and he drew all the artwork for every one of their flyers.

RAYMOND PETTIBON: My first drawings were editorial, I was doing political cartoons for the opinion section of the UCLA *Bruin*. I was going to UCLA on the cusp of the punk thing in '77, the year I graduated. By 1979 I was doing flyers for Black Flag, my brother's band. For better or worse, my work was displaced historically. I wasn't attempting any journalistic treatment of what was going on at the time. These drawings just represented what I was thinking. Except for a few instances, the flyers weren't done as commercial art or advertising. You could have stuck anything on a photocopy machine and put the band name and made an advertising flyer, but these weren't done like that. I was vehement about that as much as my personality allowed. I didn't need suggestions, although there were a few cases where Black Flag members had some great idea that was so good I had to draw it, but I never could do it according to assignment—that would have been the equivalent of going into commercial art or illustration. Nothing happens in a vacuum, and punk was, of course, an influence on my art. To me my work was the equivalent of a band like Black Flag or any other band who was righteously self-protective of their recordings. I would give them original art and it would come back to me scrawled upon and taped over or whited out, and I'd always ask nicely, "Could you please make a copy of this first and then do that?" Their master tapes were deemed sacrosanct, while my work was seen as completely disposable, but I'm not venting or complaining, just stating fact.

GARY PANTER: Pettibon's stuff was astounding. It was just astounding.

KEITH MORRIS: We were riled up and protesting against what was going on socially and musically. We were all basically nice guys. We were like *Straw Dogs* people. You've got Dustin Hoffman, this mild pacifist guy who gets pissed off and ends up killin' 'em all after his wife gets raped. You get somebody like this passive little guy and you get him mad enough, this is how he'll react. We reacted in a very aggressive, energetic, hateful, spiteful manner. Because we're from SoCal and we've grown up surfing and skating and skiing, we have a bit of aggressiveness to us. If you look at the slam dance itself, if you look at the configuration, it's basically a kid riding a skateboard.

MUGGER: Pogoing, which started a few years earlier, was kids just jumping up and down, and if you fell, somebody picked you up. Slamming, which started around the hardcore scene, was kids smashing into each other full-on football style with nobody picking you up anymore. I think it's human nature, you always wanna take something to the next extreme. Everyone's just trying to get a little more radical. There was a gradual evolution from pogo to slam. A football-playing friend of mine said he would just go to the Fleetwood 'cause it was all a football game to him. He didn't even care about how the bands sounded or if the music was any good. He'd go just to show people who's tougher. I don't know when they stopped calling it the "slam pit" and it started to be called the "mosh pit." That term came about after I got out of the scene. I think it came from heavy metal. It's not punk. It never came from Flag or any of the early Orange County hardcore bands that I remember.

GREG GRAFFIN: My theory about the origin of stage diving is that kids always liked to get up onstage, but then Mugger was always there ready to chase 'em off, so they had to jump off super fast to get away from him!

JOE NOLTE: The South Bay remained this fascist long-haired scene that felt totally threatened by punk. I was lucky if I only got ten catcalls walking down the street . . . I didn't look outrageous or anything, I had short hair that maybe wasn't combed nice and I wore a black T-shirt and straight-leg pants. By adopting this punk rock musical ethos, we deliberately disenfranchised ourselves—it was almost as if we'd turned black overnight. We deliberately placed ourselves outside of society; we had a choice, but we put targets on our shirts for the police by daring to look different.

MUGGER: The cops were picking on us, we were just having a good time. They were picking on the artistic revolution as opposed to the killers and the other criminal shitheads.

KEITH MORRIS: The LAPD didn't get it and they never will.

chapter 25

The Spike ruins everything. As usual. Photo Credit: Sue Brisk

JOHN DOE: A couple of years into the scene, around '79, heroin started coming around. It had an obvious negative impact, especially for the people that died.

BELINDA CARLISLE: When heroin came into the scene, that was the great divide. Either you did it or you didn't. In the beginning they were my friends. I like drugs, but the heroin thing scared me. At the Canterbury, there was pills and lots of booze, there were these girls bringing in Demerol. That got really icky. Everybody nodding out.

CHARLOTTE CAFFEY: I was a total junkie but I thought I kept it hidden well.

JANE WIEDLIN: We totally knew.

GINGER CANZONERI: I wasn't aware of Charlotte's drug problem to that extent. She did hide it, but Jane would always come up to me and say, "Ginger, go talk to Charlotte, her eyes are dilated." Or "Ginger, go talk to Charlotte, her eyes are pinpoints." And I'm like, "Well, what are they? Are they dilated or pinpoints?"

ELISSA BELLO: Charlotte was doing heroin and I didn't even know. She used to call up rehearsal all the time and say she had food poisoning from the Mongolian barbecue and I kept saying, "Gosh, she should stop eating there. She's really getting sick."

TRUDIE ARGUELLES: One of my worst memories of those days was walking into this party and seeing Darby sitting with these people going, "Trudie, Trudie . . . come over here. Come do some heroin." It was like a new thing on the scene. It was new for me and new for him, that's why he was bragging. "Come, do some heroin with us." And I was like, "No, I don't think so. Heroin is way too creepy." This was around '79. Darby always was trying to get people to do the same thing that he was doing. I don't know if it was a control thing or he just wanted this big surrogate family around him.

MAGGIE EHRIG: People were selfish and wouldn't give a fuck about the people around them and would hoard their drugs for themselves, but even those folks were sharing freely with Darby. Know what I'm talking about? Friends of mine who were into drugs would hog it for themselves, but for Darby they'd be like, "Hey, Darby, look what we got for you."

GERBER: Things started getting really physically violent between Darby and I. He was strung out, and I'll say one thing—I hate fucking Amber. I don't hold Amber responsible for his addiction, but I hold her responsible for not caring whether he lived or died. She had ulterior motives, man! She wanted to be the sugar mama. She wanted fuckin' Nicole Panter's seat. I think she lusted for his idol status, and putting enough dope in him got it for her. It's like someone's strung out, hand them five hundred dollars' worth of dope, "Fuck, yeah, suck my dick, I don't care." I mean I think that's what it was, totally, he used her. Like he used all those girls, you know?

AMBER: I put my foot down and told Darby if he wanted to get high to get a hotel room or get his friends together and have a party, but don't take it in the street because he was going to pass out in front of the wrong person and wind up in jail and get fucked. So we agreed that when he would do drugs it would be under thinking conditions. I knew just about every dealer of heroin and hard drugs in that area and would go with Darby to score.

HELLIN KILLER: Amber was a creepy monster person who wanted Darby around her, and she could afford to pay for whatever he wanted, and she would pay for him to get as fucked up as possible.

chapter 26

The Germs shut down (*left to right:* Lorna Doom, Don Bolles, Pat Smear, and Darby Crash), circa 1979. Photo Credit: Sue Brisk

DARBY CRASH: I'm not in to making records . . . not really. Only as a medium to get something else done.

✳ ✳ ✳

BOB BIGGS: Around 1978, Samiof left *Slash* to do a magazine called *Stuff* and I was stuck with the magazine, which was not making a lot of money, so I decided to do a record label. You spend a couple of thousand dollars making a record but it was better in the long run than trying to put a magazine on the stands that got yellow in two weeks.

PENELOPE SPHEERIS: I was there for the transfer of *Slash* from Samiof to Bob Biggs. It was all very palsy-walsy. After Samiof gave Bob *Slash*, they moved *Slash* out of the Santa Monica and Fairfax offices to the Beverly Boulevard offices and I moved in there to make my *Decline* movie. Bob always just rolled over everybody with his megalomaniac power trips. All that he was ever after was the money. He was still figuring out whether the magazine or the label was going to make more.

NICOLE PANTER: Rumor had it Biggs was a coke dealer. He did know all the *Saturday Night Live* people. I never knew. He'd tried being a performance artist.

BOB BIGGS: Anyone in a position of some power is gonna be vulnerable to people talking about stuff like that, but I was never a drug dealer and I defy anyone to find some proof. It was in a party context! There was never any wholesale dealing going on. I wasn't any more deeply involved in cocaine than anyone else. It was the '70s! At *Slash* we were just dealing with those kinds of people. I mean I once saw Darby shoot up with gutter water!

JUDITH BELL: Bob Biggs was an all-American UCLA guy who was . . . always very good at making money. He had a lot of cash that he had to put in something, 'cause you know if you have all that cash, the bank has to inform the IRS and then they become aware that something's fishy, so he wanted to invest in a business and that's when he invested in *Slash* and took over the business side of the thing. Bob was a very good-looking guy and had been approached by a lot of modeling agencies. He actually did one modeling gig but the gay guys freaked him out too much.

PENELOPE SPHEERIS: Claude would have much rather had the money put into the magazine than into recording because that's what he did, Claude was a writer, he got nothing out of the records.

NICKEY BEAT: When this Don Bolles guy came around to drum for the Germs, I started giving him lessons. Teaching him how the songs went. I stopped giving him lessons when he said, "Punk rock is supposed to be sloppy. It's supposed to have a certain amount of mistakes." I was trying to teach him to be like Paul Cook from the Sex Pistols or Jerry Nolan from the Dolls.

JOHN DOE: Don Bolles was known as Cactus Head 'cause he came from Arizona. He was just a wide-eyed, "What kind of trouble I can get into?" guy.

BOB BIGGS: I knew a lot of the bands, but I didn't have any experience running a label. I didn't think I needed any experience. The magazine had a following and all the mom-and-pop-variety record stores had already been carrying it. I knew of the Germs, so I thought it'd be a good thing to do them first. I said, "Hey, do you wanna do a single?" and they said okay. So they recorded "No God," "Circle One," and another song for six hundred bucks. Darby was a little standoffish and sarcastic. He was like a wise-ass teenager. Pat was more willing to engage you and to talk about something straight without making fun of you, so I dealt with him more than Darby. The very first thing that Darby did whenever he saw me was ask for money. I'd say, "Darby, would you cool it, you idiot? I'm not giving you any money."

DON BOLLES: We just wanted to do the stupid album and not get completely fucked. We sort of trusted Nicole. We trusted our friends. We were laissez-faire about all the business stuff. That's why we had Nicole. She was a really smart girl with a little legal acumen, a little knowledge of the music industry.

NICOLE PANTER: A friend manager scores drugs for the band, which I never did. I was a real manager, and I may have learned on the job, but I think I did a pretty decent job in what was a difficult situation at best.

BOB BIGGS: Nicole Panter was the Germs' management and she knew absolutely nothing about business. When people don't know what they're doing, they overcompensate by getting hysterical and they overstate with passion over some two-cent issue. The band would say that everyone was stealing from them, but no one was stealing from them because they didn't have anything to steal.

NICOLE PANTER: Darby and I discussed the fact that it would be a selling point to have a celebrity credited as producer. Darby's first choice was Mark Lindsay from Paul Revere and the Raiders. I couldn't even begin to guess why Darby wanted him. We told Biggs, and Bob got back to us saying that Mark Lindsay had asked for ten thousand dollars, which made it out of the question because the budget for the entire thing was only five thousand dollars. It occurred to me then and now that Biggs might have been humoring us and never even bothered contacting Lindsay. Knowing our options were pretty limited by finances, Darby and I sat down to figure out other possibilities, and so we got Joan Jett.

DON BOLLES: Mark Lindsay was my idol when I was a kid. I used to buy copies of *Tiger Beat* magazine just to see pictures of Mark Lindsay and copy his hair if my mom would let me.

JOAN JETT: When they were ready to record, the Germs asked me if I would produce, and I took it real seriously. I really wanted to do a good job. Except we partied a lot. At one point I passed out, and Darby wrote about it in one of the songs, "Shut Down." He mentioned that I was passed out on the couch and I was, but only for that one song. They had been playing around L.A. for a few years by then, so they'd worked up their songs. They were really tight. The album was basically their set list. I just had them set up and I told Darby to sing like he was onstage, except right into the mic, rather than separating him and having him sing to a track . . . and then Pat Burnette rolled tape.

DON BOLLES: Joan is a rock goddess. She knew rock 'n' roll. She understood it. It was her lifestyle.

BOB BIGGS: The Germs cut the *GI* record at a place called Quad Tech on Sixth and Western. It took about three weeks and cost six thousand dollars. I was a glorified baby-sitter, trying to get the sessions going. Giving them a ride there. Giving them a ride home.

JOAN JETT: I think the record captures the energy really well. It was really pretty straightforward—there wasn't the time or the budget or the technology for it to be anything else other than the way it came out. Sure, I doubled tracks here and there and had them do things they'd never done before. I had Darby doing harmonies. Darby took it pretty seriously. We didn't have to do a lot of takes. He was certainly not out of control in the studio. He respected me. Did what I asked him to do. They were trying to get something done and they were very serious about it. It was a controlled nuttiness at that point.

DON BOLLES: Quad-Tech on 6th and Western was a very utilitarian studio that had all the good workhorse analog shit. Pat Burnett the engineer was a young guy. He was a descendant of the famous musical Burnett family. He was like only about 30, but he seemed really old to us. Although he was really into the Germs as a band he wasn't into wearing spiked wrist bands or wanting to get drunk with us or any of that punk shit stuff. I was the only person in the band who knew about sound and recording and I communicated with Pat Burnett and Joan. Pat [Burnett] was more than just the engineer, he was really the uncredited co-producer with Joan, although Pat [Smear] knew exactly what he wanted his guitar to sound like. So everybody was pitching in at one point . . . and Joan was very cool and open to all suggestions. Joan is a rock goddess because she understood rock 'n' roll. Darby knew he could never capture what he had onstage. We all drank a little but we stayed incredibly focused. We were a hard-working little unit determined not to fuck it up. I'm sure it must've been quite touching to watch the Germs toiling away with such dedication to do the best we possibly could. It wasn't perfect, but it worked. The result was pretty much what we were trying to do—just getting down on tape who we thought we were with some professional guidance from Joan and Pat Burnett.

NICOLE PANTER: I came up with the design for the album cover. Biggs wanted to spell out *Germs* in rotten meat and jelly beans and I told him I wanted it to look different from any other punk record, I told him that I wanted it to look like a Pablo jazz release, understated and classy: Darby's blue circle on black, with simple type.

PENELOPE HOUSTON: It wasn't until their record came out and I actually saw Darby's lyrics on paper that I realized he was thinking some interesting thoughts.

RICHARD MELTZER (REVIEW OF GI IN L.A. TIMES): [Darby Crash] didn't miss a beat in out-Iggying the Ig . . . lyrically Darby left Lou Reed and Jim Morrison so far behind they resembled coffee table poets . . . the album of 1979 . . . the most staggering recorded statement so far from the American branch of new wave.

RIK L. RIK: Darby Crash made the cover of the *L.A. Weekly* in this big feature story on the boho-punk scene . . . they called the article "Who Is Darby Crash Anyway?"

NICOLE PANTER: The band never went on tour in support of *GI* because Darby didn't want to. He knew they wouldn't travel well.

BRENDAN MULLEN: Around the time *GI* came out, Danny's Oki Dog on Santa Monica Boulevard became the hot postgig gathering place for the new suburban hardcore kids who were coming up in droves to Hollywood all the time for shows at the Starwood and the Whisky. Oki Dog became the big Tuesday night hotspot, the consolidated gathering of the intercounty SoCal teen punk tribes during the summer and fall of '80. Many of these new kids would hang around Oki Dog and try to emulate Darby with his pre-Mohawk look . . . a single footlong braided ponytail hanging from the back of the neck with chains and bandanas wrapped around the ankles of U.S. Army combat boots. Oki Dog was the newest, coolest place yet to get your Germs burn and to watch Darby hold court with his minions squatting openmouthed on the ground around him while he practiced his "Gimme, gimme this . . . Gimme, gimme that" mantra. I'd hear him say, "Hi, I'm Darby Crash and that shirt would look real cool on me. Give it to me, please." It was a litany of gimmes. Gimme your shirt. Gimme that button. Gimme that bracelet. Gimme a beer. Gimme two dollars. Gimme a ride to Whisky. Gimme a ride to the party. Gimme a ride home. Jesus wept!

RODNEY BINGENHEIMER: My favorite Germs song to play was "My Tunnel" from the *Cruising* soundtrack. I played it all the time.

BOB BIGGS: The *Cruising* soundtrack sessions were a difficult thing. Jack Nitzsche was music supervisor for the movie and he was very into using the Germs on the soundtrack. I thought it would be interesting to see what a producer like Jack, who is not a typical producer producer, would do with the Germs. So they went in with Nitzsche and I don't know how they felt about it, whether they felt good about it or it was a bad thing. I felt it was generally a good thing for the maturation of the band. It was fine to create *GI*, but the next one had to have a progression. I knew that Jack's demand for new material was going to stress Darby out to some extent, but I thought that that was a good thing because Darby had to go somewhere, he couldn't be *GI* forever. So even though I heard about him stressing I wasn't really that concerned about it. In fairness to Darby, first of all, any band that's been on the street for two or three years, you gotta figure their first record is going to be the best one for a while because they've got all this material tight as a drum 'cause they've had all that time to work it out live. Maybe Jack's a junkie, maybe he's this or that, but he'd produced and arranged things with the Rolling Stones, he'd worked with Phil Spector, he'd produced this and that, a lot of different classic stuff, a big history—the guy was kind of a real musical genius in many ways, but I don't know if Darby completely understood that. I thought this was a good thing because Jack was someone that Darby wanted to be like in some ways, an outlaw bad boy. I was over the moon. Here was the perfect way to ease Darby back into creative work mode without pressuring him for the follow-up to the *GI* album. I knew they didn't have any more stuff, so I was thrilled to see them go into the studio with such a wild-card iconoclast like Jack who probably had the ability as much as anybody to pull stuff out of them.

DON BOLLES: Nitzsche was an idiot. He didn't understand shit about what we were doing. He didn't live in the same world we did. We rehearsed in the studio for a couple of days with him, and it sucked.

NICOLE PANTER: William Friedkin, who directed *Cruising*, was very aware of the punk scene and what was going on. He came to the studio a few nights and pogoed around the room.

BRENDAN MULLEN: The late Donnie Rose, who was close to Darby and was around the studio during some of the *Cruising* sessions, once told me he thought it was a major turning point in Darby's downward spiral into alcohol, hard narcotics, and depression. Donnie told me his theory was up to that point Darby had been creative at his own nonprolific pace; now the heat was on to deliver new material instantaneously. Nitzsche was demanding five new original songs, not just cover songs or remakes of older tunes. Donnie said it was the most creative pressure he'd ever seen Darby sweating under. Darby was blanking badly on lyrics, and to the alarm of the band, he disappeared for several days and took a ton of booze and drugs before returning to complete the sessions, pretty much on schedule, but the strain had taken its toll.

NICOLE PANTER: I even tried to find them professional management after *Cruising*. I'd married Gary Panter and he was after me to quit. I asked Jack Nitzsche for advice, but he thought Darby didn't take it all seriously enough for a "real" management company to be interested.

BRENDAN MULLEN: Gay organizations called for a boycott of Billy Friedkin's *Cruising*. They felt the film negatively depicted gay male culture as nothing more than a bunch of crazed fist-fucking S&M freaks performing violent sex in the darkened back rooms of creepy leather stud bars across America. Darby went around town telling everybody not to see the movie because it was shit.

chapter 27

Career suicide? Tomata du Plenty in Rene Daalder's film *Population One*.
Photo Credit: Rene Daalder

TOMMY GEAR: The Screamers greatest downfall was that we were easily bored.

K.K. BARRETT: Following a nine-month hiatus the Screamers returned to the Whisky in May '79 for six sold-out shows over three nights. We augmented the regular lineup, which now included Paul Roessler on keyboards, with two violinists and a backup singer named Sheila Edwards, sometimes known as Sheila Drusela.

RENE DAALDER: Sheila Edwards was an amazing wailing punk diva right off the L.A. streets.

PAUL ROESSLER: We'd hooked up with Rene Daalder, a very tasteless and talentless guy who could raise money and talk them into doing stuff but was unable to create anything that had any impact or was at least decent art. Rene played the members of the band against each other, and he finally just isolated Tomata from everybody, making Tomata the star of a terrible movie, *Population One*. I've seen it. It's retarded.

TOMATA DU PLENTY: It's a story about the last person left on the planet after a nuclear holocaust.

RENE DAALDER: Tommy and Tomata were thinking about where to take their act next. They didn't feel much like performing in the future. I had this strong conviction that music videos were going to be big in the near future, and I was still thinking a lot about the Pistols/Russ Meyer misadventure, wondering how a marriage between the drama of punk rock and film could work. I had gotten ever deeper involved with the punk scene, which among other things seemed highly cinematic. The Screamers had already solved one of the main problems of rock-and-roll movies, which invariably corrupt the raw energy of the musical talent by the inevitable stylization a fictional film imposes on them. The Screamers had already taken care of that stylization themselves.

PAUL ROESSLER: I was the new guy, and they were fairly secretive with me. The Screamers' image and mystique was something they had really carefully cultivated. Tommy and Tomata had been in all these theater troupes, doing avant-garde and gay theater. I was just a kid, a trained musician who'd had my head twisted by hanging around Darby Crash and the early Germs scene at Uni High.

RENE DAALDER: We decided to build a studio to make music videos to replace the opening acts at club performances. We also planned to record music for the soundtrack to a low-budget musical movie. But for something like that to work, everybody has to be respectful of each other's creativity. The Screamers were organized a little different. For one, Tommy was accustomed to being a rather authoritarian and autocratic taskmaster. The Screamers were ultimately a much more important concept to him than they were to Tomata, who—even though we didn't realize it at the time—had become kind of exhausted of the whole experience. All the screaming had been taxing his voice to the point that it became increasingly difficult to put out the inordinate amount of energy it took to project the raw energy everyone expected from his stage persona.

Apart from having no real control over his voice, it was even more difficult at times to put out that energy because, as opposed to say Johnny Rotten's conviction, the Screamers really was an art project for him. He certainly didn't carry an ounce of the same aggression he expressed onstage.

K.K. BARRETT: We were trying to make music videos. If we'd just stayed with the music, I think we would have been right on course, but getting stars in our eyes sunk the boat.

PAUL ROESSLER: They thought they'd never really be able to capture the experience of the Screamers just with recordings. They wanted to do film and video years before MTV. They hooked up with Rene Daalder, but in the process it broke up the group, after he tried to turn it into something that was no longer a rock band.

RENE DAALDER: We were assembling a sort of repertory company that would become the cast for the movie *Mensch*, which would take place in a *Cabinet of Dr. Caligari*–like German expressionist setting. Musically it was going to be a reinterpretation of the original Screamers material. The cast would be the Screamers, Penelope Houston of the Avengers, and many other stalwarts of the punk scene, as well as Beck's grandfather, Fluxus artist Al Hansen. As we were waiting for everything to come together I directed a bunch of videos art-directed with great economic resourcefulness by K.K. We didn't have the financing for the movie, so we were reduced to shooting scenes on and off. It seemed high time to do some live shows again after a nine-month hiatus.

GEZA X: Rene Daalder utterly destroyed the Screamers. Butchered 'em. That's a fact. Rene came in and filled their head with these notions. They already had a lot of problems with grandiosity, and how that band maintained equilibrium was a very delicate equation to begin with, where Tommy played leather bitch to Tomata's puppet, and the two of them had worked really hard at creating this image. I was just their employee, their sound guy and roadie. I admired Tommy and Tomata for working so hard and becoming so successful, but Tommy was the ruler with an iron fist, and when he did, things worked. That was the implicit agreement between Tommy and Tomata—they had this deal going, that was the way the band would work. When Rene came along, he gradually eroded Tommy's control and first got Tomata into his orbit, and then

Tommy also came under his spell based on his premise that they were gonna make rock videos, before there were rock videos . . . he was gonna get them a "video record" deal, but you have to understand we're talking nearly two years before MTV.

RENE DAALDER: I raised the money to build Rhapsody Studios on Melrose, a soundstage facility which included a state-of-the-art recording studio, from the father of Joe Kaufman, who was one of the producers on John Carpenter's *Assault on Precinct 13.* My friend Carel Struycken, who's since become famous as a character actor, built the studio with his own hands. It was a unique opportunity for everyone. Everybody could use the studio for whatever they wanted, but nobody ever booked a recording session. Top Jimmy and the Rhythm Pigs, the Blasters, Chris D.'s Flesh Eaters, and others recorded there, but not the Screamers, unless I proposed a video- or film-related context. It was not clear exactly where this lack of initiative came from, but it certainly was not for lack of encouragement on our part. We had built the Screamers their own multimedia studio, but they didn't seem much inclined to take advantage of it to do something together.

TRUDIE ARGUELLES: When the Screamers got together with Rene, they thought, "Maybe we'll be movie stars as well." And during the production of this *Population One* film, things started to break down between them. Tomata was the star, Tommy was doing the music, and K.K. was doing the art direction. Soon they realized this guy wanted things done his way, and then he wanted this, and then he wanted that, and suddenly it wasn't the Screamers anymore.

RENE DAALDER: One of the reasons the Screamers didn't do anything together was the fact that Tommy and Tomata hardly talked to each other anymore and had had a falling-out, the exact nature of which none of us ever figured out. Even though Tommy was trying to come up with new material, without his muse Tomata, very little came out of him.

TOMATA DU PLENTY: I haven't seen Tommy in over twenty years. And I don't foresee seeing him in the next twenty. It's just not a part of my life anymore.

K.K. BARRETT: Tommy left in the middle of filming the *Population One* movie. Who knows what happens—when bands have a lot of creative energy in the beginning, then when the focus is on them and they're trying to crank something out, it may not be as good. At one point, there was only two of us left, me and Tomata. We did a show at the Roxy called the Palace of Variety . . . we were trying to use canned video, canned music, and a script. It was the worst thing we ever did—bad all around. The music was poor, the performance was poor, it was a complete technical failure. Nothing was in sync.

RENE DAALDER: The Palace of Variety was a combination of old material and recent songs, some of them featuring Sheila as Tomata's female counterpart. Instead of an opening act there was a video show with highlights of the stuff we had done at Rhapsody. We played the Whisky and the Roxy, and Hurrah's in New York. Some evenings were spectacular, on others things didn't quite ignite. A few weeks before the first performance Tomata worried that he wouldn't have the energy to go through with the shows. His occasional lapses into exhaustion had definitely become more obvious by this time. Later on, he told me and my wife, Bianca, that he was HIV positive.

GEZA X: When Rene became involved, the artistic vision of the band got derailed. Rene brought in an acoustic piano and all this highfalutin monkey bullshit. He had them playing to loops, run off of a tape recorder—an extremely interesting idea, granted, kind of an early industrial techno twist to that—but it really wasn't the Screamers anymore. The Screamers' magic when they rocked out with those Tinkertoy synths slowly turned into this low-budget multimedia nonextravaganza which wasn't really that good, and the band started withering behind it. Rene became drunk on power, and I remember getting into bloodcurdling arguments with him behind the mixing board at the Roxy. He'd come up to the console during shows and break my concentration . . . he'd push faders up and down at random while I was mixing for the house . . . and he really didn't have a clue about audio—he had no idea what the hell he was doing—yet he'd insist on doing crazed, irrational things like that all the time. I saw the band going under, and I sometimes looked at myself as the only buffer zone to keeping some of it the way it was . . . I'll lament for the rest of my life that I never got to record the definitive Screamers album during their prime. I have some tapes, but they're almost unlistenable.

K.K. BARRETT: There was no plot to *Population One*. It was a lot of proselytizing, very dull, and in between there were music videos tying it together.

PAUL ROESSLER: Rene was from Holland and he was trying to do some great statement about "what is America." That typical European art school perspective on the American experience. They're still trying to do it, as if Melville and Twain didn't already get it.

K.K. BARRETT: We wanted to do something new and we stuck our necks out; otherwise we were just another band. We were enamored with the potential of rock fame and film stardom at the same time, but Trudie knew right away it wasn't spontaneous, it was corrupt, it was gold digging.

TOMATA DU PLENTY: I could tell you all the stupid things we didn't do. Devo offered us a tour, and for some stupid reason we turned it down! Robert Fripp asked me to sing on his album, and I had to turn that down . . . oh please! I mean, these are just things . . . I was not in my right mind . . . but I was working damn hard, so it's not that I have regrets. People say, "Well, you should have done a record." I don't have regrets about it. Maybe a record will come out. I don't own the music. Tommy Gear wrote the music. It's up to him.

chapter 28

Black Flag and their new friends in front of Frederick's of Hollywood. *Left to right:* Keith Morris, Jill Jordan, Greg Ginn, Trudie, and Chuck Dukowski, 1979. Photo Credit: Frank Gargani

JEFF MCDONALD: There's a park in Manhattan Beach called Polliwog Park, and the city was putting on these family entertainment shows during the summer of '79 and they'd booked Black Flag by mistake. Through Black Flag my band, Redd Kross, also got on the bill. We went over okay 'cause we were just little kids, no one hassled us, but when Black Flag played, people were throwing watermelon and picnic lunches. People in the South Bay were really hostile. If you weren't a surfer or a hippie, people would throw bricks at you. Keith Morris was really drunk and Black Flag was playing this noisy, art-damaged thrashed-out punk rock, and they'd never heard anything like it before, so people started heckling. When Keith responded with foul-mouthed lingo, it became a free-for-all. It was actually very funny, it was fun for both parties.

The families were tossing food at Black Flag, and Keith was just being funny and obnoxious and drunk. There wasn't a thousand rock fans like one newspaper report said. It was a small outdoor amphitheater. It was families who lived in the neighborhood and old heshers and it really wasn't as much of a big hairy experience as the legend would have it. I saw much worse situations later on, like real full-on riots with insane cops and SWAT teams, but all the local newspapers in the area wrote up these oversensationalized accounts like there had been a major riot anyway.

KEITH MORRIS: When Black Flag played Polliwog Park, 'cause the Air Force marching band or whatever couldn't make it, and they needed a replacement, Greg told them we were a Fleetwood Mac cover band. Polliwog was a Sunday afternoon hang with little ducks swimming in the pond and palm trees and families picnicking and everybody being mellow, and all of a sudden there's three hundred people in the bandshell and we started rockin' the fuck out and the whole place turned into this big giant party, everybody jumping around dancing, and the people that were picnicking were throwing food at us. It was just raining food . . . utensils and soaking napkins. Our drummer, Robo, got pelted in the face by half-eaten pieces of Kentucky Fried Chicken. Chuck, myself, and Greg could see things flying through the air and were able to duck, but Robo had no place to go sitting behind his drums. The promoter stopped us maybe ten minutes into the set and had a janitor sweep up all the onstage garbage and scolded me for foul language. I just came out and said, "Hey, you guys, we're fuckin' real loud and we're here to make a bunch of noise, and if you're not into it, you should just go home and watch Disney." The newspapers thought we were anarchists and terrorists who came to town to ruin things. From that point on we came under police scrutiny.

JEFFREY LEE PIERCE: Black Flag at Polliwog Park was a turning point for me. The gig was wild with families throwing picnic food at them which only got them more excited. Keith shouted abuse. Chuck Dukowski was all over the stage sliding on baloney, cheese, Wonder bread, jam, peanut butter or whatever. It was great punk rock at a time when I thought I had seen it all. I wrote Black Flag up immediately for *Slash* and later went down to Hermosa Beach to watch them rehearse which was nearly as wild. I hung out at the old abandoned church which everyone lived in where I discovered Red Cross [Redd Kross] and the Descendants.

X-8: The Church bands were all great . . . Redd Kross, the Descendants, the Last . . . the Hermosa scene, which Black Flag came out of, was originally all about partying and having fun with a bunch of radical rockin' bands. But it was at the Fleetwood in Redondo where everything turned creepy around 1980. You'd be sitting upstairs watching all these zit-faced kids from Huntington approaching each other and slugging each other right in the face for no reason. Too far out . . . and it was too far of a drive just to see people fight, so I just said fuck it.

RIK L. RIK: Everyone on the scene would show up to whoever was playing, but some of the older people would shun Germs shows because they weren't that musical, although they always drew pretty well from the younger end of the scene. So the Germs started playing Orange County, and because they were so hardcore and extreme, all these surf punk and skater kids would go to the shows.

TONY ALVA: Once I was exposed to punk and started going to shows, it was just really exciting. The independent attitude toward their music, producing their own sounds and saying "Fuck everything, we're gonna do it our way," that really was the same independent spirit I related to being a surfer and a skateboarder. I felt like I had something in common with these people. Even though they were pretty freaky looking.

GERBER: I would go to Marina Skate Park 'cause my friend Rob Henley would skate there. Tony Alva would skate by me all the time, and I had blue hair, so he'd scream at me, "Punk rock sucks. Nugent rules!" So we got into this big thing and I was always getting up on him and telling him, "Alva sucks, you're a piece of shit. You're a fucking hippie." Of course he loved that. Later I saw him at a party and I decided I was going to fuck him, so I got in the car and went with him to Malibu under the pretense of interviewing him for *Flipside*. Yeah, right. What happened instead is I fucked him and chopped his hair off and Krazy Kolored it. Tony took off surfing and left his little brother there unguarded and alone with me, and so the little kid got the same treatment. Alva was fucking Kira Roessler for a while, too. Then he wanted all the really fine punk rock chicks. I was going with Alva to skate competitions, and then he met Steve Olson.

STEVE OLSON: I started in the mid-'70s, '74, '75, '76 . . . the Dogtown guys were deep into it already . . . they grew up in a different setting than we did . . . they grew up in the Venice–Santa Monica area . . . they were predominantly white although their crew included some blacks and Latins . . . it was probably the first interracial gang in SoCal. . . . it didn't matter though, as long as you skateboarded . . . there was always the territorial thing, the same bullshit in every aspect of life . . . Dogtown brought some danger to it . . . I can't sit there and go, "Yeah, they were the first to skateboard in pools" 'cause there were dudes doing that in 1963, but they definitely took it to a different place . . . there were guys in Huntington Beach that were doing it . . . the Dogtown dudes just rode in their own style and the media picked up on it . . . they had a couple of dudes up there who were artists and photographers and a little more profound in the world of art and it gave them a mystique, still they had so many good guys in their area, it's not like I'm talking shit about them or anything . . . just a lot of other people were doing it as well, but they got a lot of the attention . . . they would come into any place and destroy the place, they ripped, they were really fucking aggressive . . . they had the attitude of the whole punk thing, the whole street-hood attitude about it . . . Tony Alva, Jay Adams, Bob Biniac, all the Dogtown dudes were huge . . . the Santa Monica–Venice Z-boys. The Dogtown crew were listening to Nugent, Zeppelin, Aerosmith, Sabbath, maybe a little Black Oak Arkansas . . . *Toys in the Attic, Physical Graffiti, Cat Scratch Fever,* the list goes on.

GERBER: I convinced the fucking skateboard park owner to let me have this party—that was basically what changed the whole thing, that party. Everybody played. I told every person I knew who had a band. Once you got there, you sign the list and that's when you're playing right. The pigs were there, too, it was a big fucking thing. And from that point on, every skate competition I went to, whether I went with Alva or Olson, all these guys started skatin' to punk rock. Duane Peters, another cool skater boy, skated to the Germs first, and I loved him for it. He was so fucked up, he would do face plants and his whole nose would be bleeding. His face was trashed, but he'd just get back up . . . and he was skating to the Germs.

STEVE OLSON: You know what I thought was a fucking big thing was at the skateboarder awards thing, Tony got second and he had some funky glasses and some clothes and he still had his hair and he threw his trophy in the trash like "Fuck you, I should have won." And I got first and they were like "Speech" and I was like "Fuck you, this is a bunch of bullshit. This is jive." And I just spit at the cameras and picked my nose and flicked boogers at them and that was it and then the kids were freaking . . . our reaction was "Fuck you and your bullshit"; and the skateboard industry was like "Oh my God, these are our top dudes in the reader polls," and now this is what they're saying back to us? They were against us and didn't like the fact that we were what was representing their little wholesome sport, and the next thing you know, the popularity was just growing huge and then it all started from there . . . Seeing the Deadboys walking on Sunset Boulevard, five strong, ghost white with all-black clothes on and dark sunglasses, I liked that . . . there was a lot of shit going on long before the Marina skate park shit.

RIK L. RIK: Around this time, the crowds had gotten really violent. The Hollywood people wouldn't go down to Orange County or the South Bay anymore. It became such an ugly thing, like a really bad acid trip in hell. All these idiots and all this mindless violence fucked everything up. I think that this had an effect on Darby, it depressed him.

EUGENE: Darby wasn't part of a hard-assed gang like us—his posse was pretty soft, nearly all girls—but we knew him and we would back him up 'cause he was like a living god to some of these kids.

JOHN DOE: The scene changing and becoming more violent and Darby not understanding the new suburban audience and them wanting something else from him that he didn't think he could deliver, and his uncertainty of the future of his band . . . I would give as much credit to that for him committing suicide as I would to his apparent sexual confusion. I don't think he could see himself as being the leader of that audience . . . he was really threatened by the people coming to the shows, and alienated by the extreme violence—he didn't like it and it kind of scared him. That was just my take on it. I thought the attitude of the new audience was all wrong. When we saw somebody getting hurt, we'd stop playing—maybe that's why some of those people thought we were a bunch of hippies, but that's fine—and I'm sorry, I just didn't want to see anyone getting hurt at a gig I'm playing. I didn't want this random violence . . . and my bandmates in X all felt the same way.

MIKE WATT: Darby had nothing against Orange County. The Germs would play the Fleetwood and other places down there. Darby, as leader of the Germs, was really influential, he was the head cheese of this weird punk subgroup, but they couldn't handle him as an individual. He was too scary. He wasn't de rigueur enough.

MIKE PATTON: We played with the Germs several times at the Fleetwood, always an intense night, with SWAT teams and helicopters becoming the norm . . . people running from cops with billy clubs and visors was commonplace. One night outside the venue these riot cops showed up and we'd gotten there late and we were outside and the punks were on one side of the street, the cops were on the other, and then somebody threw a bottle at them and they charged at us head-on.

EUGENE: Why was everyone so violent? I can't speak for those guys, but I didn't like the '70s or the '80s.

DON BOLLES: Darby did not like seeing where all the violence and subversion was going with all the hardcore kids. You didn't know where it was going until you found yourself playing at the Fleetwood and turned around and realized it was like being at a Nuremburg rally with all these football jocks.

BILLY ZOOM: I thought the suburban beach hardcore thing ruined a good scene that we had all worked so hard to create.

BRENDAN MULLEN: Female attendance plummeted.

D.J. BONEBRAKE: I had mixed feelings about the Orange County thing. When I saw the new beach kids I thought, "Well, it's fast . . . pretty impressive," and I could appreciate the athleticism of the audience, really incredible stage diving, but some of the klutzy ones I didn't like 'cause they would destroy things. On the one hand it added some vitality, some people thought, "Here's this new high-energy audience and they're really digging punk rock," but the other half was like, "They're too violent." You didn't see a lot of women in the slam pit—they'd get beat up, it was a bit rough for them. In the Masque days the sexes were much more integrated, but it was kind of wimpy, too, people pretending that they were violent but they were only playacting . . . when that happens you're eventually gonna have someone who comes along and says, "Gee, guess what, I'm really violent. I'll show you how to really beat up someone."

KEITH MORRIS: We had a sprinkling of female fans. When the hardcore thing really took off, it became more of a macho testosterone overdrive thing, the stage diving and the slam pits. Most girls didn't want to have anything to do with it. I was never a womanizer; I was just happy to be playing music. I figured, hell, the punk rock princess will come along and the punk rock Prince Valiant, being myself, would ride off with her into the punk sunset.

D.J. BONEBRAKE: John and Exene stopped shows all the time . . . the weird thing was that it was kind of a yes-no thing—if the audience wasn't excited enough, we'd try to get them going, but if it got too crazy, it was like, "Come on, you're gonna get hurt"—it was trying to balance those two.

EXENE CERVENKA: A lot of the beach people were like the surfers and skaters who really hated punk rock when it first started, but now they were embracing it. It was a part of society that I had no knowledge of. Tony Alva, the skater, had us play for his birthday party in Malibu, and we had to stop playing 'cause everybody was throwing rocks and stuff. Tony felt bad 'cause he really loved X and he really loved the Germs, he really loved the whole Hollywood scene, but those surfer guys weren't really ready for it. When the South Bay scene first started happening, I really liked the new bands like Black Flag . . . then there became this divide between Hollywood and the beach scene. Greg Ginn said they wouldn't let those bands play in Hollywood so they had to create their own scene and it kind of became anti-Hollywood. I would reject this because everybody I knew wanted to see those bands play. "Fuck Hollywood" was what we were saying, too! That's why we were having shows down in a basement off Hollywood Boulevard, because we couldn't play the regular clubs, either. Somehow the South Bay scene got opposed to the Hollywood scene and the audiences started becoming anti-rock-star, anti-whatever, and if you were signed to Slash, then you were a rock star traitor and the

South Bay girls didn't like me very much. So I stopped going to the hardcore shows because I was threatened too much. They'd shove me and push me and tell me they hated me, they'd tell me I thought I was a rock star. They'd spit and hiss, "Fuck you, Exene, you suck" . . . really vicious kind of stuff. I couldn't go in the bathroom at those shows, so I'd go see Black Flag in San Francisco or something. A lot of kids believed the media accounts of spitting and fighting, that punk was really mean.

STAN RIDGWAY: Black Flag would play and not take any responsibility for what was going on in the crowd, and they frequently even went out of their way to stir things up. Pogoing became slamming. Beating each other up . . . and loving it. Digging on the violence. Man, this was some wiggy scene . . . so I headed way north of it, too.

EXENE CERVENKA: The greatest thing about punk for me originally was that it was all about creating a new art and culture, replacing something shitty with something great, and having a community, which none of us had because everybody was from bad families, so this was like the first family that some people had. Now it was all dumbing down into this mob mentality where we couldn't play a show because the audience hated us so much they wouldn't even let us finish.

MIKE PATTON: The Huntington Beach scene killed off the original open interpretation of punk concept . . . no rules, no dogma, no stereotyping, no stars, anybody just do it. The original DIY ideology, as we saw it, was that it was all about free-association creativity— punk was this terrific grassroots thing which could be about anything any individual wanted it to be. Punk rock was always a serious cultural frame of reference to us, not a high school fashion thing. Once hardcore kicked in, there were very strict ways of dressing and weird codes of social behavior.

LISA FANCHER: Jack Grisham is one of the greatest characters in any era. They broke the mold when they made that kid!

JACK GRISHAM: I was always in trouble at school. I'd been getting arrested since I was like thirteen. I was just a fuck-up. I'm just misunderstood, that's the deal. I was a surfer fuck-up, even before I was a punk. All the early surfers were like punks . . . fuck-holes who were always getting in trouble, making bombs, that kind of shit, and so I was doing stuff like that and somebody said, "Hey, I know these guys that are just like you. You should meet 'em." And so I went over and it happened to be Todd Barnes, who became the drummer for Vicious Circle. That same day that we met at this girl's house, we said, "Let's make a band." And then we ripped her off. We took her guitar and her amp and started a band. We didn't know what we were doing. We only had two strings on the guitar and we'd go around stealing instruments and ripping stuff off and learnin' how to play and that's what Vicious Circle started as, just troublemaking surfer punk kids. Our drummer was only in seventh grade. It was two of us from Huntington, two from Long Beach.

MIKE PATTON: There was a big rock club called the Fleetwood in Redondo Beach, concrete floors, real austere, and that was where Vicious Circle first played and Jack was wearing a straitjacket and I remember going, "This is fucking stupid." But with Jack and his crew came all these surfers, these brain-damaged thugs from wealthy families. We played there with them and I remember seeing people getting beaten and bloodied. We were just appalled . . . it was like, "Somebody's gonna throw a bottle at me? Shit!" That's when Middle Class said, "We're not part of this," and we scurried off into our Echo and the Bunnymen period.

JACK GRISHAM: There were a lot of fuck-holes from Edison in Huntington. A ton of them came from that high school. A lot of it had to do with surfers. If you look at early surfer history, like a lot of those guys from La Jolla, they were really like Nazi punks who just happened to be surfers . . . there's always been this punk subculture in surfing . . . you think of surfing and you think of some blond-haired guy with pukka shells, but there's always been a bunch of fuck-heads like us around the surf scene, and now we were getting into punk rock . . . a lot of surfers lived on the beach and they just spread it.

EUGENE: Vicious Circle were the most ruthless fucking people I had ever seen.

MIKE WATT: I remember Vicious Circle before they became TSOL, these big, good-looking guys coming into the punk scene. I couldn't understand it . . . "Why are you guys here?" Jack Grisham is really into this bellig style, he wore war paint—he was trying to be provocative at gigs, you know? TSOL got famous really quick—

they wanted to rise to the top of that scene . . . they had a big posse around them . . . just before they were TSOL they had this thing called Vicious Circle, which wasn't even a band yet. VC just rounded up all these psychos and guys they grew up with and then punk became a gang thing that everybody went with, the whole neighborhood went with it. I saw the same thing later with Sublime . . . before that, punk was for people who didn't have friends. Nowadays these big-assed wigga punk posses grow up around some of these big-time punk bands.

JACK GRISHAM: Our first gig as Vicious Circle was at the Fleetwood with the Germs and Middle Class, that's a fuckin' good first show. Our band was basically all about a bunch of fucked guys fightin' back. There were a lot of punkers already hangin' around the South Bay, a bunch of 'em hung around the Black Flag guys, but they weren't fight club dudes at all, they were real nice, real swell guys . . . they were those peaceful SST types, intellectual punkers who read books and had good political ideas . . . they were artistic pencil necks to the max. To them it was all about the music and recording and building up their little followings with cool flyers and puttin' their logo out everywhere. Not like us fuck-ups. We weren't nice guys, man, we were like nobody you'd wanna know, know what I mean? We were the first punks on the block to say, "Yeah, go on, laugh at my hair, motherfucker, and I'll fuckin' stab ya." That kind of in-your-face, bring-it-on thing. We basically went around beating up on hippies, but it was the longhairs who started it, and they picked us . . . dude, the worst possible thing they coulda done, 'cause the guys I hung out with were already way fucked to begin with. There weren't very many times when I was a victim . . . it was more of the opposite way around. If somebody would drive by and yell, "Hey, fuckin' Devo," we'd chase 'em down and nail 'em. Vicious Circle was more like a gang than a band, a brotherhood that just looked out for each other. Beyond that, there was no thought to the name Vicious Circle, there was no thought to anything we did.

MIKE WATT: You'd be at a punk gig and there'd be some guy watching the band and because he had long hair he'd be attacked. I think it was because on the streets the longhairs came after the punkers and stomped them first . . . and the only time the punks ever had the numbers to hit back was at a show.

MIKE PATTON: Jack Grisham had the persona, he had his crowd that followed him, but he just wasn't very credible. He had a ton of charisma, and I think he's talented, too, but he lived in an upperclass suburb. Jack was well-to-do compared to Watt or Ness or us . . . he was upper middle class. You know? He had a nice life and the super rad punk thing was his comedy shtick, and his crowd were nearly all have-it-all kids who lived in nice houses and they would go to punk shows just to act tough, you know? Jack could have easily beaten up Darby Crash—he was a big guy—but Darby had way more street cred.

JACK GRISHAM: We buzzed on constant ultraviolence in the pit while we played—that's what VC was all about, and I loved it, I fuckin' loved it, thrived on it . . . there was nothing better than torturing or stomping the fuck out of somebody, either watching it or doing it yourself. It was basically Clockwork fuckin' Orange County, that was the fuckin' deal. We were SoCal droogs who'd go around stealing cars, torturing people, ripping people off. This therapist finally said I was a sociopath and told me, "You don't know right from wrong." Fuck, man, it was true, and—even worse—it wasn't like we even had any cool political cause to justify it. We were inexcusable, it was just bare-assed FSU, as in "fuck stuff up." Another motto was "Rape, pillage, and destroy." We'd drive around at night and shoot the windows out of banks, stuff like that. We had records for auto thievin', burglary, robbery . . . we were fuck-holes who were not gonna make it any other way, whether it was gonna be punk rock or heavy metal or ska or rockabilly or whatever. We were totally fucked up in the head, it just happened we found punk first. We'd been getting our asses kicked by parents, by the schools, and the police, and now it was like, "Fuck you, we're monsters now, and you're fuckin' gonna pay for it!" I was eighteen years old, six foot three, and two hundred pounds, skinheaded, and pissed off.

MIKE PATTON: Grisham talks like a psycho . . . and I'm sure he probably is somewhat. Jack had this personality where people would let him do outrageous things to them. Jack's this really charismatic guy who always had these really weak-willed people hanging around him. He's got this element of the insane about him, this dangerous aura . . . you suspect it's a put-on, but if he really gets off on violence, like he says, then he's gotta be nuts. Jack would humiliate these people, he'd abuse them constantly, and the amazing thing was they'd come back for more.

JACK GRISHAM: I was torturing this guy in the garage of my mom's house in this nice suburban neighborhood with my whole family inside eating Easter dinner . . . and I'd got this guy tied up in the rafters with a rope around his legs and I'm beating him with a two-by-four. I said, "Hang on a minute," and put the two-by-four down and walked into the house and kissed my aunt and said like, "Oh, hi, how you doing?" I grabbed a deviled egg, told them I'd be back in a minute, and I went back out, grabbed the two-by-four, and kept workin' on the guy. I finally had to get out of Vicious Circle 'cause of the violence. There were constant stabbings and beatings and people cruising by my house at night, shooting up the neighborhood. And the cops hated me, too, and the hippies hated me, and now the punks were pissed at me, too . . . fuck, it was a nightmare, a mess. A lot of people did stupid shit like pulling knives on me, so I ended up splittin'. I did something pretty bad to somebody and they retaliated with guns. It was a big deal, I had to split to Alaska for a while, they cut the lines on my car, blew up my car . . . fuck . . . I don't wanna say who they were, but they weren't punks . . . boy, they were pissed off.

KEITH MORRIS: Stirring up all the aggro was easy for Vicious Circle to do, being from where they were from, coming up here, messing things up for everybody, then running back home to their big swell homes in Huntington. Black Flag was new to this, a lot of stuff was going by us.

JACK GRISHAM: The other guys in my band weren't considered as violent as me or the people I hung out with, like this guy Pat Brown, our drummer Todd, my friend Bill Wilson, or Scott Burson, a lot of guys who ended up drug overdoses or in prison. We fucked up that X-Head guy . . . that little sicko in the *Decline*. He wasn't shit in our world. A lot of people say Vicious Circle had a lot to do with the Fleetwood becoming the birthplace of hardcore, 'cause it got so out of control every time we played there . . . we had to break up for a while for everything to cool off, and we had to jettison the Vicious Circle name for personal safety reasons. Then we came right back with a bang as TSOL, the True Sons of Liberty.

JOHN DOE: Once X was playing at the Starwood, when that really fucked-up kid in the *Decline* movie with the X shaved into his head, Mike the Marine, was swinging a big chain, the kind of chain you would hook a vicious dog up to in a yard. He was swinging ten or twelve feet of steel chain around his head in a really crowded floor in front of the stage area, and I was thinking, "This is really fucked up. This guy is the wrong kind of misfit. This guy is a psychopath and it's really sad that the scene is attracting this kind of aberrant." If I had to put a point on it, mark a day, that would be it . . . seeing that kind of person being attracted to something that was artistic and literary and creative was the end of it for me.

JEFF MCDONALD: Greg Ginn immediately saw the emergence of the Huntington Beach hardcore scene as an opportunity to expand, since Black Flag didn't have much of a following of their own yet and they needed the numbers to have this rock band career, and so they actively pandered to that crowd. That's where it split off for me.

KEITH MORRIS: It got progressively harder to play. A lot of the clubs didn't have the proper paperwork for gatherings or dancing so they'd get shut down, and we were getting banned from clubs and shows faster than we played 'em.

MIKE NESS: I didn't understand punks fighting punks at the Fleetwood. I was always like, "Hey, if you wanna fucking fight, let's fucking go there, motherfucker . . . your call." I fought with them all. All the Huntington Beach punks. These fucked-up skinheads from rich homes. I never backed away. It went on for years. Most of the kids who were into the hardcore scene at the beaches were very cool, but there was always just a handful where we just didn't get along. They didn't like me. I didn't like them. I don't think it had anything to do with where they were from. They could have been from the beach or they could have been from La Mirada, you know? An asshole is an asshole. We had assholes in our circle, too. As for Orange County being blamed for all the violence, that ain't right. The Fullerton punk scene was never about putting that shit out, not for one fucking minute.

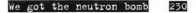

JACK GRISHAM: The one measly ethic we were able to scrape up between the four of us in Vicious Circle was that we didn't believe in punk-on-punk violence. We thought, "These guys are our team." We just believed in punk-on-everybody-else violence! I always respected the old Hollywood punkers. They were real sweet people who went through a lot to make it happen for us fuck-holes in Orange County. TSOL identified more with the Hollywood scene than with the beach scene 'cause that's what we admired when we were kids. I was really into the first-wave Hollywood bands. I fuckin' loved the Weirdos and the Germs, those were my favorites. I dug the Go-Go's, too.

KEITH MORRIS: Eventually Black Flag stopped being fun; it became more of a regimented business. We were starting to argue more, and I was constantly losing. They were getting fed up with my drunken partying behavior, and so everything started to become a little bit more tense. I just one day got fed up and walked.

The forming of my next band, the Circle Jerks, was like this natural flow that just happened. There wasn't a lot of premeditation or brainstorming. Redd Kross was auditioning drummers in the basement of the Church to replace Ron Reyes, who'd just quit, and Lucky Lehrer was trying out. Greg Hetson loved Lucky's playing but the McDonald brothers didn't. They thought Lucky was a little bit too proficient, a little too tight, a little too professional for their needs. And Greg was fed up with this attitude, so he bailed on Redd Kross. I had just quit Black Flag and all of a sudden it seemed very convenient—here's Hetson, who's getting really good, here's Lucky, this amazing drummer, and—too good to be true, almost— me on lead vocals! Raymond Pettibon had an American slang dictionary and Hetson and I came across Circle Jerks and we both looked at each other and a lightbulb lit over our heads. With the Circle Jerks, we didn't want anybody getting hurt, we wanted all the gang shit kept out in the parking lot. Let security and cops deal with that crap. The Jerks were more into creating an intense rockin' party atmosphere. For us it was all about everybody jumpin' around and havin' a good time. We thought punk should be about making new friends here, not more enemies.

We were saying, "We have enough enemies and bad situations confronting us once we leave the venue as it is . . . why poop the

party and drive all the babes away with this stupid violence shit?"
I stopped shows all the time. I'd tell 'em to cut that shit out. That
was one of the main differences between the Circle Jerks and Black
Flag. Flag liked to stir shit up without regard for crowd safety.

GREG HETSON: The difference between Black Flag and the Circle Jerks
was a sense of humor. Flag's music was very, very heavy. It was
this Neanderthal approach to manic downstroke punk thrashin'
guitar. One night these guys approached me in the parking lot at
Okie Dog's after a Circle Jerks gig . . . I think it was Greg Graffin
who said: "Hi, we're Bad Religion, we're a band from the Valley . . .
would you listen to our tape?" I said, "Sure, I will . . . and if I like
it I'll take it with me to Rodney when we go to be interviewed the
next night.

BRETT GUREWITZ: In the fall of 1980, I dropped out of El Camino Real
High 'cause I couldn't get along with anybody and formed Bad
Religion with this drummer named Jay Ziskraut and two 15-year-
old kids, also from Camino, Jay Bentley and Greg Graffin, who
wanted to be a lyricist. Graffin thought Darby's lyrics were the shit.

GREG GRAFFIN: I was greatly inspired as a lyricist by the writings of
Darby Crash. I think his writing is severely underrated as poetry . . .
even when I was a kid, I immediately thought his work was something that my father, an English professor at the University of
Wisconsin, would find interesting. Darby was hugely important in
helping me find a literary voice, my own identity. There is no
doubt in my mind that had he lived he would've surpassed his
early writings many, many times over.

BRETT GUREWITZ: We were just suburban teen musician wannabes
from the Valley trying to mix Dickies-style pop punk with the dark
lyrics of Darby Crash and the intensity of Black Flag. Later on,
we started calling it "melodic hardcore"—that's the signature
Epitaph-Westbeach sound. Greg Ginn was totally my role model in
every way. Here was this radical dude who was a musician and a
songwriter who rocked his own band and who had his own label
and took shit from no one. I was turning 18. That was it. I wanted
to be like him from that point on. It was the first time I'd heard the
term "DIY" applied to music. We began honing our live chops at
the Vex in East L.A., Bards Apollo in the West Adams district, and
at Godzilla's in Sun Valley. We launched Epitaph Records in 1980

with a Bad Religion EP . . . six songs that Graffin and I cowrote. We sold out 1,500 copies straight away because Rodney played it right away, and it went over well.

BRENDAN MULLEN: The timing was excellent—the field was wide open for a new set of players.

chapter 29

True punk takes a hit: Go-Go's founder Margot Olaverra, 1979. Photo Credit: Frank Gargani.

BRENDAN MULLEN: The major labels never wanted to touch this new stuff, let alone distribute it. The Go-Go's had to go to England to make their first single on Stiff.

MARGOT OLAVERRA: We got a gig opening for Madness and they really liked us as a band. Belinda was dating Suggs, that was the connection, and through that we got a tour to open for them in the U.K., then we were offered the Specials, who were in the same scene in England.

CHARLOTTE CAFFEY: England was spit-drenched. We were eating Madness' leftovers. We'd get off the stage every night and cry.

GINGER CANZONERI: Nobody knew who they were, everybody was throwing stuff at them, but by the end of the tour, they'd won over a substantial part of the audience, a ska audience. When they came back to L.A., they were an incredibly tight band who saw things totally differently. Punk was on its way out fashionwise and there was a whole new look coming in. They brought back new clothes and things influenced by the Belle Stars and the Modettes. Punk wasn't a force in England anymore, the younger kids were more into the mod ska look.

MARGOT OLAVERRA: There was the Go-Go's diet, imposed to fit a certain image, yeah. The Go-Go's diet was, we were on a stipend of forty dollars a week, which nobody can live on, and we would get a bonus if we lost ten pounds or something like that. I don't remember if Ginger weighed us, but it made borderline anorexics of us, including me. I remember Jane got really pimply 'cause she was doing crystal meth to lose weight. I would throw steamed vegetables in a blender and call it soup—I had no money anyway, the twenty-five-cent box of macaroni and cheese was affordable but too fattening.

GINGER CANZONERI: When we came back from London, everybody had really put on the pounds. The British heavy-starch diet.

JANE WIEDLIN: The whole L.A. scene had changed by the time we got back from England in early 1980, it had been taken over by all these real angry, young white boys, Black Flag. We were like, "What's this all about? It's really gross." We were lumped in with all those stupid bands, but we never even knew those guys. What had started as a scene of girls and gays and stuff was nearly all gone.

KEITH MORRIS: The Go-Go's were playing pop music. They were never really a punk band to begin with. They were a female vocal harmony group with rock guitars and drums. Of course they're gonna be taken aback playing a show where it's 95 percent sweaty guys jumpin' around and a little blood action flowin'.

MARGOT OLAVERRA: I went to jail again. Somebody asked me to buy them coke and Ginger had a connection. We were at the Starwood and Ginger told me to get a drink on her CBS Records tab but the bartender wasn't buying it and I'd already drank half of it so I just walked away with it and they called the cops, the same sheriffs who'd arrested me previously. I'd dumped what was left of the coke into a bush and they pulled out the coke and whatever was left blew away. They took me in, I was in jail overnight. Don Bonebrake from X bailed me out. Two lab reports came back, one for 2.5 grams . . . no way! It was totally bogus . . . so anyway, we hired a lawyer and I got something like probation, first felony offense. But one of the stories when they fired me was, "Oh, you have a

record and we want to go to Japan and you won't be able to come."
But the real reason was because I wasn't a pop songwriter. In the
same way we'd heard about Gina, they'd heard about Kathy Valentine and they wanted her in the band because she was a pop songwriter. Plus I was a really wild punk rocker and they wanted to be
a girl pop band and they knew I'd resist that transition and in fact
was already doing so . . . so maybe it was a contradiction in themselves, what they were doing in punk to begin with.

GINGER CANZONERI: Margot gradually was hanging out with different
people and had different interests and maybe took different drugs.
She became ill, type A hepatitis, and we all had to go get
shots . . . she was feeling run-down, and I think that what happened was that the band was feeling kind of fed up with her.

MARGOT OLAVERRA: Another reason why they fired me, they said, was
that I got hepatitis. I was sick. The Go-Go's diet, you know. I was
living on celery soup and then we'd go to a club and have an open
tab because now we were the Go-Go's, back from England with
"We Got the Beat" in the charts. So everyone would give me free
drinks, you know. I'd get quite drunk. Basically I fucked up my
liver. I did a myriad of drugs—I wasn't a junkie, it was part of the
scene, part of everybody's life. It wasn't that . . . if it was that and
it was used as an excuse, it was a real cop-out—that was pushed
in my face 'cause Charlotte had gone back in the closet as far as
her drug taking. Later, when I moved to New York and was living
in the East Village, I remember seeing her a couple of times walking east.

GINGER CANZONERI: We all had to get shots, I know it's contagious, and
the feeling in the band was that she was letting them down. We had
six shows that were already sold out at the Whisky . . . the attitude
was, "We better start looking around fast 'cause this girl is not
gonna be in any physical condition to play, the strenuousness of the
show is gonna be too much." So they started auditioning bass players. Kathy Valentine filled in for those dates . . . I'm not quite sure,
but the band made this decision: "We think Kathy should replace
Margot." I remember being told that because I was the manager, I
had to tell Margot, and I found that really distasteful. It was upsetting for me and upsetting for Margot. I'm not good at doing those
kind of things and I don't really want to talk about it.

TERRY GRAHAM: Margot was always a fun girl. She was great. Always laughing and smiling. She endeared herself to a lot of people. So when they kicked her out of the Go-Go's it offended many. Many people in the community felt she had been brutally violated. Any naïve ideology we might have had, that was the end of it. The end of the innocence and the beginning of the end of the scene for me.

EXENE CERVENKA: Margot was devastated when she got kicked out of the Go-Go's. I felt very sad and angry about that. I had a band mentality; you just stood by each other. You didn't replace someone like Margot. She was my closest friend in the band. I don't know why they fired her. I heard rumors. I never could figure out why. Seemed to be no reason whatsoever.

GINGER CANZONERI: I was introduced to Miles Copeland and I told him about the band and he became interested after he started hearing things back about the band. We signed a deal with IRS Records and went to New York to record *Beauty and the Beat*.

CHARLOTTE CAFFEY: We got an extremely tiny budget from Miles Copeland of IRS Records to do an album. We went to New York and stayed at the Wellington during the recording.

KATHY VALENTINE: I used to get FedEx packages of drugs sent to me.

BELINDA CARLISLE: We'd be at the kitchen table choppin' that coke out and talking about what we were gonna do that night.

CHARLOTTE CAFFEY: It's amazing we got the record done.

X at home. *Left to right:* D.J. Bonebrake, Exene Cervenka, Billy Zoom, and John Doe, 1979. Photo Credit: Frank Gargani.

RAY MANZAREK: Jim would have loved X.

JOHN DOE: X and the Germs played at this place called Hope Street Hall, which was right near Morrison Hotel, the fleabag fucking hotel where they shot the Doors album cover. Exene and I immediately went down to Morrison Hotel. They still had the same stenciled window.

RAY MANZAREK: My involvement with X came about from reading the lyrics for "Johnny Hit and Run Pauline." It absolutely reminded me of Jim. I thought, "I can't wait to hear this band." After catching them at the Whisky, I went back to the dressing room and said, "Holy shit, you guys are incredible." I said, "Listen, I'm Ray Manzarek from the Doors and I would love to help you guys out in the recording studio. Make records with you guys." John said, "Do you think we can get a deal with a big record company?" And I said,

"Well . . . I doubt it, with this kind of music, man, but surely somebody out there will take a chance on it."

D.J. BONEBRAKE: Jay Jenkins was our manager. He had a rough time getting us a deal. He wrote letters to most of the companies. A&M wrote us a rejection letter saying, "Sorry, we're just not interested at this time." I can understand from a business point of view them not wanting to sign the bands. There was no indication that any of them would be a big hit on the radio.

JOHN DOE: It was impossible to get signed at first 'cause we didn't have the knowledge or the connections to make proper introductions. We never sent around demo tapes, we didn't understand how all that worked. I think Slash was already interested before Ray became involved. They were really new as a label. They were recording the Germs' *GI* album when we agreed to sign. Having Ray attached to it was an incredible break. Here was a bona fide rock icon digging our shit and I thought for sure that we're doing something right. I couldn't believe our good luck in having this person understand the impact X was having.

D.J. BONEBRAKE: We got a deal with Slash and Ray agreed to do the record for a very low budget with his producer fee deferred. We did *Los Angeles* in early 1980. We got no advance—it cost $10,000, the basic budget, it all went into making the best recording possible. We were made to feel we were just lucky to get a record out. It was pretty straightforward, not a lot of overdubs. We didn't have the time or the budget, but we had all the songs for *Los Angeles* and *Wild Gift* well rehearsed. We'd been playing them for more than two years straight. We just chose nine that we thought would fit good on the first record, including the title song, which has become a sort of anthem by now.

RAY MANZAREK: Slash signed them and we went into the studio to do the first album with ten thousand dollars. Fuck, make a record for ten thousand dollars? That's not a lot of money! "Well, it'll only work if nobody gets paid," I said. So nobody got paid. We paid the pro technicians. Other than that, everybody in X got one union scale gig. As far as the union was concerned, we recorded the whole album in one three-hour session. The atmosphere was incredible. They didn't fuck around. They'd been playing these songs for two years straight. They knew them inside and out. They didn't have any money. Exene would bring in a bag of baking potatoes and we'd make them in the microwave oven and everyone'd be sitting around having baked potatoes with margarine and salt and pepper and drinking beer.

JOHN DOE: We'd done two years of prepping, learning how to play the songs, and Ray was smart enough not to change anything, just like the Doors did it. We did the vocals separately . . . we did some overdubs . . . it was a ten-thousand-dollar budget . . . beginning to end, it was probably about three weeks, maybe a month at the most. We didn't have any illusions about wanting to do it lo-fi or antiestablishment . . . we wanted to go in there and make the best record that we could.

BILLY ZOOM: I liked Ray Manzarek [as a producer], but I could have done better.

RAY MANZAREK: Billy was a very highly strung and volatile guy. Exene was always seeking psychic dominance, and John would be caught in the middle between his love for Exene and his friendship with Billy. He'd be the mediator, the peacemaker, with help from D.J., who was always a rock of consistency in reasoning. Billy, John, and Exene lived together in this dingy little apartment full of crazy little voodoo dolls.

JUDITH BELL: Muriel Cervenka, Exene's sister, came to L.A. with her husband and was staying at my house. They were selling their own jewelry line to customers like Madonna before she got famous. Madonna totally copped Exene's sister's look. She was wearing all Muriel's clothes and jewelry when she started. Muriel came to L.A. with her husband and they showed this movie, *Ecstatic Stigmatic*. In the opening shot, Muriel is in a coffin, which is really eerie in retrospect.

CHRIS D.: Muriel and her husband, Gordon, were in town for a screening of their *Ecstatic Stigmatic* movie, and they were staying at the Tropicana and they kind of went their separate ways during the week. Muriel was having all these affairs.

JUDITH BELL: She was seeing all these guys at the same time, and all these ex-boyfriends were coming after her again, and her husband was there. She was having a real crisis over men. She was staying with me because her husband was being a bastard who was so cheap he wanted to sleep on Chris D.'s floor. She was crying a lot and talking to all these guys on the phone. Muriel was fucking this guy Johnny O'Caine, Farrah's brother, too. Farrah bought this Volkswagen the morning of the night they drove to the Whisky when the terrible crash happened that killed Muriel.

CHRIS D.: We were waiting for Steve and Farrah and Muriel to call us 'cause we were all going to see X at the Whisky, and they never did.

JUDITH BELL: Farrah was driving. Steve Naive from Elvis Costello's band got thrown out of the car and Farrah broke her jaw. Muriel was in the backseat. The impact snapped her spine. Muriel just said, "Oh, shit." And that was the end of her. I was at the Whisky waiting for them. Johnny O'Caine showed up at the club escorted by four cops to tell Exene. Johnny told Exene, and she screamed and went in the back with John. We thought they were gonna cancel their show, but they said, "No, we're gonna play." They went out there and destroyed all their equipment and screamed and yelled and a lot of people who didn't know what happened thought it was the best show they'd ever seen.

CHRIS D.: I saw cops come in and walk backstage down that long hall and I didn't know what they were saying to her but she just dropped to the floor and everybody watching just knew something really heavy had happened. They were on their way to Judith's house. They were coming down Willoughby when the accident happened, and they never made it.

TOP JIMMY: I was at the Whisky the night Exene's sister was killed. It was in between shows, and Exene asked Ray Manzarek, "You're so fucking cosmic, what do I do now?" So Ray went and got like a whole bottle of Jack Daniel's and he came back to the dressing room 'cause he didn't have anything to say. When she went back out onto the stage, I took her out there and held her up for a while . . . she was real broken up. I think she would have gone on, because you know, tickets were sold, blah blah blah, the show must go on. I remember walking her down the steps and taking her out on the stage and holding her 'cause I didn't want her to fall down.

CHRIS D.: They were completely drunk out of their minds and crying during the songs. It was great and noble that they went on, but it was really difficult to watch. Judith and I left early to buy up as much liquor as we could and we headed over to their place on Genessee and there was this long drunken wake at their apartment.

JUDITH BELL: Afterward we went over to Exene's house and started drinking. Then the neighbors surrounded the house and pretended to be cops. When we realized they weren't cops this huge fight broke out and I spent the next day downtown bailing everybody out.

TOP JIMMY: After the show we went over to John and Exene's. We stayed up talking all night, not much to do really, just sit there and kind of look off in a daze . . . what do you do when somebody dies, there's nothing to say. It's just a bummer.

D.J. BONEBRAKE: In 1980 we went to London, the critics didn't like us at all. In New York it wasn't a triumphant premiere of this L.A. band, it was like we could have been anyone. We didn't make a giant splash. At least it made people aware that there was something going on in L.A.

chapter 31

The Blasters, 1980. Photo Credit: Donna Santisi

JEFFREY LEE PIERCE: I was raised by a Mexican mother in El Monte and had spent my entire life in her family environment. I was even briefly in a gang at Velle Lindo Junior High School. I understood Spanish and spoke a little. I have a penchant for black-haired girls and can deliver a fearsome street rap. It's all part of my Mexican upbringing. The girls of my youth were all either Mexican, Korean, Japanese, or Black. The Mexican girls were often inaccessible— property of the cholos. But the Asian girls were excellent students, and often lonely and as inexperienced as I was. Among Latinos or Asians, I always felt quite at home. I even experienced some militancy when my family moved to the San Fernando Valley . . . being unable to get along with the wealthy Anglo kids. I was always reading Eldridge Cleaver or Huey Newton, supporting the Viet Cong, who were my idols. Needless to say, I didn't have very many friends.

PLEASANT GEHMAN: Jeffrey Lee totally was into like any old blues people that were like shit-faced or doing heroin or getting beaten down by a bad woman. He was always a real drama queen about that.

PHAST PHREDDIE: After *Back Door Man* folded, I started writing a column for *Slash*, but I didn't want to focus exclusively on the punk scene because it would have been redundant. Who would've cared if I waxed poetic on X, when all of the *Slash* writers already did that? So I thought my column, "Faster than You," should be unique and attempt to open minds. It was a drag going to a punk rock party at the time, and the only records the host would have (or at least have on display) were from last week. . . . I wanted folks to know that there was music with honest expression all over the place, not just in the best punk rock.

TOP JIMMY: Before my blues band Top Jimmy and the Rhythm Pigs, I was in Top Jimmy and the All Drunk All-Stars. We were at Club 88—the band for the first gig was Billy, Johnny Doe, and D.J. Bonebrake—Brendan blew harmonica on a few tunes, and Jeffrey Lee Pierce also got up . . . he was onstage waving a Bible about, and the guy who owned the place and his wife were really upset. They were serious Christians and they thought that was real blasphemy, getting up there and waving a Bible and talking some shit.

BRENDAN MULLEN: I drove Jeffrey crosstown to Club 88 in West L.A., where we were both slated to jam with Top Jimmy and the All-Drunk All-Stars. We sat in the car outside for fifteen minutes while Jeffrey guzzled a whole pint of some cheap nasty bourbon all by himself (I had my own stash of intoxicants), and he was already well soused before he even broke open that bottle. He said he was petrified with stage fright. I did my big number, blowing the blues harp solos on some amped-up punk-rockin' versions of the Doors' "Roadhouse Blues" and Dylan's "Obviously Five Believers," and then it was time for Jeffrey to go on and for Jimmy to take a leak and get a fresh round in. Jeffrey was staggering. I don't know why he wanted to do this, but he went into this long, drawn-out version of James Brown's "It's a Man's World," this bizarrely drunken histrionic drama where he was crawling all over the dance floor in front of the stage, squawking and drooling incoherently into the mic, just like Darby seemed to be doing a lot of these days. All I could do was take it as comedy and laugh. The juiced-up audience seemed totally perplexed, but nobody got really mad.

TOP JIMMY: After a few gigs with Billy and the other X guys, I had my own band that could rock people, I had Li'l Gary Argyle on bass, the boyfriend of Lorna from the Germs, and this guitar player Eric Amble from the Accelerators, the first punk band out of Wisconsin—they ended up being the Blackhearts—after Joan Jett heisted my whole band in one day. Then I met Carlos Guitarlos, who was the back-door security guy at the Hong Kong or somethin', who was backing up some transsexual guy . . . he wanted to play, and I said sure. He knew this bass player, and I said, "What does he sound like?" and he said, "Look at this." And it was a picture of Gil T., this big fat bad-ass motherfucker and he was looking for a rockin' band and we were that band. We thought, "Damn, if this motherfucker can play bass as fat as he looks, we'll be in real good shape." We played an awful lot at the Whisky and the Roxy . . . they never gave us hardly any money but we drank it all up . . . maybe we did get paid good but we drank it . . . then we played the Cathay de Grande every Monday night for years. Some of our band and crew were pretty roughneck people, nobody you wanted to mess with for sure . . . our roadies carried shotguns to gigs when we played in some hard-assed neighborhoods in Long Beach. One of the wilder nights was when Tom the sax player beefed with Carlos, our lead guitar player. Tom went out to the trunk of his car . . . he had a little Saturday night special there and he let off a round or two into the air, then he said, "No, I'm not gonna shoot you, motherfucker, I'm gonna chop your fuckin' head off." And Tom would've, too, and Carlos ran for his life. Those were some pretty wild times. The Blasters were definitely the major catalyst for the whole roots thing after the novelty of Levi and the Rockats wore off. The Blasters had better musician skills and they had Dave as their chief songwriter so they could go for a wider range of styles than straight-ahead generic rockabilly.

DAVE ALVIN: The connection I felt with punk rock was this: I was a fry cook in Long Beach and I saw the Sex Pistols on TV and Johnny Rotten and I were the same age. And I decided, "Well, hell, if he can do this, I can do it, too." And I thought, "Well, you don't have to be the greatest guitar player in the world, either—you just have to play guitar." I have my heroes that I've always had, Freddie King, Johnny "Guitar" Watson, and Chuck Berry, that made me want to play, but it wasn't until the Blasters that I played guitar in a band. In a weird way my biggest guitar influence overall was probably Johnny Rotten.

LOUIE PÉREZ: The one specific band from the Hollywood punk scene that got all of us in Los Lobos excited was definitely the Blasters. They were the one band that made sense for us to make the trip over the river from East L.A. to play the West Side because when the roots revival began to happen in Hollywood we thought maybe there was a place for us there, too. Rockabilly stuff was happening within this roots thing, and it just seemed to make sense to try to relate musically. Punk rock itself as a musical genre was really exciting music, but it didn't make any sense to us to try to fit in with that until we heard the Blasters.

TOP JIMMY: I don't know how many times in the last twenty years people say I changed their life, that they'd never listened to that kind of music before. They tell me I first got 'em listening to classic American music . . . blues, folk, country, hillbilly, what have you. If you listen to Howlin' Wolf and those people, it's much wilder than anybody out there today.

DAVE ALVIN: Club 88, this tiny beer and wine dive in West L.A., was the only place we could get a gig.

EXENE CERVENKA: I fell in love with the Blasters and we became instant friends. Dave and Phil and John and I would stay up all night listening to records. They are legendary for their collections and knowledge. I learned most of my music history from them. I remember lots of Scotch, lots of speed, lots of crazy shit.

DAVE ALVIN: Then X asked us to do the Whisky. I'd already seen X play. The first thing that bowled me over was Billy's guitar playing. There were a lot of references in there, almost as if he was deconstructing the history of rock-and-roll guitar: He'd have rockabilly stuff flying around with surf stuff thrown in and Ramones power chord riffing.

The Vex: Los Lobos and the East L.A. Scene (1980)

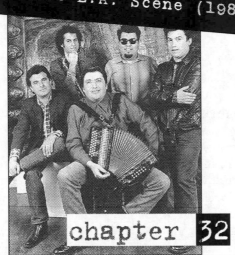

chapter 32

East L.A.'s own Los Lobos, 1983. Photo Credit: Ann Summa

SEAN CARRILLO: In 1980 Willie Herron, who was in the Illegals, and a beer distributor from East L.A. named Joe Suquette started up the Vex with permission from Sister Karen, a nun who ran this arts center, which was owned by the archdiocese, and it still is. It was called Self Help Graphics. They had a hall upstairs which they would rent for weddings and what we call quinceañeras, fifteenth-birthday parties. They told Sister Karen that they were gonna rent the hall and that she wouldn't have to do anything, they were gonna rent the hall like a normal wedding, and Joe and Willie did up all the flyers and went around East L.A. and hired every band they could find, and very quickly it took off . . . and all of a sudden bands from Hollywood started coming to East L.A. to the Vex to play, which was previously unheard of.

WILLIE HERRON: The sisters were so supportive and they thought it was such a brilliant and excellent idea.

JOE VEX: Self Help Graphics was basically a rentable space in East L.A. There were a lot of visual and performance artists coming and going, so we decided to get a project going together. We tried to get a magazine going, photographers, artists and writers, and bands. Eventually it became a place for the bands from East L.A. to play—Los Illegals, Crush, the Brat, the Stains.

WILLIE HERRON: The Brat had Theresa, and that's what set them apart. They were fronted by a Chicana. And then you had the Undertakers, who were more gothic and death metal style. And my band Los Illegals, which dealt with more social commentary issues. And then you had the Warriors, who were interesting because they were all black.

JOE VEX: We called it the Vex. Willie Herron came up with the name. He looked it up in the dictionary. It means "vexation." It fit with the space and the time.

WILLIE HERRON: Basically we wanted to just cover expenses. There was no hard cover fee. It was donation at the door. We really wanted it to be an alternative in every way possible. A cup of beer was 25 cents. Everything was very, very low key so people that didn't have a whole lot of money could come and enjoy some great shows. It was a perfect idea. We couldn't do it in Hollywood without the fear about the other clubs, the other people in the industry fearing us or maybe bombing it. So the idea was to get visitors to come to East L.A. to see us without fear of getting shot or stabbed. We did that by putting on great shows.

JOE VEX: Soon bands from Hollywood started coming down. At the time punk was going big and there was an overload of bands that needed a place to play and eventually when they heard about the Vex, they were just curious about East L.A.—they were curious about East L.A. because back then it was a notorious you-come-into-East-L.A.-you-take-your-life-in-your-own-hands kind of thing . . . a total myth, but it was that type of thinking. At the same time, a lot of other groups were really interested and curious to play there—X did a show there, the Punk Prom. So the Vex became the link between East L.A. and Hollywood. Eventually people started giving East L.A. bands recognition. I think we opened the door for a lot of those bands. Los Lobos came to the Vex and shortly thereafter they were playing the Cathay de Grande in Hollywood . . . they were doing folk and electric stuff. If it wasn't for the Vex, a lot of East L.A. bands wouldn't be playing the Whisky and the Roxy.

LOUIE PÉREZ: Our early gigs outside of East L.A. were great. You'd have punks mixed with the Blasters crowd, and people stage-diving, and we'd go to the Atomic Café to hang out after the gig, and people would be walking in with big blue mohawks.

BRENDAN MULLEN: Then, of course, there were just as many new punks who didn't want to know from the blues at all.

LOUIS PÉREZ: Los Lobos experienced a large punk crowd for the first time when we opened up for Public Image at the Olympic Auditorium. We hung on for about ten minutes until serious projectiles began hitting the stage; finally we were run off. They threw everything they could at us. We felt this incredible rush of adrenaline. We had smiles on our faces, actually. It was like, "Wow, this is different." Most people would have seen it as an incredibly negative experience. We could have just run back to East L.A. to hide, but we were like, "Let's keep going with this," while our poor families and friends were almost in tears. Talk about diving right into the deep end of the pool! It was Tito Larriva's idea for us to play that show, he pitched it to the promoter, and maybe he just thought that this would be funny or something, but it was cool. I've never confronted him with it, and I don't think I ever would ask him what exactly was on his mind.

DAVE ALVIN: Still, the roots underground was taking off. The Dils had become a countrified band called Rank and File, and then Los Lobos came out with their EP and it was obvious right away that they were going places.

LOUIE PÉREZ: The Blasters said to Bob Biggs, the president of Slash, "Hey, you've got to sign up this band," and so Bob came out to see us a couple of times, and he liked it, but frankly, I don't think he ever had any idea of the full potential. It was pretty easy to confuse anybody with our band, because basically we were playing revved-up Mexican music.

JOE VEX: Later I booked Black Flag, Circle Jerks, Adolescents . . . in East L.A. they went over really well 'cause their following followed them no matter where they went. I think the fact that they were in East L.A., the crowds knew not to go out and start trashing the neighborhood—they were respectful of what was going on. There was a lot of negativity that followed some of these bands, but you could tell they knew that you can't come down to East L.A. and start tearing up the neighborhood. There's gangs in the neighborhoods and down at the Paramount Ballroom—there was a gang shooting right across the street, a drive-by, they shot a guy in the mouth, right in front of the Jack in the Box, they killed a kid. I was upstairs and one of the punk girls came and told me they shot somebody. I crossed the street and the guy was slowly dying . . . he was about sixteen, seventeen years old . . . I looked at death right in his face . . . it gives me a chill just thinking about it right now, I can still see the guy's face. So the hardcore punks were pretty respectful.

TONY CADENA: Bands like the Adolescents, we'd get banned from places like the Starwood, mostly due to our behavior. So we started to play these halls in East L.A. We were playing in the barrios, which was an alien world for us. It was a scary experience, dealing with the gang members who didn't want us to be there.

chapter 33

The Gun Club (Jeffrey Lee Pierce, center), 1980. Photo Credit: Ann Summa

CHRIS D.: The Gun Club's *Fire of Love* is probably the definitive record to come out of this roots revival movement. So many people have come up to me about that record. It's just one of those legendary records. Several people told me that record made them want to start a band and come to Los Angeles.

PLEASANT GEHMAN: I met Jeff 'cause he was really into Blondie and he was hanging around at the Tropicana where they were staying. He was totally into pop, he'd be wearing a beret and a striped T-shirt with white jeans, or a black T-shirt with white polka dots on it, all mod and pop and beach-party-like. That was before the Gun Club . . . he was totally into pop . . . he had a band called the Red Lights that was totally poppy. I remember he had a song that was like an ode to Debbie called "Debbie by the Christmas Tree." It was about this cardboard stand-up he had of her from the *Plastic Letters* album, he had it propped up on his TV.

PHAST PHREDDIE: When I met Jeffrey he was into Blondie, Bruce Springsteen, and Bob Marley more than anything. He also quite liked soul music, having grown up a bit in East L.A. or thereabouts. If I didn't turn him on to blues and jazz, I certainly turned him on to more blues and jazz than he'd ever heard before.

PLEASANT GEHMAN: In the midst of this he discovered blues. Phast Phreddie was turning everybody on to blues. He had an amazing record collection of every kind of weird swamp and blues and 78's and Ornette Coleman and zydeco. He'd go to Phred's house and get shit-faced and start DJ'ing . . . he'd put on the Cramps' first single and it would just segue into like Charlie Christian or something. Jeff started getting into weird swampy stuff. The first band he had was called Creeping Ritual. Before that he forced me to have a band with him called the Cyclones. He wanted me to be a singer. I didn't really want to but he kept saying it and one time he saw me at a party and said, "When are you gonna start a band?" "I'm not." And he'd say, "You'd make a great singer." "I'm not interested." "Well, too bad, I'm putting a band together for you." We played one gig with the Go-Go's and the Last at Gazzari's. We opened. It was sort of rockabilly and sort of swampy and sort of just weird screaming and we were all completely drunk on Jack Daniel's and Jim Beam. Brad Dunning, who's now a famous interior designer, was on drums. Back then he had a fanzine called *Contemp Trends*. Jeffrey played guitar and I sang. We wrote a few songs and did a few covers . . . it was a total fucking mess. Jeff got into a fistfight onstage with Johnny Nation, who was Lydia Lunch's guitar player. Black Flag thought we were so punk rock, they asked us to play with them, but we broke up. Then Jeff started Creeping Ritual with Kid Congo.

JEFFREY LEE PIERCE: The Creeping Ritual were rehearsing and drinking. Drinking and rehearsing in a cheap studio on Selma Avenue. Kid Congo Powers had bought an amp and a guitar which he did not know how to play.

KID CONGO POWERS: It was a quick turning point from fan to musician. I picked up a guitar and then I was making records and going on tour. We had several different members at the beginning of the

Gun Club, including Brad Dunning and Don Snowden, now a professional music writer. We were very influenced by the Slits and no wave and blues and reggae and dub, but of course we couldn't play at all, but that was the genesis of us wanting to play . . . we wanted to do something other than basic punk rock.

PHAST PHREDDIE: An early gig at Club 88: Jeffrey dressed in a black suit with a white shirt and a black string tie and a black hat, looking like something out of a Flannery O'Connor short story. He had chains in one hand and an old Bible in the other as he sang "Preachin' Blues." At one point he threw the Bible down and jumped on it. The owner of Club 88 promptly banned the Gun Club from playing there ever again.

CHRIS D.: Bob Biggs wanted to do another little label that would be attached to Slash that he thought wouldn't be as accessible, and that was Ruby Records.

TITO LARRIVA: I found Jeffrey Lee Pierce after he threw a tape in the back of my amp, a tape of his band jamming with Kid Congo. I said, "What is this? I fuckin' love this thing." I said, "Where is this band from?" I'd never heard anything like that in L.A. And I played it for everybody and Exene said, "Oh, that's Jeffrey." And I said, "Where can I find him? I wanna do a record with him." She told me he was working at Slash, so I called over there where he was boxing records and said, "I wanna do this record with you. I'll put up the money." I worked with Jeffrey for two fucking weeks, on the lyrics, on the structure of the songs, we broke it down. I tore that whole thing apart. He was fucking drunk every day. As a matter of fact, when we cut the tracks, they sucked. When we first got to the studio, he totally froze. He was so stiff. I thought, "Oh my God . . . disaster." I went out and bought him a big bottle of cheap champagne, that's all I could afford. I said, "Drink all that and then we'll cut it, 'cause I'm not touching the record button until you're drunk." And we waited till he drank the whole thing and he drank it and he was drooling and falling down and then I hit record and they started and did every track all the way through. By that time he was so fucking wasted. He's just screaming the whole fucking time, but they're beautiful. He was just starting. He was real insecure. We cut it and mixed it in one day. We had sixteen tracks, but we decided to do mono drums. Then I took it to Biggs. I'd run out of money and I couldn't put it out myself. I said, "Do you want it?" He said no, but Chris D. liked it. We were in the office and Chris said to Biggs, "Well, let me have my own subsidiary label and we'll put it out on that." That was the beginning of Ruby Records. Chris went in with the band and cut three more tracks and we remixed the record. Pat kept going, "Where are the drums?" And I said, "They're on one fader, man. Just turn it up." He had such a hard time with that. He wanted to tweak for hours and there was nothing to tweak. I thought Chris added a lot . . . really beefy and lots of reverb and delay.

JEFFREY LEE PIERCE: When we put out that *Fire of Love* record, it got really popular in Boston and New York, so there was enough demand there for us to tour. The record was doing well there and everybody was waiting for somebody to do something different. We weren't New Romantic and we weren't like Echo and the Bunnymen or something, and we weren't like some punk band. We were doing this weird thing. And everybody on the East Coast was just ready for that. We went on this ridiculous and horrendous two-month tour of America. It was almost like volunteering for Vietnam. I remember driving through Texas thinking, "I'm just too far gone now. I'm just too far." Like going up the river in *Apocalypse Now* or something.

PLEASANT GEHMAN: Jeffrey was into this sick combo of looking like Marilyn Monroe and Elvis at the same time. Part of the Marilyn thing came from Debbie Harry, who looked like a punk rock version of Marilyn. He came over one night, it was Halloween, and they were gonna play at Otis art college downtown. He was wearing this loungey looking jacket, kind of a smoking jacket, and his hair was bleached white and it was getting kind of long and he wanted me to put this fifties kind of Marilyn Monroe outfit on him.

JEFFREY LEE PIERCE: Kid and I were always looking for some excuse to put on women's clothing.

PLEASANT GEHMAN: We all got really drunk and went down to Otis in the middle of the set, Jeff crawled under the stage and he was just lying under the stage with the microphone, screaming. Billy Person, who was playing bass, had to go under the stage and drag him out. Jeffrey's problems weren't nearly as glaring as they would have been now. Everybody was fucked-up all the time. Nobody was in a twelve-step program. Alcoholics Anonymous was for fucking fat old men on Skid Row.

WAYZATA DE CAMERONE: I knew this struggling actor named John Pochna, an Eastern-educated, near Ivy league type. Pochna, like a lot of the straight non-punker types back then wanted to hang with the cool crowd and the cool crowd was going to see the local punk bands. Bands like the Germs, X, and the Screamers. I used to run into Pochna backstage at the Whisky or Club 88. We shared drinks and had some other common interests: women and marijuana. After closing at 2 A.M. everyone wanted to know where the party was. I remember telling Pochna we should rent a hole-in-the-wall dump, buy a couple of cheap refrigerators, stock 'em with cheap beer, and tell all our friends, bands and groupie types where they could go. We could charge 'em five bucks a piece and make a little money. Pochna would always say what a great idea it was and that we should do it. I kept at him pretty steadily through the last half of '79 and into 1980 to front the cash. We finally found this store-front at 1955 Cahuenga Boulevard. The joint fronted Cahuenga underneath a seedy hotel across the street from the Hollywood Freeway southbound on-ramp. The front room was small, maybe 400 square feet, with bay windows long ago boarded up and painted over. We decorated the rear room with what would become the essential look of coffeehouse chic in the early 90's: old ratty couches, spindly throwaway tables, and mis-matched lamps.

JOHN POCHNA: The Zero opened the first weekend of 1980, and it was an immediate hit. Basically, the idea came about a month or two before that. I was over at Disgraceland and we were all talking about how we needed a place where we could all hang out, because after these gigs, these guys were like, wide awake, so was I. Nobody wanted to go to sleep after the regular clubs closed, but someone was always calling the cops at the house parties, and I thought, "Well, I always wanted to open an art gallery, and we could do this at night at an art gallery." It took two months for any art to show up on the walls because it was a mail art show, where people mailed in erotic postcards and crap that they made, and it just took us so long to get all the mail in. The mail art show was a big hit.

PLEASANT GEHMAN: The way the Zero Zero operated was, you'd come from another nightspot which closed at 2:00 A.M., you'd pay your five bucks to become a "member" of this "private club," then join the seventy or eighty other scenesters inside, getting trashed until the wee hours. Since the whole thing wasn't legal anyway, there were no ID checks or door searches, and all the patrons' pockets would be clanking with smuggled booze bottles, plus whatever joints, pills, and powders they had access to. Everyone was fucked up beyond belief—that was the point! But this was no callow underage crowd: The Zero Zero attracted a boho elite of artists, photographers, actors, models, writers, filmmakers, club bookers, Eurotrash intellectuals, and, of course, musicians. There was even a board of directors, though it's doubtful they ever met anywhere besides the club itself. On the board were John Doe and Exene from X and Tito Larriva from the Plugz, plus members of Los Lobos and the Blasters. Regulars included ex–Warhol superstar Mary Woronov, among others. David Lee Roth in particular took a shine to the Zero, and it was rumored that he was an "investor." Whatever the case, he'd always be found holding court in the notorious back room. You had access to that place only if you were super-duper hip or had a lot of blow to share.

JOHN POCHNA: David Lee Roth showed up at the Zero one night very early on and just loved it. He showed up the first time in a limo, and he had these two chicks with him and Eddie Anderson, his personal security guy. The chicks thought that they were going to some fancy place . . . one of those classy, high-end rock places that Rod Stewart would hang out at. They completely freaked out when they saw the look of the place and this raw, totally fucked-up downscale crowd. The chicks were so bummed that David just sent them back out into the limo and then he'd continue to hang out and pick up other chicks . . . and then he'd send those chicks back and so it would go on and on until the limo was eventually stuffed to the roof with them. David wasn't covering the rent in the beginning. He didn't do that until later. Every once in a while, somebody would really look at the art and buy a membership card . . . I think Roth still has his Zero Zero membership card in his wallet.

PLEASANT GEHMAN: I remember El Duce, of the most politically incorrect band on earth, the Mentors, and Top Jimmy (the namesake of the Van Halen song "Top Jimmy") were the janitors, cleaning up for free so they could imbibe all the "high school" beers set down by the drunken revelers, and maybe, if they were lucky, find someone's stash on the floor.

JOHN POCHNA: El Duce's real name was Eldon Wayne Hoake. I saw his license or maybe it was an ID card. It had his picture on it from the state of Washington. He had a pear-shaped, classic beer belly look. Watching Duce's body language while he swept a broom across the floor was just a sidesplitting crack-up because it was something he obviously didn't do too often.

BLACK RANDY: The Mentors were three gross trailer park farmboys in black executioner hoods who said they played rape rock, and of course we had to have them for our opening act. Their leader was El Duce, who had two dildoes for drumsticks. They did sick songs about butt-fucking whores, Peeping Toms, and one about goin' through a girl's purse, a song about bringing a girl home and robbing her. We loved it because it was so raw and it was going to be so unfashionable and utterly incorrect. The people who found X and *Slash* magazine palatable would hate the Mentors, so we had to get them in there, and they outdid themselves. It was monstrous. Duce pissed into a glass jar onstage then pulled out a bloody tampon from some stripper's pussy, dipped it in and started sucking it dry. All these chicks were losing it . . . throwing things and screaming sexism. They hated it. Duce was singing the Four F's— "Find Her, Feel Her, Fuck Her, Forget Her"—and calling out "You coke pigs! Little coke whores! Bow down to your master! On your knees!" And so on. He really got into it like one of those bad guy wrestlers. He'd growl and rasp like a wrestler. "This is a song about an Indian girl who eats a skinhead in Seattle! She got thrown out of the teepee because she fucked Darby and not me." Stuff so off the wall. It was a great show.

TOP JIMMY: The Mentors would wear their hoods all the time. I finally got El Duce to de-hood and he says, "Man, if you looked like this, you'd wear a fuckin' hood too." I took one look at him and I says, "Motherfucker, you put that hood back on, right now!"

chapter 34

Some of the Adolescents at Disneyland (Steve Soto, Frank Agnew, friend Michelle Baer, and Tony Cadena), 1980. Photo Credit: Frank Gargani

TONY CADENA: Fullerton, California, is the home of Fender guitars, which was certainly a badge of honor for the musicians who lived there.

MIKE NESS: I think there was a Fullerton sound. We had a lot of the same influences. The Adolescents and Agent Orange and my band, Social Distortion . . . we found a sound we all liked, pop punk—we were listening to a lot of Generation X and Buzzcocks. Those guys grew up with Chuck Berry and the Stones and the Beatles—that's why that first wave of punk, whether it's Johnny Thunders or the Ramones, the very blues-based rock and roll with pop melodies but done punk style, is what I listen to. But we played it differently because we're American. I love the British stuff so much but at the same time I realized, "Well, fuck, man, I'm not fucking English! I don't know anything about the fucking queen! I don't know anything about the working class over there. But I do know what's happening here." So it was very important to establish our own identity as being American, and part of being American was digging into our roots, everything from the old black blues and the old big bands and the old country and rockabilly and doo-wop and primitive rock and roll—everything—and that's what I really liked about X so much, they felt the same way . . . Woody Guthrie . . . I've done intros to songs where I've said, "Johnny Cash was just as important as Johnny Rotten was."

TONY CADENA: If you look at a map of Orange County, it's a huge area. If you go west, there's this affluent beach community, but Fullerton was more of a working-class environment. Some of us came from very stable families, but there was also a lot of turmoil, a lot of divorce, a lot of kids literally running their households.

MIKE PATTON: The Fullerton scene had its own vibe, separate from the rest of Orange County, separate from Hollywood, separate from the South Bay and the Church scene, with no beach scene affiliation whatsoever.

JEFF MCDONALD: The Fullerton bands got lumped into the beach hardcore scene just because they weren't from Hollywood, but they were totally different. The Adolescents, Agent Orange, and Social Distortion—bands like that were more eccentric and arty. They were from Orange County, but it wasn't a fascist thing.

MIKE NESS: Some of the Hollywood punks were like, "Oh, Orange County." There was this misconception that it was plush. I remember this tall skinny Adam Ant wanna-be—he'd been to London and got this look and brought it back to Hollywood. He'd say to me, "You guys are from Orange County. You don't know what's fucking happening." And I bet the guy had like—I bet his family was still together and paying his rent, you know? I just remember I told him I'd stick a Les Paul up his ass. Just because we live in a suburban setting, what? There isn't alcoholism in the home? There isn't child abuse? There isn't fucking abandonment? There isn't fucking addiction? You're fucking confused, man.

MIKE PATTON: The Black Hole was this crash pad that the Fullerton kids hung out in. Some of them would come to Eddie Joseph's place to practice because Eddie had a PA and all this cool gear and amps, but I never really hung out at the Black Hole. It was Mike Ness's apartment and you'd hear stories about how they thrashed it all the time . . . it was a disaster area where they all hung out and partied. I think it was probably Tony Adolescent who named it. The Black Hole was more pure than Eddie's place 'cause there weren't any older degenerates orbiting around. Eddie would just buy bags of pot, sheets of acid, tons of speed, and we'd all just go over there to jam and do free drugs. He just went though this incredible amount of inheritance money in a very short time. It was a very interesting spiral to participate in.

MIKE NESS: This guy Robert Omlit was my roommate at the Black Hole. He was an odd fellow and we used to take his Throbbing Gristle records and throw them across the street. I had a little phonograph that folded out. Dennis Danell and I used to listen to the Hersham Boys and Sham 69. It was my first apartment, and to help out with the rent I got Robert and this guy Kirby to move in. We spray-painted all the walls. It still amazes me that the neighbors weren't more aggressive in getting us out sooner 'cause it seemed like it lasted forever. The night of the downfall was the night I almost cut off my index finger and had to be rushed to emergency handcuffed to some girl and they kept me overnight for psychiatric evaluation. After I left, everyone just decided that that night was the night it should end, so they trashed the place and somebody stole my two-tone cowboy boots. It was called the Black Hole because there was fungus growing on the windows and shit. A real classy dump.

TONY CADENA: I was a sixteen-year-old high school kid when I met Eddie Joseph, leader of the Tubaflex Brothers and Brine, a rock oldies cover band who was playing a gig at Cypress College, and we became friends. Eddie single-handedly helped nurture a punk band scene in Fullerton. His generosity in loaning out professional amps and PA equipment to penniless high school fledgling bands like us [the Adolescents] earned him patron saint status of the Fullerton punk scene, which would eventually create its own Big Three: the Adolescents, Social Distortion, and Agent Orange.

MIKE ATTA: Fullerton bands like Agent Orange and the Adolescents started producing these great punk singles like "Blood Stains" and "Amoeba," which nobody could really deny them.

LISA FANCHER: "Amoeba" by the Adolescents is the song. Definitely was a phenomenon. "Amoeba" is a masterpiece of a single from any era of rock music.

TONY CADENA: I think bands like us and Social Distortion and Agent Orange were able to put out stuff that stood out from the hardcore scene because we had these diverse influences. I grew up listening to oldies radio. AM stations that played stuff like "Summer in the City" by the Lovin' Spoonful. So when you start learning to write songs, you gravitate toward what you're familiar with. We gave Rodney a tape and he started playing it on his show, which was really encouraging for us. Then it became a huge local hit. It made our scene explode. KROQ even had an "Amoeba" contest.

DARRELL WAYNE: Listeners were supposed to send in their interpretation of an amoeba. We got naked pictures, Barbie dolls in vats of Jell-O, and a box of human feces. The human feces was delivered with the morning mail and sat on the receptionist's desk until I came in at noon. All in all we received several hundred entries, some of them not smelling as bad as others.

TONY CADENA: We had radio hits because the songs were structured like fast pop music with a melody but a lot of anger, too. Another thing about Fullerton is its proximity to Disneyland. You couldn't walk down the street without getting called a faggot or getting beat up, but you're right next to the "Happiest Place on Earth." And they wouldn't let us in. Mike Ness and Dennis Danell and a bunch of people from Fullerton tried to go one day because Dennis's brother worked there and, they were like, "We're sorry, you can't come in."

MIKE NESS: I was fighting a lot 'cause I'd be walking down the streets of Fullerton with vermilion red hair and a leather jacket and a carload of construction workers would drive by and say, "Faggot." And you'd flip 'em off and then they'd turn around and you gotta box! You gotta fight!

TONY CADENA: It was a beautiful irony when they opened up the House of Blues at Disneyland last year and Social Distortion was one of the first bands to play it. And sold it out. You can't imagine how vindicating that was. I haven't talked to Mike in a long time, but I hope he had the same smile on his face that I had when I opened up the paper and saw the ad for the show!

chapter 35

Rob Henley at the premiere of the Penelope Spheeris film *The Decline of Western Civilization, Part 1,* 1981. Photo Credit: Gary Leonard

CLAUDE BESSY: In late 1979 or early 1980, I approached Penelope and said, "Let's make a fucking film of the scene." I came up with the title *The Decline of Western Civilization,* and Philomena talked to the bands and got them on, my idea totally.

PHILOMENA WINSTANLEY: We thought she did an excellent job.

CLAUDE BESSY: Yes, fantastic, 150 percent fantastic. The only problem I have is that she shoots them and leaves them no money.

PENELOPE SPHEERIS: This guy Ron told me that he had some buddies, a couple of insurance salesmen from the Valley who had a few extra bucks, that wanted to do a porno movie and would I be interested in directing it. I said, "No, absolutely not, but how about a punk rock movie?" So they wanted to look-see, and I brought them to the Starwood. We saw Darby and I said, "Is this crazy or what? It's fuckin' nuts here," and they said they wanted to do the movie. Initially it was only going to cost around fifteen grand because I was shooting in Super 8, but after we looked at some of the footage we agreed that the subject was more important, that it had to be shot in 16mm and blown up to 35mm. I told them that I thought the cost would go up to about eighty grand and they said, "Okay, we'll do it." It ended up costing about $120,000 altogether.

JENNY LENS: The *Decline* was an interesting but unfortunate view of the scene that was nothing like the one I knew. Most of the kids that Penelope interviewed were not central in my book . . . they were mostly a bunch of slobbering chauvinistic idiots and psychos from Orange County. They were no people I knew or had been photographing for the past four or five years. Penelope's movie focused on the homeless, aimless, self-destructive aspects as opposed to the creative, educated, even self-educated, fun people that I knew.

PENELOPE SPHEERIS: We went along and shot more and more shows, these guys would come out there, Jeff Goodman and Gordon Brown were their names, to see what was going on—and I remember the night we shot the Germs, they were scared that they were going to get sued because people were getting thrown around and stuff, it felt like utter mayhem. It was in this really little soundstage, Cherrywood Studios, they were really nervous because that was the craziest night of the shoot. And this wasn't even the last performance I had to shoot, so I was afraid they were going to pull the plug on me, but they didn't, they hung in there. Besides, nobody really got hurt there or at any of the shows; I think Darby got hurt more than anybody else.

JOHN DOE: I didn't realize Penelope Spheeris had an agenda until later. For better or worse, I think she got a good movie out of it, but she definitely supplied anybody and everybody with whatever kind of drug or alcohol they wanted, and I think she knew that she would get what she wanted by doing that. Get someone fucked up and roll the camera. And one of the biggest mistakes, that would have only added to the movie, was not having a little banner running underneath saying where, when, and under what circumstances the bands were filmed. When they filmed Darby, I heard they got him a bunch of smack and said, "Okay, go." It was early in the morning, and he never got up in the morning.

PENELOPE SPHEERIS: It's possible that Darby got extra fucked up for the filming. I don't really know. But there's a point where you say,

"Oh, he's fucked up, isn't this interesting and entertaining?" and then there's a point where it's "No, you can't even do this." Gary Hirstius, the audio engineer, is back there going, "Darby, the mic! Pick up the mic!" because he couldn't even pick up the microphone. You know, I didn't think back then that Darby got fucked up, I just thought that was how he was. I remember thinking, "This is unusable," because he wouldn't put his mouth up to the mic—I needed to get the lyrics on tape. I didn't really realize the impact of that performance until later, when it dawned on me that this says something bigger than the music itself would've said even if it had been recorded correctly. This is making a statement that's more important!

JOHN DOE: When they filmed X, Penelope's crew set up in Exene's and my house while we were out playing. We knew we'd be filming from two in the morning until the sun came up so we were drinking and snorting speed. We were all fucked up as well. Nobody gave a shit. Nobody cared. Nobody was looking at it as a career move. Didn't really think it would have any impact. Didn't care.

EXENE CERVENKA: I think *Decline* is a really important movie, but I think that the things that aren't in that movie are more important than the things that are. It makes me sad that you freeze a moment and that's the whole extent of its reality. That's what people believe it was. And it was just so limited. Penelope had an idea of what she wanted to portray and she portrayed it. A lot of stuff was left out . . . certainly a lot of the bands were left out.

JOHN DOE: The only regret is that the movie didn't show the true picture of the Los Angeles scene at the time. Penelope was very selective in the bands that she chose. The Screamers and the Weirdos were huge bands then. The Plugz were also very popular. They were much more musical and artistic in a pop art sort of way, but she picked all the really hardcore bands, the element coming out of Huntington Beach, and everybody in the original scene hated that crowd because it was all about uniformity and pointless violence.

EXENE CERVENKA: We played a show and came back to our house, and there was a film crew there. They had these big lights set up and our house was small, maybe six hundred square feet, little tiny bathroom, kitchen, bedroom, and there was nowhere to go, nowhere to hide. There was a light set up in the backyard, shone into the window of the bathroom, so the bathroom was all lit up . . . you couldn't get away . . . and they brought cases and cases of beer and speed and I think we kind of thought the movie wasn't gonna come out anyway. It was funny to us that anybody thought we were worth documenting. It got very grueling and they were still filming us at seven o'clock in the morning. I was in a blackout at that point. I had no idea I was even on camera, so I feel like there I was, this wild drunken girl, which I was, mouthy and kind of fucked up all the time, but there was another part of me that didn't get across and that makes me sad. Penelope was showing the dark side, she wanted to show the real, real dark stuff, and, of course, I was too young (twenty-four? twenty-five?) and naive to realize that I was in control of the situation and I could have asked them to leave or I could have left or I could have shut up. It was just, "Who are all these annoying people in my house when I'm trying to party?"

EUGENE: I didn't want to be in the thing, but Penelope kept on bugging me because there were no other skinheads in it. I said, "No" at first, and then finally relented. I said, "This is like some project for somebody's school, right? Like nobody's gonna see this thing, right?" She was like "No, nobody's gonna see it." Little did I know, a year later, I'd be stopped in the street all the time, there were thousands of posters with my picture. . . . I'd end up going home with some nice young girl and she'd have a poster of me on her fucking wall.

LEE VING: Fear played at the Fleetwood, and the footage she shot of our audience was used for all the bands once Penelope cut the movie together.

EUGENE: When she filmed at the Fleetwood when the fights were going down, I kind of un-directed that. I told everybody, "Okay, they got cameras in here, on tripods." Those big tripods were standing above the crowd, and I said, "Just drag your fights *behind* the cameras" 'cause there was some serious fighting in there that she wasn't even able to show 'cause it was so fucking gnarly.

Ant fashion victim: Darby Crash, just back from London, 1980.
Photo Credit: Jenny Lens

chapter 36

DON BOLLES: In 1980 Darby was about to go to London and he decided Rob Henley was in and I was out as the drummer. His excuse was that I was also playing with this band Vox Pop and Darby considered it a joke band.

BRENDAN MULLEN: In 1980 Darby booted regular drummer Don Bolles from the Germs to create a place for Rob Henley, his most recent regular squeeze. Henley was a sixteen-year-old beach urchin surfer who, like Darby, was a bit of a womanizing gigolo except he worked them with his dick in counterpoint to Darby's ability to work their minds. Henley became a sort of hetero-lecher version of Darby as he perpetuated the punk-slut-boy-on-drugs archetype left over from the glam era. Rob was Darby's penis in absentia for all the girls that wanted Darby. I overheard Darby once cussing out Robbie to deadly rival Gerber (who eventually wrenched Robbie away, as she'd done with his previous big romantic affairs with hitherto straight boys). Darby was despairing that his love was "fuckin' off sluttin'" somewhere in Beverly Hills, *again,* where-upon the shit-faced Gerb slurred with her drink splashing out of the glass, "How the fuck do you think I feel? I'm fucking him, too!" Henley regaled me on several occasions with numerous sordid tales of his dog-boy toilet sodomy exploits with several young heiresses in Beverly Hills and Bel Air. Rob was the secular end of Darby's mystical Circle One orbit. He was an adorable acne-faced kid straight outta one of those Larry Clark–Gus Van Sant chicken hawk fantasies, a real cutie proto–River Phoenix type. Darby announced he was going to London and instructed Lorna and Pat to teach Henley to play drums so the Germs could resume without Bolles on his return. He accused Don of disloyalty and of embarrassing the Germs by frequently appearing in public naked or dressed in women's clothes and dispatched Bill Bartell to tell Bolles he was out.

DON BOLLES: Darby was so heavily narcoticized that he was apparently unable to see irony in wanting to be the leader of the world's most outrageous punk band, yet he is embarrassed by someone's appearance in his band?

HAL NEGRO: Darby, it seemed that last year, was not having any fun. Everything about him became so serious and dark. It was like, "Lighten up." To be that serious 'cause your band wasn't going where you wanted . . . nobody's band was going where they wanted, but it was fun to play anyway.

BRENDAN MULLEN: There had to be other, deeper personal reasons, and claiming "embarrassment" seems more of a smokescreen for the real reason. It was said by several Germs insiders that Darby simply didn't much like Bolles' personality but kept him on for so long because it was less hassle than reprising the rigmarole the band went through during their first year to find a decent permanent drummer. Whatever the reasons, however, the two musicians—

Pat and Lorna—who had spent three years honing instrumental chops resented having to revert to their primitive garage-thrash beginnings when they weren't able to play at all, and after gamely attempting to teach some rudiments, they were dismayed to realize that the situation was hopeless—their student had absolutely no drumming instinct or musical talent whatsoever, not even by punk emotion-over-technique standards. Lorna quit in disgust first and Pat followed suit, thus ending the Germs as a band.

HELLIN KILLER: When he came back from London he was all like Mr. Adam and the Ants. I guess Amber introduced them.

GREG HETSON: Black Flag once showed up at Tower Records and totally disrupted Adam Ant during his big in-store appearance . . . they bombed the place with thousands of flyers saying BLACK FLAG KILLS ANTS ON CONTACT! This was how Black Flag greeted the New Romantic hype from London. It was great! L.A. punk rock ruled!

NICOLE PANTER: I couldn't understand why he was emulating someone as lame as Adam Ant. He came over to visit me in that getup and I was like, "Why?"

SHAWN STERN: During the summer of '80, just after he got back from England, Darby hung out at Skinhead Manor. He was rehearsing there with the Darby Crash Band. Darby would come over and party and get fucked up, he was hanging out with this little gay kid. I don't remember who was in his band . . . Bosco, and I don't remember who else. He wanted to start a new thing, but he was just getting fucked up all the time. He was partying a lot, and there were people shooting up speed at the Manor all the time. It was horrible.

MAGGIE EHRIG: I thought that Casey Cola was Darby's enabler. It just seemed like that was why they were friends. She enabled him, she got cash all the time, I don't know if it was from her mom or whatever, and she picked up for everything after Amber was removed from the picture when they got back from London. Casey had hard cash everywhere in her room . . . in socks, inside clothes, there was just money everywhere, in drawers, under the bed . . . everywhere you looked there was cash, and we were always rifling through her shit.

HELLIN KILLER: I barely knew Casey Cola personally, but her rep as a big heroin addict preceded her. That's always an easy way to get somebody to stick around, it's like, "Here, I'll get you dope . . . hang out with me and get high." It was all about "Let's go get a whole bunch of dope and I'm gonna do it all." He realized that all the people he'd been really close to, people that he'd loved and had loved him, had kind of written him off and moved on and he'd gone in a different direction. Nobody could help him.

BRENDAN MULLEN: The Starwood was an oversold sweatbox mess. It was wall-to-wall newer kids yet again. New recruits to suburban punk were multiplying at such a fast monthly rate, most of them may not have even known this gig was a Germs reunion since there was no public announcement whatsoever [till October '80, and then only in an obscure fanzine] that the Germs had even disbanded. None of these kids read nor cared about *Slash;* most of them had probably never even heard of it. Due to the influence of key skateboarder icons like Tony Alva, Duane Peters, Steve Olson, the punk word was spread throughout the outer 'burbs of the entire SoCal basin. Many of them had only just heard about this insane punk band the Germs, and they'd heard all the rumors about the Circle One cult of Darby, which held court at the Temple of Oki Dog. It had been about six months from the time of the trip to London, through the DC Band fallout, and the *Cruising* sessions, right up until now, early December 1980. This was the first chance many of these new kids had ever had to catch the Germs live. Pat Smear showed up with a spanking new guitar, beaming proudly that it was the first one he'd ever actually owned. The Germs finally rocked the way they were meant to live. This meant that Darby actually went out on a high note blast when he did himself in a few days later, but he really didn't seem that plastered onstage that night, another reason the show was so damned great.

DON BOLLES: Our reunion was great in almost every way. Me, Lorna, and Pat were so happy. It was like we were in love and had the best sex in our life. Me and Darby had been so civil to each other in rehearsal. I thought we could be a real band again.

RODNEY BINGENHEIMER: I DJ'ed the Germs' last show at the Starwood. They really packed the place. They were great that night.

JOHN DOE: When the Germs played the Starwood for the last time there were probably six hundred suburban kids and we didn't know everybody in the audience personally anymore.

DONNIE ROSE: Darby told people before the show the purpose of the Germs reunion was to demonstrate to the new punks how it was, what it was really all about in the old days. The reunion was a big success, and everybody in the band and the audience thought it was one of the best Germs shows ever. Darby should have taken the cue to quit screwing around, finally, and should have gone back to his writing to come up with a new Germs album . . . but he'd already insisted on going solo. But instead of doing either he decided to go ahead with this plan to kill himself—literally days after this gig.

JOHN DOE: If there was a bad audience or an audience he didn't understand, it would change again, you know? I was trying to give him more life experience 'cause he obviously hadn't had a lot of that. Darby had never had a day job since he left high school, he never really lived as a regular person. I was trying to tell him how many fucked-up jobs I'd already had and how writing and playing music was really a good job and it could be for him as well. There was no real reason given for why he felt that way, other than everyone at some point in their lives feels that way. We knew he was doing a lot of heroin, but it was before the point where people would consider doing an intervention. We didn't know about NA or anything like that back then, we knew what alcoholism was, but we didn't care. He was a gourmand . . . he became a bit of a gourmet, mostly doing heroin.

DON BOLLES: Darby was always talking about killing himself. In almost every interview, he always said that he would never be old. He was going to kill himself. When he was done doing what he wanted to do, he wanted to die. He said it so much, people thought he was a crying wolf kind of boy. He actually said at the rehearsal that he was only doing the reunion show to get enough heroin to kill himself.

GERBER: The last thing I said to him was, "I'm so fucking tired of you threatening to kill yourself! So you know what? Why don't you just stop fucking with me and stop fucking with everyone else and stop threatening. If you're gonna fucking do it, why don't you just go do it and stop trying to take people down with you." He said it to me all the time. I'm talking all the fucking time, man. He told me for years that he would "check out" by twenty-two.

CASEY COLA: I've been referred to as self-destructive, but, um, it's really odd because they would get mad at me for like getting too drunk and driving too fast and for them, they can walk into walls and cut up their arms and stuff, and it's not the same thing. Self-destruction is a means of showing, if you're cutting up your body and marking or whatever, it's your own, it's one thing that you can call completely and totally your own, and so much of people's identities is being taken away, and even being a punk, a lot of that's just sameness . . . you still need a personal identity . . . and where everybody's coming from, they're just seeing the same thing happen to them that's happening to their parents, the same wasted life, so they claim something as their own . . . their body is their own, they can always mark on that or cut on that or push up against somebody or shave their heads or color their hair, it's a mark of "This is my body."

PAT SMEAR: We had always talked about suicide and doing it at this certain time, this certain time in your life. So it was not a surprise. When his timetable came up, he was, coincidentally, fucked up enough in the head to want to do it anyway. He had a choice. He could either have been happy and said, "What a stupid idea that was," and just gone on with his life, or he could go, "Well, since this is the time I was going to kill myself anyway, and since I'm so unhappy, and my life's so fucked up, I may as well really do it." I don't know. That's sort of my theory.

CASEY COLA: We both just looked at each other and it was such a bad night we told people we were going to go kill ourselves. We said it and like nobody believed us, you know, but once that had been done, we were just going and we got started and we were doing it. Some people really have doubts about whether we really thought we were gonna die. People will swear to me that Darby didn't think he was going to die, and I know for a fact that he wanted to die. He wrote a suicide note, he knew how much drugs he was doing, and he did think he was going to die, and he did also think that I was going to die.

JOHN DOE: I'd talked to him a couple of times before that, because he was obviously unhappy, and Lorna had asked me to talk to him to try to keep him from doing this. I remember telling him that he was an amazing person. He just needed to get through it. I tried to encourage him to not be so sad. It obviously didn't work. I do remember saying that life was worth it even if it didn't seem like it.

I put my arm around him and tried to show him that people really cared for him. He had lost that belief.

CASEY COLA: Darby and I had the same kind of mood swings. If we were drinking, we'd forget the same things and we'd remember the same things. We'd been kidding around about it—we always talked about how we would kill ourselves and stuff. The time came and, um, we did it, and, um, he died, um . . . there are a lot more details. He died and I didn't. I did technically die for about three minutes, two and a half, three minutes—I read the police report. For me it was really hard because a lot of people said that Darby didn't mean for me to die and that he did it on purpose and stuff like that, which is untrue . . . he did mean for me to die 'cause I was dead for a few minutes. We'd worked out already that the drugs moved slower through my veins because we'd done drugs before and we knew what was going on . . . we'd talked about committing suicide together before, but not in a serious way.

GEZA X: Darby Crash was a premeditated would-be apocalyptic cult leader. He chose to do that, he chose his doomsday, and he did a bang-up job on it, I gotta say. It's lived on as the stuff of mythology. He flat out said he was gonna do it, and I think he did it exactly when he said he'd do it, according to something he wrote in 1975. He used to say, "I'm gonna kill myself in five years." He'd put some twisted spin on the Bowie song "Five Years." That's how he had all those girls weeping onstage 'cause they knew he was gonna die. He preyed on the female instinct to save things, especially certain types of female who go for guys who seem doomed, where the infatuated female is led into believing she will be the one who saves him from himself, or whatever. Darby was unhappy and he had it planned out that he was gonna get as far as he could and then off himself.

CASEY COLA: Darby and I had been doing consistent drugs for a month and a half. We'd really been trying to put our lives together. Everything was fucking up with our plan for this great house we were living in. He was supposed to be writing [but] he hadn't done anything, and he was supposed to be recording in January. We looked around the courtyard of the Hong Kong and said, "Man, fuck it, let's do it. Fuck this shit, it's not gonna ever change, it's not gonna get better. It's going to go on and on, we're going to be doing this same shit next year." We talked about whether we could get enough drugs, and that if he hit me up it would be murder—I can't do myself, because I have a manual-dexterity problem. We were each asking, "Are you sure? Are you sure?" He didn't coerce me, and I didn't talk him into it. We never talked each other into anything. I didn't make Darby die. I got water and a spoon. He wrote a note, which he didn't show me, but which I think said, "My life, my leather, my love goes to Bosco." He hit me up first and said, "Are you okay?" and I said, "Um, yeah." He put his hand at the small of my back and he said, "Just hold it, just stay there, just wait for me, okay? Just wait for me." He held me up for a second, then he hit a vein and laid himself against the wall and pulled me to him. It was almost like he forgot what we were doing, and he goes, "Wait a minute." And then he kissed me and said, "Well, bye."

GERBER: I think it was maybe about three-thirty in the morning and Pat called me, he said, "Are you sitting down?" I said no, and he said, "Sit down." He said, "He's gone."

NICOLE PANTER: I found out that morning. Someone called me on the phone and woke me up out of a dead sleep. I thought it was those assholes from Dangerhouse playing a phone prank, something they were famous for.

PHAST PHREDDIE: I remember going to the *Slash* offices on that Monday after Darby OD'd. Everyone was crying. Chris D. and I had a long conversation about death. Little did we know that John Lennon was being shot as we talked.

BELINDA CARLISLE: I was living at Disgraceland, when I got the phone call [that Darby died]. Then John Lennon died. It was a bit of a blur. Really bizarre.

RODNEY BINGENHEIMER: When Darby died, it was the same time that John Lennon died. I did a whole show of Beatles and Germs back and forth. One Beatle song and one Germs song as a tribute to Darby and John. Darby picked the wrong time to die. John Lennon kind of upstaged him.

BOB BIGGS: Darby was ambitious, but not so ambitious that he didn't kill himself. Darby wanted to be a rock star like Bowie, but he had such disdain for the institutions that would enable him to become that, so he settled for cult hero, and I think that was enough for him. He just didn't want to go through all the machinery and relentless ego maintenance that it takes to first become a rock star and then to stay one.

PENELOPE SPHEERIS: The night that I found out that Darby died, Bob Biggs and I were sleeping and the phone rang and I answered. I thought it was a joke, that people were fucking with you like they always did, a Germs joke. But no, it was really true that he had died. And then I thought, "Oh, my God, people are going to think that I'm terrible because I just did this movie and I have 5,000 posters sitting on the floor at *Slash* with him lying on the floor looking like he's dead." I felt so bad, but it was just ironic that I had chosen that particular frame as the advertisement for the movie because he looked dead, eyes shut. I felt sort of guilty, because I had done this movie and it was supposed to be all really fun and funny and then somebody that was supposed to be the hero of the whole scene had died. It sort of took the fun out of it. All of a sudden it had a terrible feeling to it. It had this slap-in-the-face kind of reality to it of "Oh, you little bastards, you wanted to play mean and gnarly and bad and be as perverted and as sick as you could be. Okay, slap-in-the-face reality: Well, how's death for ya?" That was the way it felt. It was kind of fucked. It also felt like the end of an era. That's what you thought: "Okay, now that the symbol of the whole movement is gone, I guess the movement's over."

NICOLE PANTER: If you saw *Suburbia*, you saw the funeral basically. It was this really sad little punk rock funeral. Darby looked like they'd put green clay on his face and his hair was dyed black.

JUDITH BELL: After Darby died it was really depressing. "This just isn't fun. It's not cool, and these people are just a really sorry lot." When Claude left L.A. for Europe never to return, too, that was it. Claude was the one with the humor and he took a lot of that with him.

chapter 37

The Go-Go's celebrate signing with IRS Records with Miles Copeland, 1981. Fame, fortune, and MTV lurk. Photo Credit: Gary Leonard

BRENDAN MULLEN: By October-November 1981, *Beauty and the Beat,* the Go-Go's debut album, hit number one on the *Billboard* album charts. It would go on to sell millions of copies.

MILES COPELAND: IRS's target was to sell 100,000 Go-Go's records. We figured that if we could do that, that was a good starting point, and we'd build from that. It just so happened that the song kinda clicked and the timing was right, momentum was there. It was good solid pop and it was refreshing and it was the summer and it just clicked.

HAL NEGRO: When I saw the Go-Go's on the cover of *Rolling Stone,* I was stoked. These were girls I knew. I felt like it enhanced my stature with my little sister's friends. Fourteen-year-old girls were impressed.

MARGOT OLAVERRA: I had no indication that it would be that successful. My mind wasn't set on those heights. I was really pissed off. *Beauty and the Beat* was number one and I was squatting in an East Village apartment full of holes. I was still being recognized in the club scene as a Go-Go. That sucked, it really sucked. I had great resentment and hostility. Of course, when the album came out, all of the songs were songs I'd collaborated on. I was written off of the copyright, just erased from "How Much More"—I couldn't get a lawyer at first until the record hit number one. Then I had lawyers calling me!

ELISSA BELLO: I was in this mall in Buffalo when I heard "Crazy" playing in a record store. This is a song I'd played for two years and here I was in this mall in Buffalo three thousand miles away listening to it. Then I got an eyeful of this poster with all the girls on it. It was bizarre. It was like somebody hit me on the back of the head. When you move from a place you're born and raised in, it's like your history, your past is back there and it's never brought out, and then when you go back and there's something you were doing that nobody there knows about, it's so weird . . . it brought my two worlds together at that moment. They were playing at Madison Square Garden with the Police and I wanted to go see them and Belinda pretended she didn't know who I was.

EXENE CERVENKA: What they were doing was so different from what I was doing that it wasn't like a personal thing when they exploded. We were doing fine with what we were doing—we had all that critical acclaim, which we didn't know how to process. They had a lot more commercial potential than we did. I was just amazed. I couldn't believe that that band that used to play at the Masque was suddenly on the cover of *Rolling Stone*. It was unbelievable. But then a lot of odd things had happened. I'd rather that the Go-Go's were on the cover of *Rolling Stone* than Darby commit suicide. I guess it would be in the positive column.

MARK MOTHERSBAUGH: When it launched in 1981, we thought Music Television, MTV, was gonna change music for the good. Like artists are going to be back in control and there'd be a renaissance period. Instead, MTV helped turn pop culture into some big marketing device. MTV took something that we took as very personal and integral to our art form and, about six months after its inception, made it part of their home market network for the record companies. MTV did a very big disservice to pop music. The pre-MTV days will be remembered as the end of a renaissance period for the arts and pop culture in the West.

GINGER CANZONERI: A lot of the Go-Go's early success came from MTV. That first video for "Our Lips Are Sealed." Miles Copeland was shooting a Police video at the time and he borrowed the camera-man and said, "Here, go out with the girls, just go for a few hours." And the first video was just them driving around in a car. But I think it was a really good call on his part.

MILES COPELAND: Prior to MTV, the game was all about radio. And TV was actually something you did not do. I remember the manager of ZZ Top saying to me that he's never going to put his group on TV. Wanna see the group? Gotta buy tickets to the show. And he actually had this philosophy and he did not do TV and ZZ Top did not do TV. They did not do MTV for a long, long time. Most of the pro-gressive rock-era bands refused to support MTV. Everybody who was an established act turned their noses up to MTV. So MTV basically went to whomever they could get—beggars can't be choosy—and so MTV paid attention to the Police, to the punk bands. And in return, the punk bands paid attention to MTV because they were one of the few people who would play their stuff. And the Go-Go's totally benefited from this. The Go-Go's, when you saw them, they were fun and disarming and all that. And you could listen to them at the volume that you wanted to, and you could put forward the visual that you wanted it to be because you were controlling the camera and whatever. So you're sitting and there's an audience tuning in and, "Gee, this stuff is actually quite good. I quite like this stuff." MTV coincided with the new generation, with the punk generation, and the marriage worked. Then everybody woke up in the industry to what the power of MTV was, and then all of a sudden ZZ Top said, "Shit, we're going to make videos," and bang, look what happened to them. All of a sudden there was a rebirth of a lot of those bands. The ones who actually got into what MTV was and came up with a kind of a thing. So all of a sudden ZZ, with these long beards, they start selling shitloads of records, because they figured out that this vehicle was a whole new way of selling stuff.

EXENE CERVENKA: In life, no matter what you do, you have to deal with the reality outside the perfect world that you're trying to create for yourself and your friends and your family, so going to see the Blasters and the Gun Club play and drinking all night and listening to 78's is a wonderful thing, but then in the morning there is such a thing as MTV. Nobody liked it. Nobody wanted to be part of it.

Everybody was dragged kicking and screaming into it. The more noble people, the hardcore bands, could just say "fuck you" 'cause they already had a really strong network of kids who would go see them play and buy their records and follow them and it was more like a huge underground thing, where our underground thing, which was never that big, we were gonna have to play on TV and get people to find out about us . . . and no, we didn't really want to do MTV and it would have been really nice if the whole world could have found out about that scene without having to compromise any of it, but it was just a necessary evil and everybody had to do it.

BRENDAN MULLEN: Although obviously nowhere near as commercially successful as the Go-Go's new wave pop, hardcore kept going somehow. In 1981 Black Flag recruited their fourth lead singer, a former Washington, D.C., Type-A ice cream parlor manager named Henry Rollins.

HENRY ROLLINS: The Go-Go's never really figured into my thinking. I had nothing against them and thought they were a sturdy pop unit. They were playing pop music and it was a KROQ thing and we were on Mars with what we were doing. I joined Black Flag by showing up at an audition in New York City in the summer of 1981. I sang two sets with them in a small practice place and they gave me the job. The first days were a jolt because they were living hard and low to the ground and I had no experience like that before. It was a bend in the road as they say. I had worked hard all my short life at multiple jobs. I thought I was quite the hard-working taskmaster type. Ginn was ten times this. When I first joined the band, we got into a rehearsal regimen that was quite an undertaking. We were at it hours a day. I thought that a few days in, I was ready. Ginn told me that I was nowhere near ready. I month later, I saw that he was right, of course. By the time we hit the stage for real, there was no real nervousness on my part. I knew my stuff. It was not a warm-up show. We went out there and kicked their asses.

BRENDAN MULLEN: With Rollins in front, Black Flag released *Damaged*, which consisted mostly of songs written by Greg Ginn and Chuck Dukowski before Dukowski left the band. To this day, *Damaged* is still their best-known album, and probably one of the most influential in hardcore. They toured relentlessly in support of it.

HENRY ROLLINS: Black Flag was a committed band of people who wanted to create and perform totally unrestrained musical expression. This is not the kind of thing that got you let in the front door. In fact, there was a struggle. I think that Greg is one of the most unique figures in the indie record world. He had a route he wanted to take and he went for it and a lot of people benefited from his determination. I'm sure that there is a chance that we inspired some bands in other towns by coming through and playing. I think American hardcore probably opened some doors and shook up the record industry a great deal.

JOHN DOE: X survived because we had that larger life experience. Exene had it. And so had Billy and so had I. Billy had played with Gene Vincent. And D.J. [Bonebrake] was a drummer without being a dummy.

RAY MANZAREK: We got ten thousand dollars to make the second record, *Wild Gift*. Basically it was the same thing. We went to another studio, paid the engineer, and did the second one with Clay Rose. Unfortunately, nobody made any money. I never got paid till the third album, after they went to Elektra Records. By the third album, I was actually able to get a producer's fee. Then our budget went from ten thousand to a hundred thousand and the record sounded the same! You listen to record one, two, three, four, you're like, "Yeah, that's X, man. That's the X sound." Whether we made it for ten thousand or a hundred thousand, it didn't matter. And Elektra was never able to sell any more records than Slash. The only difference between the first two and the last two was that we all got paid.

EXENE CERVENKA: More money [for a record budget] means you can decide to stop and go eat sushi and go drink Irish coffee for four hours and come back and go, "Where were we?" Yeah, we had a little clubhouse thing going on a lot.

D.J. BONEBRAKE: X was the first unsigned band to headline the Greek Theater—that was in '81. In L.A. we were a phenomenon. We were unsigned . . . and we headlined the Greek, which had a capacity of 6,500.

RAY MANZAREK: We did the Greek Theater. I played with them. It was like the X All-Star Show and Revue. I came out, Top Jimmy came out, and we closed the whole thing off with "Roadhouse Blues." I thought, "This is it, man. Punk rock is gonna take over. X headlining the Greek Theater." Man, it was fucking electrical. I left the stage and took the microphone and said, "Keep the fire burning." And the audience just screamed, "Yeah." God, what a fuckin' night that was.

TOP JIMMY: After playing the Greek I found myself at four-thirty in the morning walking down Vine Street and Fountain and barely having enough for a cup of coffee and a doughnut at the Winchell's there. But a few hours before, man, I'm king . . . I'm in front of all these thousands of people at the Greek, and a few hours later, I'm just walking down the street . . . back to the real world.

Pat Smear with Nirvana (*left to right:* Krist Novoselic, Dave Grohl, Kurt Cobain, Smear) on MTV, 1994. Photo Credit: Frank Micelotta/ImageDirect

GREG HETSON: The Dark Years of Punk were from '84 to '90. That was when the audience for punk rock had basically dwindled to nothing. A lot of it had to do with the violence at gigs. In Los Angeles, especially, it was completely outta hand . . . and it didn't help when cops overreacted every time . . . and then the violence fed off the violence and then people were afraid to go. It was also the time when speed metal took over on one side . . . and the big hair MTV bands were on the other . . . and so punk rock sort of fell between the cracks . . . it was written off as extinct since they thought they had already assimilated the entire "punk" culture with all the big New Wave radio pop bands: the Cars, Blondie, the Knack, Devo, the Go-Go's . . . and punk was shit out of luck as far as getting any serious commercial airplay outside of Rodney on the ROQ till Nirvana.

BRENDAN MULLEN: The mid-to-late '80s was a weird no-man's-land for punk rock . . . there were very few punk bands still knocking around that meant anything outside of small bars and clubs and a tiny youth center or two. Even Fugazi or No Means No didn't yet have the medium-sized concert audience they enjoyed later on.

The speed metal bands like Slayer and Metallica who roared up around '82–'83 may not have tried to emulate the L.A. hardcore bands—they always claim it was the so-called 'New Wave of British Metal' musically, but these guys took the independent DIY aspect from the SoCal hardcore punkers—the zines and the tape trading—and ran with it . . . without giving 'em any credit or props for priming new, young rock audiences to be receptive to super-intense sped-up metalloid punk rock à la Fear, Black Flag, and their ilk. But it was Suicidal Tendencies that really kicked the doors down with their punk/speed-metal hybrid classic "Institutionalized," which was all over MTV. Slayer eventually did a TSOL cover years later when someone probably told 'em it was a good career move to acknowledge that the L.A. hardcore sped-up punk chord thrash thing existed years before thrash chord metal. Many mistook Metallica for a Punk band during their early days . . . and that's my theory—dumbed-down speed metal played with precision chops took away all the kids who would theoretically have latched onto Black Flag and Co.

GREG HETSON: But the Jerks were nose-diving anyway, the Dead Kennedys had peaked, the Adolescents had broken up, Black Flag was in its last gasp . . . TSOL had gone big-hair bandana rock with a line-up of no original members . . . SST as a label was evolving away from strict punk and Ginn was really into recording Hüsker Dü, the Meat Puppets, Sonic Youth, and many other early pre-grunge art bands.

BRENDAN MULLEN: REM became the Beatles of that whitebread soft-handed "cool alterna-geek" college radio set, many of whom were trust-funded babies who could afford to work as interns at major labels to a point later on where they damn near took over the record biz until studio gangster rap, aggro rock-rap, nu metal, and the boy dance troupes smoked most of 'em out by early 2K.

GREG GRAFFIN: By 1985–86 there weren't any rock-media-defined "punk rock" bands left. There were very few new punk labels. That was the big picture context; it was also one of the reasons Bad Religion was hailed as fresh when the *Suffer* album came out in '87—hardly anybody else was playing melodic punk with a hardcore edge anymore. We were still well below the mainstream radar as we still are.

GREG HETSON: Serious rock critics ignored us. It's also accurate to say, without seeming too biased, that our good friend Brett was really getting Epitaph up and running as a viable enterprise for getting the records well distributed.

GREG GRAFFIN: In Germany Bad Religion was feted at the time as the "saviors of the punk flame" . . . we were able to tour 1,000-seater venues in Europe after *Suffer,* but could only get booked in tiny punk clubs in America outside of L.A. County if we were lucky . . . but then things changed after *Suffer* and, of course, there was a before and an after for punk rock when Nirvana popped up on MTV a couple of years later.

BRETT GUREWITZ: In 1990 I was still working out of Westbeach, with no formal Epitaph offices, when I signed Down by Law, Rancid and the Offspring. The Offspring's *Smash* album sold nine million worldwide, a landmark feat for an indie with no help from a major label to keep up with pressing and distribution.

BRENDAN MULLEN: Together with multiplatinum and gold sales from the Offspring, Rancid, and other strong catalogue titles from the likes of Down by Law, Pennywise, NoFx, and, of course, Bad Religion, Epitaph grossed $64 million in 1994.

BRETT GUREWITZ: Since that time I've received countless offers from major corporate conglomerates to sell.

✳ ✳ ✳

BRENDAN MULLEN: I was working as a paid consultant to facilitate the opening of the Viper Room circa 1993. The club was right across the street from the SST Super Store on Sunset where Pat Smear was a store clerk. The Strip was absolutely the wrong location for this store, which would have been better off down on Melrose. It was a business hawking 100 percent SST Record releases and Black Flag shirts, one for every record sleeve . . . Black Flag baseball hats, woolen ski caps, shorts, you name it. Everything but Black Flag lunch boxes. But there were never any customers. During lunch breaks, I'd go over there to share a joint with Pat and buy a CD to give him something to do. He'd invariably sit on a stool enthusiastically chain-smoking joints like cigarettes, surrounded by at least three or four little girls who'd wandered in off the street and were squatting lotus style on the floor in front of him. I was fascinated. It was that special voodoo, something Pat had that only the little girls understood. Suddenly the spirited, giggling hijinks was silenced for a second when the phone rang. When Pat got off a few minutes later, his look was completely changed. He was absolutely poker-faced. All stoned mirth completely vanished. I said, "Okay? Anything wrong, Pat?" He lowered his voice away from the little girls on the floor. He seemed stunned. "What is it?" "That was Kurt Cobain on the phone. He says he wants me to play in Nirvana . . . and I don't think it was a prank. He wants me to go up to Seattle to play with the band. But please keep it quiet. Please don't mention this to anybody in case it doesn't work out. This is a band I actually like."

MIKE WATT: When Pat Smear joined Nirvana he was as happy as can be. His whole dream was to be Bowie's guitar player or Brian May from Queen and here he was playing the Forum. And Kurt's on the other side and his eyes were like, "I do not want to be here . . . this is shit . . . this is jive." Kurt really wanted to be a little punk band. He wanted to be in the van. Kurt loved Black Flag, loved the Germs . . . all the SST bands. The past shaped me into what I am today . . . I'm forty-three, I'm going up against cats who weren't even born then, but whenever there's a Warped tour, they ask me to do a week. If they're gonna sell punk rock, they gotta deal with some of the ghosts, I guess. I'm not just doing a fucking sentimental journey. I haven't changed at all . . . zero . . . I got grayer hair, the health is not as strong, but I've even started playing with a pick again. I still think of punk as a state of mind and not a style, so how can it go out of fashion? "Alternative" and "new wave" were horrible terms, totally limiting words. "Punk" can mean anything. That's how it started out—it was whatever you want to chain it to—but understand this: It's always gonna bust out on its own, there's always gonna be something that's kind of wild and you're gonna call it punk. It's like what the Renaissance cats had to do. Pettibon had me read this autobiography of Cellini, he's in the 1500s and he's trying to get his own thing going despite these huge institutions . . . this has always been around . . . I was lucky.

KID CONGO POWERS: The last time I saw Jeffrey Lee, he was really wasted at one of Pleasant's benefit concerts. He was going through a kind of cleaned-up period and then it went really bad. We had done some Gun Club reunion shows—the band was really good but he was really wasted . . . he looked terrible. We'd played four or five months earlier at the Viper Room and he was great, in great shape, everyone was like, "Wow." But he would very quickly fluctuate—you could tell by his appearance. It's not a fond memory—that was the last time I saw him. The last time I talked to him we'd been offered good money for a reunion tour. We talked about it and said, "This is too horrible." We knew people would come, but it seemed horrible to us, like going backward. We had kind of lived through it already, we knew it was kind of bogus, so we decided not to do it. Jeffrey was gonna move to New York. I'd already just moved there, and I'd been talking to him by phone. He'd gone to his father's in Utah, which was where he died. He was trying to finish his book, *Go Tell the Mountain*—he'd call me and read me stuff, we'd laugh—we thought the book was hysterically funny. We'd been talking about doing stuff here in New York, so we'd been calling each other. One time when his mother answered the phone I said, "That's weird, why's his mother answering?" And Marge said, "Oh, you heard then?" And I said no. And she said, "Jeffrey died." And I just . . . whew . . . I can't even believe it. I was calling to tell him I'd gotten these musicians to do something if he'd just get over here, so I was really mad 'cause I'd been in New York a week and I had to fly back to L.A. to go to his fucking funeral. You bastard! But he was a sweetheart, too. It was like my brother dying or something.

BRENDAN MULLEN: Claude and Philomena moved to England, where they spent seven years in London and Manchester. Claude worked as a VJ at the Hacienda Club in Manchester and for Rough Trade in London, writing sleeve notes and producing videos for the Throbbing Gristle and the Fall. He also produced this amazing William S. Burroughs video made up from some rare footage of the old mummy himself.

PHILOMENA WINSTANLEY: Claude was hired at Rough Trade to do promotion work, but he wouldn't promote any of the bands he didn't like. He hated the Raincoats, for example. And they told him,

"Look, you're supposed to be our promo person!" But he wouldn't do it so they fired him.

BRENDAN MULLEN: After that Claude and Philly moved to Barcelona, Spain, where Claude took up drawing and painting, and teaching English.

JAVIER ESCOVEDO: When the Zeros played Barcelona in '95, we had dinner with Claude and Philomena, and at the end of our show we got him up on "Pushin' Too Hard." He was so ripped it came out like "Pussin Too Hard"! "Pussin too hard" became our battle cry for the rest of the tour. I had a feeling that he wasn't into old punk bands getting back together, but he seemed to have a blast that night anyway.

BRENDAN MULLEN: In '99, Claude died from lung cancer at his home in Barcelona. Philly was by his side. He was 54.

STEVE SAMIOF: It's really unbelievable it wasn't his liver that quit him. Unbelievable. He taught me how to drink with abandon; he was my guru. He taught me red wine, and he taught me brandy. And when we'd get loaded, we'd lament all the assholes in the world, wishing they'd fuck off and die. And while I hadn't seen him in fifteen years, it broke my heart to hear the news: The asshole, he fucked off and died.

TOMATA DU PLENTY: One day I found this little kiddie paint kit in an alley off Hollywood Boulevard. I lived off Hollywood Boulevard. And I just started drawing. First I drew a picture of my cat. Then my boyfriend. Then my landlady. Just people you know? Then Bob Forrest of Thelonius Monster said, "You should show this stuff." And he was great. He brought me to the Zero Gallery, which is also on Hollywood Boulevard, and they let me hang all my little ten-dollar paintings.

PLEASANT GEHMAN: The last time I saw Tomata was at this, uh, art show he had at Beyond Baroque. I was reading and Vampira was reading and Tomata looked like he was really sick but he was great. He looked more gaunt than usual, but he was still awesome. He was working and productive right up until the very end. During his memorial everyone was crying but laughing hysterically, too, 'cause of all the stories people were telling. Vampira was there and this '50s female wrestler called the Cheetah Woman. And like all the Screamers were there, a bunch of crazy drag queens in their

'60s or '70s that had known him in many different weird ways. It was a crazy collection of people. Tomata would talk to anybody, and he'd cultivated friends from a million circles of people.

EXENE CERVENKA: I'm very unaware of my own age or place in life. I'm very present-tense-oriented. So for me it's like, "What are your goals . . . what do you hope to achieve?" And now they're asking, "What did you think would happen? Give us your whole overview of the past and what do you think will happen in the future." Which to me is just not interesting . . . I just kind of go along.

HELLIN KILLER: I got married, had kids, and kind of stepped out of it. I made a conscious decision . . . one day I said, "This isn't what it used to be anymore." I'm going through the motions of trying to hang out and I think I'm beating a dead horse . . . I'm just not into smashing windows anymore.

source notes

Pg. 2, 4 Jim Morrison, from the Doors' first Elektra Records bio, 1967. Courtesy Danny Sugerman.

Pg. 7 David Bowie, from an interview with Lance Loud (*Details* magazine, 1992). Used with permission.

Pg. 7, 10, 17 Zory Zenith, courtesy of Chuck "New Wave" Nolan.

Pg. 9, 10, 25 Tom Ayres (see above).

Pg. 9 Terry Atkinson (see above).

Pg. 10 Kristian Hoffman (see above).

Pg. 11, 13 Lori Lightning (see above).

Pg. 11 Steve Priest (see above).

Pg. 12 Amy Freeman (see above).

Pg. 20 Leee "Black" Childers, from *Too Much, Too Soon: The Make Up and Break Up of the New York Dolls* by Nina Antonia (Omnibus Press, 1998).

Pg. 19, 20 Syl Sylvain (see Leee "Black" Childers).

Pg. 36 Paul Beahm, aka Bobby Pyn, aka Darby Crash, from *Flipside,* used by permission.

Pg. 41, 42, 43, 45, 46 Joan Jett, from an interview with Jaan Uhelski, used by permission.

Pg. 44 Micki Steele, from an interview with Ben Edmonds, *Mojo,* used by permission.

Pg. 48 Joan Jett, from the *New York Rocker,* used with permission from Andy Schwartz.

Pg. 49 Gary Stewart, used with permission from Ben Edmonds.

Pg. 39, 40, 42, 43, 56, 67, 68, 73, 74, 135 Pat Smear, from *Lexicon Devil: The Fast Times of Darby Crash and the Germs* (Feral House). Used by permission of Adam Parfrey, courtesy of Bill Borley.

Pg. 50, 60, 99, 100, 101, 102, 138 Black Randy, used with permission from Charles M. Young from his own interview.

Pg. 60 Tom Lambert, *Los Angeles Times,* December 6, 1976.

Pg. 64, 65, 87, 88, 90, 212, 214, 216 Tomata du Plenty, courtesy of Jack Rabid (The Big Takeover).

Pg. 67 Bobby Pyn, from an interview with *Flipside,* used by permission.

Pg. 76 Editorial, *Slash,* July 1977, used with permission from Bob Biggs.

Pg. 103, 107, 164 Gorilla Rose, courtesy of Doug Cavanaugh.

Pg. 111 Claude Bessy, excerpted from *Slash,* used with permission from Bob Biggs.

Pg. 120 Johnny Stingray, from sleeve notes to *Controllers* CD, courtesy of Dionysius Records.

Pg. 127 Claude Bessy, excerpted from *Slash,* used with permission from Bob Biggs.

Pg. 127 Darby Crash, from an interview with *No,* January 1979. Courtesy Chris D. and Bruce Kalberg.

Pg. 144 Pat Smear, Bobby Pyn, Lorna Doom from an interview with *Flipside,* used by permission.

Pg. 152 Lamar Saint John. Excerpted from *Punk '77: An Inside Look at the San Francisco Rock 'n' Roll Scene, 1977.* Published by Re/Search Publications (www.researchpubs.com). Used with permission from James Stark.

Pg. 167, 169, 171 Terry Graham, courtesy of Doug Cavanaugh.

Pg. 176 "Local Shit," excerpted from *Slash,* September 1979, used with permission from Bob Biggs.

Pg. 185 Pleasant Gehman, from *Escape from Houdini Mountain* (Manic D Press © 2000). Used by permission.

Pg. 198 Darby Crash, excerpted from *No,* circa January 1979. Courtesy Chris D. and Bruce Kalberg.

Pg. 201–202 Richard Meltzer, excerpted from the *Los Angeles Times,* December, 1979.

Pg. 212, 236, 246 Jeffrey Lee Pierce, excerpted from *Go Tell the Mountain: The Stories and Lyrics of Jeffrey Lee Pierce,* copyright 1998, used by permission of the Jeffrey Lee Pierce Estate, courtesy of 2.13.61 Press.

Pg. 248 Wayzata de Camerone, excerpted from "The Zero Chronicles," an unpublished memoir by Mark Boyd.

Pg. 265, 266, 267 Casey Cola interviews courtesy of Ella Black (Kari Leuschner) and Rene Daalder.

cast of characters

X-8: Cofounder, *Flipside* fanzine

Eugene: Star of *The Decline of Western Civilization*

Gerber (aka Michelle Bell):

Pooch (Pat di Puccio): Cofounder, *Flipside* fanzine

Mugger: Former roadie, Black Flag

Phranc: Former member, Nervous Gender, Catholic Disciplines; America's Favorite Jewish Lesbian Folksinger

Robo: Drummer, Black Flag

Trifle: Plunger sister

David Allen: Graphic designer, *Slash, Art Trouble*

Kittra Allen: Former manager, the Go-Go's

Dave Alvin: Former member, the Blasters; solo artist

Trudie Arguelles: Former Plunger sister; housewife, mother

Skot Armstrong: Guerrilla theater, mail activist, founder of *Science Holiday* magazine

Ron Asheton: Former guitarist, the Stooges

Chris Ashford: Founder, What? Records

Terry Atkinson: Journalist

Mike Atta: Guitarist, the Middle Class

Tom Ayres: Record producer; co-owner, Rodney's English Disco

Alice Bag: Lead singer, the Bags

Barry Barnholtz: Co-owner, Rodney's English Disco; movie mogul

K.K. Barrett: Drummer, the Screamers, Black Randy, and the Metro Squad; art director

Paul Beahm (aka Bobby Pyn, aka Darby Crash): Former lead singer, the Germs, the Darby Crash Band (deceased 1980)

Nickey Beat: Drummer, the Weirdos, the Germs, the Bags

Judith Bell: Graphic designer (the Gun Club's *Fire of Love*)

Elissa Bello: Original drummer, the Go-Go's

Claude Bessy (aka Kickboy Face): Founder, *Angeleno Dread* fanzine; chief writer, *Slash* magazine; lead singer, Catholic Discipline (deceased 1999)

Bob Biggs: founder and president, Slash Records

Blank Frank: Junkie, street hustler (deceased)

Rodney Bingenheimer: Partner, Rodney's English Disco; disc jockey, KROQ; "Mayor of Sunset Strip"

Don Bolles: Drummer, the Germs

D.J. (Don) Bonebrake: Drummer, the Eyes, X

Billy Bones: Former lead singer, the Skulls

Black Randy: Former lead singer/songwriter, Black Randy and the Metro Squad; cofounder, Dangerhouse Records (deceased)

David Bowie: Musician; songwriter; actor; producer; Internet entrepreneur; Godhead

Angela Bowie: Former wife-muse of David Bowie; musician; author (*Backstage Passes*)

David Brown: Former keyboard player, the Screamers; founder, Dangerhouse Records

Denny Bruce: Manager, former A&R director

Tony Cadena: Lead singer, the Adolescents

Charlotte Caffey: Bassist, the Eyes; guitarist, the Go-Go's

Ginger Canzoneri: Former manager, the Go-Go's

Belinda Carlisle: Lead singer, the Go-Go's; solo artist

Sean Carrillo: Artist

Gerry Casale: Guitarist/keyboardist, Devo

Peter Case: Former singer/guitarist, the Nerves, the Plimsouls; solo artist

Exene Cervenka: Singer, X; poet

Leee "Black" Childers: Former MainMan publicist; former manager, Johnny Thunders

Casey Cola: Former friend of Darby Crash

Kerry Colonna: Photographer

Miles Copeland: Founder, IRS Records

Richard Cromelin: Journalist

Cherie Currie: Former lead singer, the Runaways

Chris D. (aka Chris Desjardin): Former lead singer, the Flesheaters; *Slash* magazine contributor; founder, Ruby Records

Rene Daalder: Writer, director, *Massacre at Central High, Population One*

Martha Davis: Lead singer, the Motels

John Denney: Former lead singer, the Weirdos

Wayzata de Camerone: cofounder, Zero Zero club; teacher

Michael des Barres: Former lead singer, Silverhead; actor

Pamela des Barres: Former groupie; author

Levi Dexter: Former lead singer, Levi and the Rockats

John Doe: Singer, bass player, X; actor

Maggie Ehrig: Former friend of Darby Crash

Lisa Fancher: Founder, Frontier Records

D.D. Faye: *Back Door Man* contributor

Doug Fieger: Lead singer, the Knack

Robbie Fields (aka Posh Boy): Founder, Posh Boy Records

Jed the Fish: Disc jockey, KROQ

Lita Ford: Former lead guitarist, the Runaways; solo artist

Kim Fowley: Producer/songwriter, the Runaways; solo artist

Jackie Fox: Former bass player, the Runaways

Amy Freeman: Former regular, Rodney's English Disco

Pleasant Gehman: Cofounder, *Lobotomy* fanzine; columnist; author; former member, Screamin' Sirens

Paul Greenstein: Former promoter, collector, historian

Terry Graham: Drummer, the Bags, the Gun Club

Jack Grisham: Former lead singer, Vicious Circle; lead singer of original TSOL

Matt Groening: Artist

Bibbe Hansen: Former actress; Andy Warhol star; daughter of Fluxus artist Al Hansen; Beck's mother

Fayette Hauser: Friend of Tomata du Plenty

Willie Herron: Member of Los Illegals; cofounder, the Vex club

Greg Hetson: Cofounder, Circle Jerks; guitarist, Bad Religion

Kristian Hoffman: Former keyboard player, the Mumps

Gus Hudson: *Flipside* scribe, producer

Steven Hufsteter: Former lead guitarist; songwriter, the Quick; film composer

Amber Hunt: Former friend of Darby Crash

Barbara James: Former scenester

Joan Jett: Former singer, rhythm guitarist, the Runaways; lead singer/guitarist, Joan Jett and the Blackhearts; actress (*Light of Day, The Rocky Horror Picture Show*)

Mary Kay: Former bass player, the Dogs

Tony Kinman: Singer/bassist, the Dils, Rank and File

Hellin Killer: Plunger sister; bloodied Sid Vicious In Dallas, '78

Bunky Kirchenheimer: Former promoter

Kari Krome: Songwriter, the Runaways

Harvey Kubernik: Music journalist; publicist; spoken word record producer

Bobby Lambert: Former member, Les Petites Bon-Bons

Tito Larriva: Former lead singer/guitarist, the Plugz, the Cruzados; cofounder, Fatima Records; film composer; actor

Stan Lee: Guitarist, the Dickies; owner of Iggy Pop's *Raw Power* jacket

Jenny Lens: Photographer

Robert Lopez: Former guitarist, the Zeros; solo artist (as "El Vez," the Mexican Elvis)

Jeff McDonald: Singer/guitarist, Redd Kross

Laurie Maddox (aka Lori Lightning): Former groupie

Russell Mael: Lead singer, Sparks

Toby Mamis: Manager, Alice Cooper, the Runaways, Blondie

Ray Manzarek: Former keyboard player, the Doors; producer (X's *Los Angeles, Wild Gift,* and *Under the Big Black Sun*)

Susan Martin: Cofounder, SSB (Some Serious Business), an independent arts promotion company

Kristine McKenna: Journalist; art historian

Keith Morris: Founding lead singer, Black Flag; lead singer, Circle Jerks, Midget Handjob

Mark Mothersbaugh: Lead singer, Devo; film and television composer

Brendan Mullen: Founder, the Masque; drummer, Arthur J. and the Gold Cups, Hal Negro and the Satin Tones; author; disc jockey

Hal Negro: Lead singer, Hal Negro and the Satin Tones

Mike Ness: Lead singer, guitarist, Social Distortion

Joe Nolte: Former lead singer, the Last

Margot Olaverra: Cofounder, former bass player, the Go-Go's

Steve Olson: Professional skate boarder; original skate punk

Gary Panter: Artist; *Slash* magazine contributor

Nicole Panter: Former manager, the Germs; author; professor

Mike Patton: Former bassist, the Middle Class

Louie Peréz: Drummer-songwriter, Los Lobos

Raymond Pettibon: Artist

Leonard Phillips: Lead singer, the Dickies

Phast Phreddie (aka Fred Patterson): Cofounder, *Back Door Man* fanzine; *Slash* contributor; song plugger

Jeffrey Lee Pierce: Former lead singer, the Gun Club; author, *Go Tell the Mountain* (deceased 1996)

Tomata du Plenty: Former lead singer, the Screamers (deceased 2000)

John Pochna: Cofounder, the Zero Zero Gallery; founder, the Zero One Gallery

Genesis P. Orridge: Artist; former member, Psychic TV, Throbbing Gristle

Kid Congo Powers (aka Brian Tristan): Former guitarist, Gun Club, the Cramps; solo artist

Steve Priest: Former bass player, the Sweet

Joey Ramone: Former lead singer, the Ramones; actor (*Rock 'n' Roll High School*) (deceased 2001)

Stephen Randall: Journalist

Mary Rat: Plunger sister

Stan Ridgway: Former lead singer, Model Citizens, Wall of Voodoo; film composer (*Rumblefish*); solo artist

Rik L. Rik: Former lead singer, F-Word (deceased 2000)

Paul Roessler: Former keyboard player, the Screamers

Henry Rollins: Former lead singer, Black Flag; lead singer, Rollins Band; spoken word artist; author; actor

Poison Ivy Rorschach: Guitar player, the Cramps

Danny Rose: Former friend of Darby Crash (deceased circa 1998)

Gorilla Rose: Performance artist (deceased)

Steve Samiof: Founder, *Slash* magazine

Sky Saxon: Singer/guitarist, the Seeds

Gina Schock: Drummer, Edie and the Eggs, the Go-Go's

Gene Sculatti: Journalist; coined phrase "Radio Free Hollywood"

Andy Seven: Saxophone player, Arthur J. and the Gold Cups, Trashcan School

Greg Shaw: Founder, Bomp Records, *Who Put the Bomp* fanzine

Pat Smear (aka George Ruthenberg): Former guitarist, the Germs, Nirvana, Foo Fighters

Penelope Spheeris: Filmmaker (*Decline of Western Civilization 1–3, Wayne's World*), real estate mogul

Sabel Starr: Former groupie

Chuck E. Starr: Former disc jockey, Rodney's English Disco, the Sugar Shack, the Odyssey

Micki Steele (aka Michael Steele): Former bass player, the Runaways; bass player, the Bangles

Shawn Stern: Cofounder, Skinhead Manor; member of Youth Brigade; cofounder, BYO (Better Youth Organization)

Mark Stern: Cofounder, Skinhead Manor; member of Youth Brigade, cofounder, BYO (Better Youth Organization); brother of Shawn Stern

Johnny Stingray: Cofounder, the Controllers

Danny Sugerman: Doors archivist, author

Phil S. Teen (aka Phil Miller): Former booking agent, the Screamers

Top Jimmy: Singer, Top Jimmy and the Rhythm Pigs (deceased 2001)

Kathy Valentine: Bass player, the Go-Go's

Dave Vanian: Lead singer, the Damned

Joe Vex: Cofounder, the Vex club

Lee Ving: Lead singer, guitarist, Fear; actor

Don Waller: Cofounder, *Back Door Man* fanzine; journalist

Mike Watt: Former bass player, the Minutemen, fIREHOSE; solo artist

Chuck E. Weiss: Singer/songwriter, Chuck E. Weiss and the Goddamn Liars; inspiration for Ricki Lee Jones hit "Chuck E's in Love"

Sandy West: Former drummer, the Runaways

Jane Wiedlin: Guitarist, the Go-Go's; solo artist; actress

Rick Wilder: Former lead singer, the Berlin Brats; lead singer, the Mau Maus

Philomena Winstanley: Former *Slash* magazine editor/contributor

Geza X: Former guitarist, the Deadbeats, Geza X and the Mommymen; producer

Billy Zoom: Guitarist, X, the Billy Zoom Band

about the authors

Marc Spitz is a senior contributing writer at *SPIN* magazine. He spent his twenties in post-punk Hollywood and now lives in Greenwich Village, New York.

Brendan Mullen founded the Masque, the Hollywood underground club/rehearsal space hailed as the birthplace of the Los Angeles and Orange County punk scenes. He is currently a contributing writer for *LA Weekly*.

Printed in the United States
by Baker & Taylor Publisher Services